Beyond
Se Habla Español

Beyond

Se Habla Español

Q Abogado| ✕

13   "HOW LAWYERS

14   WIN

15   THE HISPANIC

16   MARKET"

17

18   < NATALIE FRAGKOULI

19   & LIEL LEVY />

20

HOUNDSTOOTH
PRESS

BEYOND SE HABLA ESPAÑOL
How Lawyers Win the Hispanic Market

ISBN   978-1-5445-2167-1 *Hardcover*
       978-1-5445-2166-4 *Paperback*
       978-1-5445-2165-7 *Ebook*

*A todos los hispanos en Estados Unidos que
mantienen nuestra cultura viva.*

< CONTENTS >

< PART 3 >
Win with PPC

< PART 4 >
Measuring Results

< **PART 5** >
Measuring Success

< **CONCLUSION** >

< INTRODUCTION >

Welcome to the one-and-only guide you will ever need on how you can use pay-per-click (PPC) to turn the internet into your law firm's personal lead-generation machine.

Sound good?

Sound *too* good to be true?

We totally get it.

The last thing the internet needs is another expert boasting about how much they know. Chances are, we're not the first experts you've heard from either. Maybe we're not even the second, third, or fourth.

Whatever the case, let us first say, "Thanks." We appreciate you giving us a chance to share our knowledge with you.

However, we also want to take a moment to introduce ourselves and, more importantly, actually prove that we are real experts who know what we're talking about (a novel idea—we know).

Before you read a single word in Part 1 of this book, we want you to have 100 percent confidence in the authors behind it.

< **xii**   Natalie Fragkouli & Liel Levy >

MEET YOUR DIGITAL MARKETING EXPERTS

Hi. I'm Liel.

And I'm Natalie.

From now on, we'll just refer to ourselves as "we."

But *we* are a husband-and-wife team who run our own digital marketing agency based in Austin, Texas. This agency focuses specifically on helping law firms that concentrate on the burgeoning Hispanic American market.

WHY WE WROTE THIS BOOK

The simple answer would be that we wrote this book because we love what we do. In fact, one of us often has to remind the other not to incessantly rattle on about digital marketing when we're talking with friends and family (we're not naming names here).

Over the years, we've published newsletters, written blog posts, and even recorded podcasts about our beloved profession. We've covered countless topics, many of which we're also going to include in this book.

But the reason we decided to finally go this route is that we wanted to package more than a decade's worth of expertise into one resource. We wanted to give law firm owners like you a single asset they could read and reference to increase the effectiveness of their marketing efforts.

No tracking down blog posts.

No relistening to podcasts.

We wanted to create a book about digital marketing for law firms that includes *everything* you need to enjoy massive success.

< Introduction **xiii** >

WHY WE'RE QUALIFIED TO COVER SUCH AN IMPORTANT TOPIC

"That's all well and good, but why should *I* listen to *you*?"

Good question!

And, again, we get it: there is no lack of people out there who claim to understand online marketing, *especially* where PPC is concerned.

But there is absolutely no one who is more qualified to explain the intricacies of using digital methods to market to Hispanic Americans who need help from legal professionals.

No.

One.

The two of us transitioned what was already a renowned Spanish legal service brand from a traditional marketing approach to a full omnichannel marketing strategy. Since then, we have leveraged the full power of digital marketing to target the Hispanic market like no law firm, legal directory, or referral service has ever been able to accomplish.

That's not all.

We were actually the very first professionals to pull off this kind of undertaking. While many firms have followed—not all of them have done so successfully—we were the trailblazers who knew it was possible. We were the ones with the expertise to pull it off before anyone else had even tried.

The agency we're referring to wasn't ours. The owner simply knew of our reputation and entrusted us to pull off this ambitious goal. Someday, maybe we'll write a book that delves into that story and explains how our expertise was able to make the transition happen.

< **xiv** Natalie Fragkouli & Liel Levy >

In any case, that same expertise is now at your service in this book. So, whether you're just looking to add a new segment into your law firm's current marketing strategy, or you're looking for a completely new start to your marketing efforts, we're here to help.

That's what we've been doing for more than a decade. Since our humble beginnings, *a lot* has changed about the digital landscape.

Facebook has gone from a questionable marketing investment to one that few companies can afford to ignore.

Google has tweaked its algorithm countless times and flat-out overhauled it more than a dozen. It's also revamped and reinvented a number of different ways for companies to use its network for advertising.

Video ads have become the norm for Fortune 500 companies, small businesses, and everything in between.

Despite all of this, the two of us have continued to thrive. We understand the complex world of digital marketing and have been able to find success for the firms we partner with no matter what changes.

More importantly, we've kept our eye on how the Latinx market is changing, growing, and evolving. We know which tactics—both digital and traditional—still work and which ones you should stop investing in.

A BRIEF RUNDOWN OF OUR CREDENTIALS

While we can't mention any clients or past agencies for which we've worked, we *can* tell you about our own personal resumes.

First, Natalie is an MBA who specialized in marketing and has more than ten years of experience serving firms that need help marketing to the Hispanic American demographic.

Liel grew up watching—and eventually helping—his uncle

< Introduction **xv** >

build one of the country's largest legal brands. He was there for every step of their marketing plan. Sometimes, this meant handing out balloons at fiestas where they knew potential clients would be. Other times, it meant finding new markets to introduce to his uncle's brand. It was an intense education through constant participation.

Together, Liel and Natalie cofounded Nanato Media with the goal to help law firms run relevant, expert campaigns targeting local Hispanic markets. By leveraging the power of Nanato Media, law firms don't need to pay for their own team of multicultural marketers. By hiring us, they save money without sacrificing results.

In fact, any law firm we've partnered with would tell you we brought them the best results they've ever seen.

WHY DIGITAL MARKETING FOR LAW FIRMS MEANS SO MUCH TO US

Earlier, we mentioned that digital marketing is our passion. It's what we love and, yes, even obsess about.

Hopefully, you can relate to this with how you feel about law.

Nonetheless, we know that a lot of people wonder where we find this kind of commitment to such a niche world: using these tools *specifically* to generate Hispanic leads.

The answer is that we are a Hispanic family who lives in the United States. As such, we understand the lack of inclusion and the presence of biases that exist when it comes to marketing to Hispanic and Spanish-speaking communities.

Large national brands have the resources to create a multicultural marketing division within their organizations, but we

< **xvi**   Natalie Fragkouli & Liel Levy >

know that this generally isn't the case for law firms. It just isn't remotely realistic.

We also know that this creates two problems.

First, it means many Hispanic Americans go without the representation they need during what is often the most difficult times in their lives.

Second, it also means that many law firms struggle unnecessarily. They either don't know how much promise this market holds for them, or they don't know how to tap into it.

Or both.

By writing this one book, we are aiming to solve these two problems.

We can also help you avoid a third, which occurs when some law firms decide that they don't need any help from multicultural experts. They know they're totally capable of running their own ads, even those that will target a specific demographic within the Latinx community.

At best, they simply waste *a lot* of money.

At worst, their marketing is so tone-deaf that it not only fails to generate new leads, it actually turns away people who may have decided to hire them in the future. Those people will remember that disappointing ad and simply take their business elsewhere.

HOW WE LEARNED THE LESSONS WE'RE ABOUT TO SHARE WITH YOU

Now that you know what makes us tick, let's answer another very important question:

"Why should I listen to you?"

Aside from our ten-plus years of experience in this dynamic

< Introduction **xvii** >

field, we also have experience working with one of the largest legal brands for the US Spanish market. We learned a lot of invaluable lessons during this unique opportunity.

We have had success at building a Google Premier Partner in-house agency from the ground up. This is only possible because of our deep understanding of digital marketing.

Speaking of unique credentials, we've actually worked hand-in-hand with Google at their Mexico headquarters. We were chosen to help them with betas and tests aimed specifically at the US Hispanic market.

We also participate in conferences like Google Marketing Live, an invitation-only gathering for the top Google Ads experts, and we frequently conduct *Grow with Google* digital skills workshops at Google Austin. This program was designed specifically to help Black and Latinx small local business owners leverage the power of Google and digital platforms to grow their businesses.

Among other things, working with Google like that has given us insights that *still* keep us ahead of competitors and at the very forefront of digital marketing innovations.

As an agency, we attend important legal marketing conferences. Some popular examples of these conferences include the American Association of Justice, Great Legal Marketing, and The Powerful Innovative Legal Marketing & Management Association (PILMMA), just to name a few. These ongoing events are another way we stay at the forefront of all legal marketing conversations.

Furthermore, we are very involved in our local community and take pride in supporting nonprofits around Austin, such as Think Bilingual, which promotes multilingualism among families. Another one we love is Bleu Lotus Project, which seeks to enhance the quality of life for African Americans in the Austin area.

That's hardly where our experience ends, though. At Nanato

< **xviii** Natalie Fragkouli & Liel Levy >

Media, we've developed a reputation for constantly learning about, experimenting with, and developing new ways to help our clients reach new heights.

"WHAT IF I DON'T WANT TO FOCUS *SOLELY* ON MARKETING TO HISPANIC CLIENTS?"

That said, before we show you what you have to look forward to in the pages that follow, we do want to answer a very common question we get from many law firm owners.

While we are definitely very passionate about helping law firms engage their local Hispanic markets, it's not a requirement that you do the same in order to benefit from the information in this book. As long as you are excited about using digital marketing to build your law firm's profits, you'll find the chapters in this book to be extremely helpful.

That said, we encourage you to keep an open mind on the topic.

In the first chapter of Part 1, we're going to cover exactly *why* we believe modern law firms need to treat Hispanic clients as priorities. Over the years, we've partnered with a number of different firm owners who had no interest in the idea until we explained its numerous upsides. Many of them now focus almost entirely on Hispanic prospects these days.

< Introduction **xix** >

WHAT YOU'LL FIND IN THE FOLLOWING PAGES

Still interested in turning your firm's web presence into a lead-generation machine?

Glad to hear it!

We know how valuable your time is.

We also know that it's probably in *very* short supply.

So, we truly take it as quite an honor that you've found the time to read our book.

We also want to make sure you know that the time you spend with it will be time *very* well spent. It will be time that can absolutely change the entire trajectory of your law firm. This will, among other things, mean understanding how to attract more qualified prospects *without* investing more of that valuable time into generating them.

If you're already excited about that possibility, by all means, jump into Part 1 and start learning about how digital marketing can transform your firm's future.

However, if you're still not 100 percent sure about putting the time into reading our book, we get it. Nothing personal. No offense taken (at least not *much* offense).

In that case, allow us to show off a bit. We've used our ten-plus years of experience to compile the absolute last word on digital marketing for law firms. Here's what you're about to become a master of by reading it.

< **xx**   Natalie Fragkouli & Liel Levy >

AN EXPERT'S GUIDE TO DIGITAL MARKETING FOR LAW FIRMS

We organized our book into four distinct sections and sixteen chapters. Starting with the groundwork for our strategy, we'll walk you through every aspect of successfully marketing online to Hispanic Americans.

By laying it out this way, we also know it will be easier to come back and reference different sections as necessary when you build, deploy, and refine your own law firm's strategy.

PART 1—MEET THE US HISPANICS

- **Why Every Law Firm Must Focus on Hispanic Clients—** Before we look at *how* to market, we want to make a case for *whom* your firm should be marketing to. Hispanics aren't just the fastest-growing ethnic group throughout the entire country. We'll explore a number of other reasons it pays— *literally*—to focus on this group.

- **The Evolution of Media Consumption Among US Hispanics and Its Effect on Law Firm Marketing—**Many of the firms we partner with came to us *after* an unsuccessful attempt to market to the Latinx community. We'll make sure you understand how to avoid the common mistakes these firms made.

PART 2—LEARN TO PRIORITIZE

- **Getting Started with Your Hispanic Marketing Strategy—** Here it is: we start laying the groundwork for the online marketing strategy that will transform your firm by generating a regular source of Hispanic leads.

< Introduction **xxi** >

- **SEO vs. PPC**—Search engine optimization (SEO) and PPC, arguably, are the two most common acronyms in all of online marketing. But here's the thing: they don't deserve equal billing in your law firm's online strategy. We're going to explain why this is, so you never divide your budget the wrong way again and you start seeing profitable results from your strategy a lot faster.

PART 3—WIN WITH PPC

- **What Law Firms Need to Understand About Google Ads**—As a business owner looking to market their company online, Google Ads will either be one of your greatest assets or your shortcut to a broken budget. In this chapter, we use our own experience with Google Ads—including actually working with Google—to show you what it takes to make this powerful tactic work.

- **Law Firm Campaigns: Google Ads Keyword Research and Segmentation**—Once you understand the ins and outs of Google Ads, we're going to jump right into the kind of keyword research that powers successful campaigns. Then, we'll show you how to segment your market effectively, so you're *really* dialing up that return on investment (ROI).

- **How to Write Conversion Copy for Your Law Firm's Google Ads Campaigns**—That's right. We're going to turn you into a copywriter! Here's the thing: it doesn't take years of practice to get good at writing successful Google Ads. Once you understand the fundamentals of writing winning ads, you will be able to quickly and effectively do it all on your own. At the very least, if you really don't have the time to write

< **xxii**   Natalie Fragkouli & Liel Levy >

them for your firm every month, this section will give you the knowledge required to hire a copywriter with confidence.

- **How to Create Landing Pages That Convert for Your Law Firm**—In our experience, the vast majority of law firm owners simply have no idea what makes a landing page convert. What should be one of their greatest marketing assets hardly brings in any business. So, in this section, we're going to break down the fundamentals of a high-performing landing page.

- **How to Set Up a Google Ads Search Campaign for Google Ads**—Let's put it all together and build your law firm's first Google Ads campaign focused on Hispanic Americans.

- **Advanced Google Ads Strategies for Your Law Firm**—After you know how to build a successful Google Ads campaign, we're actually going to take it several steps further by introducing you to advanced strategies. These are tactics your competitors don't know about, but they'll soon become *very* familiar to you.

- **Why Advertising with Google Display Ads Is a Must for Law Firms**—If your law firm isn't currently using Google Display Ads—or simply isn't investing in them enough—you're leaving money on the table. In this section, we'll explain what makes Display Ads so powerful and what to do to take full advantage of them.

- **The Ultimate Guide to Facebook Ads for Law Firms**— Facebook Ads. Just about every law firm owner tries them at some point, but most find them woefully lacking. We're going to make sure you *love* them by actually showing you what it takes to use them successfully.

< Introduction **xxiii** >

PART 4—MEASURING RESULTS

- **Measure the Results of Your Law Firm's PPC Campaigns**—If you don't know how to effectively measure the results of your law firm's PPC campaigns, you won't know if there is room for improvement or by how much. We'll tell you what needs to be measured, so your campaigns are *constantly* improving.

- **Make the Most from Your Law Firm's Business Metrics**— Easily the most important step that you can take toward this kind of constant improvement is knowing which business metrics matter the most to your law firm's success.

PART 5—MEASURING SUCCESS

- **Everything You Need to Know to Improve Your Law Firm's Intake Process**—All the leads in the world won't account for much if your intake team doesn't know how to process them so they're on their way to becoming clients. This involves very specific steps when you decide to focus on Hispanic Americans.

- **The Ultimate Guide to Law Firm Review Generation**— Nothing will do more for your law firm's lead-generation efforts than an enviable reputation. If Hispanic prospects don't already know about yours, we'll walk you through what it takes to gain favorable reviews *and* make sure they get in front of the people who are looking for your help.

< **xxiv**   Natalie Fragkouli & Liel Levy >

BEGIN YOUR JOURNEY TOWARD A WINNING DIGITAL MARKETING STRATEGY

Now that you know who we are, why we're experts, and what we plan to teach you, there's nothing left to do but get started.

Without further ado, we'd like to introduce you to the fastest-growing ethnic group in the United States and the most important demographic for your law firm.

< PART 1 >

MEET THE US HISPANICS

< CHAPTER 1 >

WHY EVERY LAW FIRM MUST FOCUS ON HISPANIC CLIENTS

Everyone knows that growing a business means understanding which demographics will help it grow the most.

And yet, many law firms don't segment their markets to include important cultural differentiators. Instead, most only focus on age, gender, and location.

This is a huge mistake, though, as the US Hispanic population is arguably the most important cultural demographic for law firms looking to grow.

The subject can be a complicated one, but we've included all the pertinent details you need to understand *who* makes up this population, *why* they deserve extra attention, and how to give it to them.

< **4**   Natalie Fragkouli & Liel Levy >

WHAT YOU HAVE TO KNOW ABOUT MARKETING TO THE HISPANIC MARKET

While "Hispanic" is an accurate umbrella term, there are more specific ones that apply to unique groups under that umbrella. To market to each of them, you need to understand how they prefer to be addressed.

In fact, if you're already running Google Ads for Hispanic prospects and *aren't* seeing many clicks, it could be that you're simply using the wrong terms.[1] Making this one important change could be all it takes to turn your campaigns around and see that positive ROI.

After all, imagine a company was trying to target attorneys. Maybe it's a marketing agency. Maybe it's a marketing agency based in Austin, Texas, with *a lot* of experience helping law firms generate qualified leads through PPC. Maybe they're also really nice, easy to talk to, and a lot of people even say they're very good-looking.

They sound like they'd be a lot of help, right?

But what if their ads were addressing you as law professionals?

Does that sound right?

Or legal service providers?

Those terms may *technically* describe you, but they don't inspire a lot of confidence, do they?

Of course not.

It sounds like the company doesn't *really* understand you, so you're probably not going to click on their ads.

---

1   "Why Law Firms Must Run Spanish Google Ads," *Nanato Media*, March 23, 2020, https://nanatomedia.com/blog/why-law-firms-must-run-spanish-google-ads/.

< Meet the US Hispanics **5** >

(**Note:** This was a hypothetical. If you thought we were talking about ourselves, we weren't. We actually know how to target prospects and would never make this mistake, but the rest of those traits do apply to us, especially the one about our looks.)

Alright, with that said, it's time to meet the Hispanic population of the United States.

WHO ARE LATINX?

In the next section, we're going to detail five very important segments of the Hispanic population.

However, before we do, it's worth noting that many people who may have formerly been considered Latina or Latino no longer identify with that term.

Instead, many have adopted the identifier, "Latinx."[2] This alternative to traditional terms Latino and Latina is defined by *The Oxford English Dictionary* as:

> "A person of Latin American origin or descent (used as a gender-neutral or non-binary alternative to Latino or Latina)."[3]

The term may have originated as far back as 2004 according to Google Trends data, cited in *Latinx: A Brief Handbook*, but it largely flew under the radar at first.[4]

---

2   Katy Steinmetz, "What 'Latinx' Means—and Why the Label Is Taking Off," *Time*, April 2, 2018, https://time.com/5191804/latinx-definition-meaning-latino-hispanic -gender-neutral/.

3   "Latinx: Definition of Latinx by Oxford Dictionary on Lexico.com," Lexico Dictionaries, accessed May 18, 2020, https://www.lexico.com/definition/latinx.

4   Arlene Gamio, "Latinx: A Brief Guidebook," Academia.edu, Summer 2016, https://www.academia.edu/29657615/Latinx_A_Brief_Guidebook.

< **6** Natalie Fragkouli & Liel Levy >

It's been in the last few years that Latinx has seen a resurgence among Hispanic people throughout North America.

But why did the term become necessary?

The popularity of "Latinx" as an identifier mirrors the growing movement among people of all ethnicities, sexual orientations, and genders to choose how they want to identify themselves.

In the Spanish language, "Latina" only refers to cisgender females. "Latino" only identifies cisgender males. Those traditional labels feel outdated to many people, especially among millennials and Generation Z.

The problem is made all the worse by the fact that a group of Hispanic individuals is referred to as "Latinos," even when it includes women.

"Latinx" gives people the ability to refer to individuals or groups without relying on traditional gender descriptors. It's similar to the English version of the singular "they," which was Time's Word of the Year back in 2015 for this very reason.[5] Other attempts in the past to overcome the traditional restrictions of Latina and Latino came up short for pronunciation reasons. In text, there was "Latina/o," but that doesn't translate well to communicating aloud. "Latin@" was another valiant effort but failed for the same reason.

Don't worry. We'll cover pronouncing Latinx in just a moment, so you know exactly how to say it.

Although adoption of Latinx has been especially widespread throughout the LGBTQIA+ community, one misconception around the term is that it refers to sexual orientation.

It doesn't.

Joseph M. Pierce is the assistant professor in Stony Brook

---

5   Katy Steinmetz, "The Final Word of the Year: Gender-Neutral 'They'," *Time*, January 9, 2016, https://time.com/4173992/word-of-the-year-2015-they/.

< Meet the US Hispanics **7** >

University's Department of Hispanic Languages and Literature and describes the distinction this way:

> "It does not imply any particular sexuality...Nor does 'Latinx' apply to everyone as an identity category. Instead, it expands the possibilities for expression that people have at their disposal. People who have been marginalized because of the gendered dynamics of Spanish view this shift toward the 'x' as one of inclusivity and openness."[6]

That said, not every member of the Hispanic community is comfortable with this label.

LATINX MAY NOT BE FOR EVERYONE

Although the whole point of the term is to be inclusive, many Hispanics don't like to be called Latinx. Some actually find the term offensive, a form of reverse appropriation. As one Latino man put it in an interview with *Latina*:

> "So instead of taking something from Spanish...they are putting a distinctively American—and really, it's mostly found at elite college institutions—viewpoint into a language without appreciation or reverence for it. That's reverse appropriation, where we blatantly force our worldview into another culture."[7]

When it comes to marketing your law firm, our suggestion is to use both in your ads and see which your market seems to

---

6   Irina Gonzalez, "Most People Don't Know What the Term 'Latinx' Means, a Recent Survey Suggests," *Oprah Magazine*, October 6, 2020, https://www.oprahmag.com/life/a28056593/latinx-meaning/.

7   Raquel Reichard, "Latino/a vs. Latinx vs. Latine: Which Word Best Solves Spanish's Gender Problem?" *LATINA*, March 30, 2017, http://www.latina.com/lifestyle/our-issues/latinoa-latinx-latine-solving-spanish-gender-problem?page=2%2C1.

< **8** Natalie Fragkouli & Liel Levy >

prefer. It might be that you need to use Latinx for some segments and Latino or Latina for others.

As far as our agency is concerned, we understand both sides: those who feel strongly about making Spanish less gender-centered and those who think it impacts the integrity of the language.

For the sake of neutrality, we will use Latina, Latino, and Latinx throughout this chapter. We hope this will be taken in the spirit of respect with which it's meant.

You may want to do the same on your firm's website or even make mention that you're trying to use language that is both inclusive and respectful.

HOW DO YOU PRONOUNCE LATINX?

Lastly, before we move on to describing the different demographics of the American Hispanic population, we want to make sure you know how to pronounce Latinx.

Putting it on your website and in your ads is one thing, but if you mess it up on the phone, you might alienate a prospect.

Fortunately, it's simple. According to *Merriam-Webster*, the way to pronounce Latinx is:

> "The most common way to pronounce Latinx is the same way you would say Spanish-derived Latina or Latino but pronouncing the 'x' as the name of the English letter X. So you get something like \luh-TEE-neks\. 'Latinx' is a gender-neutral word for people of Latin American descent."[8]

See?
Simple.

---

8 "'Latinx' And Gender Inclusivity: How Do You Pronounce This More Inclusive Word?" *Merriam-Webster*, accessed May 18, 2020, https://www.merriam-webster.com/words-at-play/word-history-latinx.

< Meet the US Hispanics **9** >

UNDERSTANDING THE DIFFERENT MEMBERS OF THE HISPANIC COMMUNITY

According to the United States Census Bureau, the Hispanic population in the US is estimated to be a little over *60 million* people.[9]

That's *a lot* of people.

Might be worth getting to know them a bit better then, right?

This is especially true if you, like us, are based here in Texas. More Latinx live here than anywhere else in the country. The Texas cities with the largest Latinx populations are:

- Houston

- Dallas-Fort Worth

- San Antonio

- Rio Grande Valley

That's why we've pulled information from Claritas' *The Hispanic American Market Report* to help better acquaint yourself with this growing market.[10]

Because, at more than 60 *million*, this population is actually made up of five very distinct groups. Trying to market to all of them the exact same way is bound to end in low—or even nonexistent—ROIs.

So, take a moment to get to know each group:

---

9 "US Census Bureau QuickFacts: United States," United States Census Bureau, accessed May 18, 2020, https://www.census.gov/quickfacts/fact/table/US/RHI725219.

10 Cesar Lizano, "The Hispanic American Market Report 2019," Claritas LLC, November 24, 2019, https://www.slideshare.net/cesarlizano/the-hispanic-american-market-report-2019.

< **10** Natalie Fragkouli & Liel Levy >

1. LATINOAMERICANA

Someone who is Latinoamericana emigrated to the United States within the last ten years. They speak Spanish but almost no English. Latinoamericanas feel a much stronger bond to their native country than they do to the US. As such, they still participate in many Hispanic cultural practices.

Claritas found four main tendencies that are common among this group. They tend to:

- Be the least educated of these five groups.

- Work as migrant laborers.

- Shop at Hispanic grocery stores.

- Use the internet the least of the five groups.

2. HISPANO

Hispano simply means "Hispanic" in Spanish. It's a very appropriate term for this group as it refers to the demographic that emigrated to the United States more than ten years ago but still prefers to speak Spanish. Generally, Hispanos do speak some English, though. They still partake in many Hispanic cultural practices, as well.

Claritas reports that, on average, most Hispanos:

- Are blue-collar workers.

- Have larger families than the other groups.

- Enjoy watching late-night Spanish TV and Mexican soccer.

< Meet the US Hispanics **11** >

3. AMERICANIZADO

Americanizado means "to Americanize" making this a very accurate term for a demographic that is made up of Hispanic people who were born in the US, just like their parents and grandparents.[11] Many have family roots that go back even further. English is their native language and they speak little, if any, Spanish. Despite their heritage, they participate in very few Hispanic cultural practices.

This group represents 17.1 percent of the American Hispanic population. That's about 11,022,030 people.

Given their Americanized identities, it should come as no surprise that many of the tendencies *Claritas* identified among this group are common across other ethnicities in this country. Americanizados tend to:

- Watch MTV2, VH1, and UFC.

- Be single and never married.

- Work in tech.

- Shop at Whole Foods.

In many ways, then, marketing to this group of more than 11 million people wouldn't be *so* different from marketing to other demographics in the United States.

4. NUEVA LATINA

The fourth group you have to know about is Nueva Latina. This refers to the majority of the American Hispanic population. A Nueva Latina is someone with equal footing in American

---

11 "English Translation of 'Americanizado'," *Collins Portuguese-English Dictionary*, accessed May 18, 2020, https://www.collinsdictionary.com/us/dictionary/portuguese-english/americanizado.

< **12** Natalie Fragkouli & Liel Levy >

and traditional Hispanic cultures. They're second-generation Americans who *prefer* English but can speak at least some Spanish.

Because of this dual identity, many Nueva Latinas experience what is known as retro-acculturation.

> "A term coined by Hispanic marketing researcher, Carlos E. Garcia, it refers to the conscious search for ethnic identity or roots, especially by second, third, or fourth-generation Latinos who feel they have lost their cultural identity."[12]

Nueva Latinas make up 29.2 percent of Hispanic Americans or about 18,829,098 people.

According to *Claritas*, this group tends to:

- Go to school or work in office and administrative support.

- Watch *Universo* and *Telemundo*.

- Shop at Sam's Club.

So, while Nueva Latinas either have strong Hispanic cultural ties—or are working to reconnect with them—they're still integrated into the larger fabric of America.

---

12   Mario Carrasco, "The Persistence Of Hispanic Culture In The Digital Age," *MediaPost*, September 1, 2016, https://www.mediapost.com/publications/article/283902/the-persistence-of-hispanic-culture-in-the-digital.html.

< Meet the US Hispanics **13** >

5. AMBICULTURAL

Someone who is Ambicultural has "the ability to functionally transit between Latino cultures and the American, giving them a unique position in the consumer landscape."[13]

Abasto magazine also provides the following statistics about this segment of the American Hispanic population:

- Eighty-five percent call themselves Latino and American.

- Eighty percent look forward to dinner with their family every night.

- Thirty-seven percent consider themselves to be more connected to their culture of origin than their parents.

- Seventy-five percent state that it is important that their children continue with their cultural traditions.

- Seventy-two percent say that their cultural heritage is an important part of who they are.

- Seventy percent would like to learn from cultures of other countries.

- Forty-eight percent feel good seeing celebrities in the media who share their cultural heritage.

- Seventy percent consider themselves to be sociable people.

Ambiculturals are able to speak English and Spanish at about the same level. They emigrated to America either as a child or young adult and—as we just touched on—participate in many Hispanic cultural practices.

---

13 "Ambicultural: The New Identity of Latinos," *Abasto*, April 1, 2016, https://abasto.com/en/news/ambicultural-new-identity-latinos/.

< **14** Natalie Fragkouli & Liel Levy >

Claritas also notes that they tend to:

- Live with their parents.

- Enjoy watching boxing.

- Attend US soccer games.

- Shop at Walmart.

Representing 25.8 percent of the American Hispanic population means there are 16,590,556 Ambicultural Americans in our country. They are the second-largest group on our list.

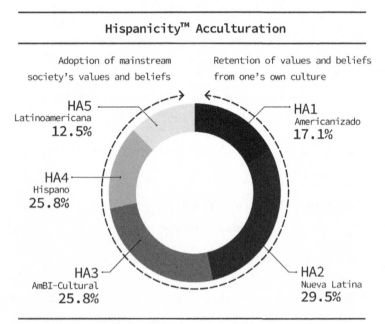

Hispanicity™ Acculturation

Adoption of mainstream society's values and beliefs

Retention of values and beliefs from one's own culture

HA5
Latinoamericana
12.5%

HA1
Americanizado
17.1%

HA4
Hispano
25.8%

HA3
AmBI-Cultural
25.8%

HA2
Nueva Latina
29.5%

Source: Claritas LLC, 2020

< Meet the US Hispanics **15** >

THE FUTURE OF THE HISPANIC MARKET

Understanding *all* five of those terms will help your law firm better market to the Hispanic population.[14]

For Latinoamericanas and Hispanos, this requires marketing to them in Spanish, the language they'll use when they search for help online. Your campaigns should also stress the fact that your firm doesn't just create Spanish marketing materials. You should also have attorneys who can speak with them in their native language or at least staff who can translate on their behalf.

Latinoamericanas and Hispanos may not represent the largest Hispanic demographics in this country, but they *do* represent promising client segments for your firm if you know how to properly market to them. Just like anyone else, they get in car accidents and need personal injury attorneys. They get hurt at work and need help with workers' comp.

In short, they need law firms like yours to represent them. Show them that they'll be comfortable coming to you for help—just as you would with any other demographic—and Latinoamericanas and Hispanos will quickly grow your firm.

However, there are actually two *other* segments of the Hispanic population that are especially important to your firm's future because they're slowly making up the majority.

While you still want to know the other three as they could come up in conversation or it may still make sense to target them, these two deserve the most attention from your marketing efforts.

They are Ambicultural and Nueva Latina.

What makes them so vital to the future of your law firm?

---

14 "How Your Law Firm Can Get More Latino Clients," *Nanato Media*, May 30, 2019, https://nanatomedia.com/blog/three-tips-on-how-law-firms-can-get-more-latino-clients/.

< **16**   Natalie Fragkouli & Liel Levy >

1. AGE

Ambicultural and Nueva Latinas represent the younger generations of American Hispanics. Learn to target them now and your
law firm's marketing strategy will have a nice, long life. While we'll
talk about the growing population of *all* Hispanic Americans,
these two groups are the largest contingencies of millennials and
Generation Z.

2. INTERNET USAGE

It should come as no surprise, then, that this younger group is
also *very* internet-savvy. In fact, they're even savvier than other
groups of the same age.

Again, we'll delve into the Hispanic population as a whole
in just a moment, but the point is that if you start prioritizing
Nueva Latinas and Ambicultural prospects with your internet
marketing right now, you'll see results in the very near future.

Of course, the distant future looks good for your efforts, too.

3. COMFORT WITH ENGLISH

Finally, this younger group is the most comfortable with English,
which is a huge advantage when you look at structuring your
firm's marketing campaigns.

To be clear, it may still make sense to use Spanish in some of
your marketing materials.[15] Having a bilingual staff member can
be extremely helpful, too. We're definitely not saying *never* target
those other demographics.

It's just that both your English and Spanish ads will work with
Ambicultural and Nueva Latina populations. Of course, you still
need to target this group correctly. This includes the messaging

---

15   "Why Law Firms Must Run Spanish Google Ads," *Nanato Media*, March 23, 2020,
     https://nanatomedia.com/blog/why-law-firms-must-run-spanish-google-ads/.

< Meet the US Hispanics **17** >

you use in your campaigns. Even if it's in English, it must still reference the culture of Nueva Latinas and Ambiculturals. You need to back this message with proof of your bilingual bonafides to show that your company really *does* walk the (literal) talk.

WHY YOUR FIRM MUST MARKET TO HISPANIC PROSPECTS

Alright, so you now understand the different terms that apply to the Hispanic population.

You know why they're significant and how to properly use them.

You even know the two demographics that deserve the most attention in the years to come.

Pat yourself on the back.

In this last section, we're going to show you *why* all of this information is so important (besides, you know, just understanding other people's cultures is never a bad thing).

So, stand up. Have a stretch. Get yourself another cup of coffee if you need to.

And let's dive in.

Unless otherwise noted, the statistics in this section were drawn from the *absolutely massive* 2019 Nielsen report, *Descubrimiento Digital: The Online Lives of Latinx Consumers.*[16]

---

16 "La Oportunidad Latinx: Cultural Currency and the Consumer Journey," The Nielsen Company, August 12, 2019, https://www.nielsen.com/us/en/insights/report/2019/la-oportunidad-latinx/.

< **18**   Natalie Fragkouli & Liel Levy >

1. LATINX ARE THE FASTEST GROWING DEMOGRAPHIC IN THE COUNTRY

If you had to choose between a market that isn't growing, one that's actually declining, and one that is skyrocketing in size, which would you choose?

We'll give you a minute.

If you picked the third option, we agree, but then your law firm needs a plan for engaging the Latinx community.

They are, *by far*, the fastest growing demographic in the country and it isn't even close.

Currently, Hispanics account for more than half of the US population growth that has taken place since 2016. By 2040–2045, experts believe they'll account for as much as *80 percent*.

To put that into perspective, here is how the *Claritas* report sees population annual growth for multicultural groups between 2019–2024:

- **Non-Hispanic Whites:** -60,156.

- **Non-Hispanic Blacks:** 315,492.

- **Non-Hispanic Asian and Pacific Islanders:** 483,004.

- **Hispanics:** 1,536,315.

If you want to build a sustainable marketing campaign for your firm, the numbers make it clear: Hispanic prospects are *and will continue to be* on the rise.

2. TECHNOLOGY. TECHNOLOGY. TECHNOLOGY.

It's not just their growing population that makes Latinx such an important demographic for your digital marketing strategy.

< Meet the US Hispanics **19** >

It's that they are on the internet *a lot*.

Sixty percent of Hispanics were either born or have grown up during the Internet Age. For non-Hispanic Whites, that number is just 40 percent.

Ninety-eight percent of Latinx own a smartphone compared to 95 percent of the rest of the population. This number takes into account everyone from the age of two and up.

They actually over-index the rest of the population by 9 percent when it comes to owning smartphones, which explains why an incredible *99 percent* of Hispanic households rely on wireless phone services. These households are *well ahead* of the curve there.

Toddlers aside, if you focus on *actual* adults, you'll be interested to know that, among Hispanics thirty-five and older, their smartphone ownership exceeds that of the rest of the US population by 5 percent.

On average, Latinos spend *twenty-seven hours a week* on their smartphones visiting websites and using apps.

Fifty-seven percent of Latinos say they are interested in watching videos on their smartphones over-indexing non-Hispanic Whites once again by 22 percent.

So, if explainer videos would help better engage your prospects, make them with this growing population in mind.

Finally, it can't be emphasized enough how important it is that 27 percent of Hispanics live in multigenerational homes. This means younger generations are helping older ones keep up with technology. In fact, those who are fifty or older over-index non-Hispanic Whites when it comes to using electronic gadgets by *36 percent!*

< **20**   Natalie Fragkouli & Liel Levy >

3. SOCIAL MEDIA IS *VERY* POPULAR
AMONG LATINOS AND LATINAS

This love of technology means Latinx also love social media.

Fifty-two percent of Hispanics spend *at least* an hour a day on social media, compared to just 38 percent of non-Hispanic Whites. Twenty-four percent of Hispanics actually spend three hours or more on social media a day compared to only 13 percent of non-Hispanic Whites.

Twenty-seven percent of Latinx report that finding out about products and services is one of the *most important* reasons they visit social media sites. So, by all means, run social ads knowing you're not interrupting their experiences.

If you want to know *where* to run them, here are the social-networking sites and apps *Nielsen* says Hispanics report using in the past thirty days at the time of their report:

- Facebook: 74 percent.
- Snapchat: 32 percent.
- YouTube: 68 percent.
- Twitter: 22 percent.
- Instagram: 45 percent.
- LinkedIn: 12 percent.

4. LANGUAGE IS AN EASY
MEANS OF CULTURAL CONNECTION

As you probably know all too well, a big part of your job as a lawyer is about building trust with your prospects—*fast*.

One simple—but effective—way you can do this with Latinos is by using Spanish when marketing to them.

Consider the following from the *Nielsen* report:

- Seventy-two percent of Hispanics and 75 percent of Hispanic households speak Spanish at home.

< Meet the US Hispanics **21** >

- Seventy-three percent of US Hispanics agree that it's important to them that their children continue their family's cultural traditions.

- Seventy-three percent of US Hispanics agree that their cultural ethnic heritage is an important part of who they are.

Along with understanding the accepted terminology for each group, showing that you appreciate how important language and culture is to Hispanics is a great way to make the right first impression with potential clients.

5. LATINX CLIENTS ARE LOYAL CLIENTS

Lastly, focusing on Latino clients might be one of the best ways to reliably grow your law firm's business for one very important reason. It's not just that they represent such a large percentage of the population or that they're so comfortable with the internet.

It's also that they're extremely loyal to the companies that earn their business.

When *Customer Communication Groups* analyzed Latinx buying habits, they found that:

> "The 2019 study found that 53 percent of Hispanics report they tend to find a good source for their purchases and stick with it. This is compared to 37 percent of Americans overall and 46 percent of African Americans who said they stick with a good source for purchases once they find it."[17]

Obviously, giving their business to a law firm is different than a retail company, but there's no reason to think that kind

---

17 Sandra Gudat, "Insights on Hispanic Brand Loyalty," *Customer Communications Group*, September 12, 2019, https://www.customer.com/blog/retail-marketing/hispanic-brand-loyalty/.

< **22**   Natalie Fragkouli & Liel Levy >

of loyalty doesn't hold in other circumstances—provided they are happy with the service received.

Furthermore, as we've covered a number of times now, the Latino population is family-focused and very social among their communities.

This is a huge advantage for your law firm because *Nielsen* reports that 38 percent of Hispanics say they like to share their consumer experiences *online* with reviews and ratings.

In other words, give your Hispanic clients incredible service, and they'll do a lot of the marketing for you.

EFFECTIVELY MARKET YOUR LAW FIRM TO HISPANIC PROSPECTS STARTING NOW

By now, we hope it's clear that you should do everything possible to show Latino prospects all that your firm has to offer.

If you want to grow your business, you need to grow your strategy to include specific campaigns that are laser-focused on this growing market.

< CHAPTER 2 >

THE EVOLUTION OF MEDIA CONSUMPTION AMONG US HISPANICS AND ITS EFFECT ON LAW FIRM MARKETING

For decades, the most important marketing mediums for law firms were television and radio.

Of course, a few other options deserved attention, too.

The sides of buses and the benches people sat on when waiting for them were always popular.

Obviously, billboards did really well in certain markets, too. But nothing compared to getting in front of potential clients using TV and radio ads.

Then, the internet came along, became widespread, and eventually led the way for social media and mobile devices.

Nowadays, these two formats reign supreme for law firm marketing, *especially* if you want to engage Hispanic prospects. This demographic has quickly transformed from one that was

< **24**   Natalie Fragkouli & Liel Levy >

ideal for radio and TV to one that is *perfect* for social media and mobile marketing.

The sooner you understand why and adjust your methods accordingly, the faster you'll grow your firm.

WHAT LAW FIRM MARKETING FOR HISPANICS USED TO LOOK LIKE

Before we dive into what *currently* works best for marketing your law firm to Hispanics, let's take a moment to understand why TV and radio used to be the easy choices.

Even though we believe these mediums are past their prime, we know that some of our clients wondered if they should still make room in their marketing budgets for them.

So, why *were* TV and radio so effective at engaging with Hispanic prospects in the past?

The easy answer is simply that, before the internet, these were the two most popular electronic mediums for delivering entertainment and information.

However, just like TV and radio stole the spotlight from books and magazines, these two mediums are now losing users because of the internet.

Radio and television aren't just dropping in popularity among Hispanics, either. They're dropping among *everybody* because the internet has largely made them obsolete.

< Meet the US Hispanics **25** >

THE DOWNFALL OF TELEVISION

One of the most dramatic illustrations of this phenomenon is how TV networks have actually *increased* the number of commercials they show even as viewers flee to YouTube and streaming services to avoid them.

Why?

Because this massive migration is giving networks no other option to make up for lost profits:

> "As TV viewership declines and more consumers jump to streaming services like Netflix, media companies have only a couple of options to generate the advertising revenue that Wall Street expects: They can raise prices, run more commercials or do a little of both."[18]

That's not exactly a recipe that inspires confidence, is it?

Not surprisingly, many experts have predicted that "the future of television" is in streaming services, where fewer, if any, ads are necessary to post profits.[19]

After all, when's the last time you've looked forward to ads? (The Super Bowl doesn't count.)

Back in 2018, the writing was already on the wall—loud and clear. At the time, a *Forbes* article reported that TV ad spend was falling in the US while digital ad spend was climbing all the way to $107 *billion*:

---

18   Gerry Smith, "TV Networks Vowed to Cut Back on Commercials. Instead, They Stuffed in More," *Los Angeles Times*, August 3, 2019, https://www.latimes.com/business/story/2019-08-02/tv-networks-vowed-to-cut-back-on-commercials-instead-they-stuffed-in-more.

19   Blake Morgan, "What Is The Future Of Television?" *Forbes*, July 5, 2019, https://www.forbes.com/sites/blakemorgan/2019/07/05/what-is-the-future-of-television/?sh=585a5db559de.

< **26** Natalie Fragkouli & Liel Levy >

"Last year, TV ad spending in the US saw a first-time drop since 2009. With the double-digit growth of digital video, TV ad spend will continue to decline this year with TV's share of total US media ad spending dropping from 33.9 percent in 2017 to 31.6 percent."[20]

This was *before* Disney bought a controlling interest in Hulu, Disney Plus debuted, Apple TV+ launched, and a number of other streaming services made things even *more* difficult for TV stations.

THE IMMINENT DEATH OF RADIO

It looks as though radio is guaranteed the *same* fate for the *same* reason. As a post on *Digital Music News* proclaimed, the evidence is undeniable, "Radio Is Dead in 10 years."

...that was three years ago.

The summation of the article paints a stark picture:

"Young people have fled terrestrial radio. The medium now brings in less revenue than streaming platforms. People purchase smart speakers to listen to 'better music.'"[21]

The article, which looks at a study performed by Larry Miller, Director of NYU's *Steinhardt Music Business Program*, actually lists

---

20 Dana Feldman, "US TV Ad Spend Drops As Digital Ad Spend Climbs To $107B In 2018," *Forbes*, March 28, 2018, https://www.forbes.com/sites/danafeldman/ 2018/03/28/u-s-tv-ad-spend-drops-as-digital-ad-spend-climbs-to-107b-in -2018/?sh=2ebf3e157aa6.

21 Daniel Sanchez, "Radio Is Dead In 10 Years. This Study Proves It," *Digital Music News*, August 31, 2017, https://www.digitalmusicnews.com/2017/08/31/radio-dead -musonomics-study/.

< Meet the US Hispanics **27** >

eight compelling reasons radio is on its last legs.

One that is particularly interesting is that car manufacturers have begun to abandon radio:

> *"...Miller notes that in-car media screens allow easier access to platforms like Spotify, Pandora, and iTunes."*

In the actual report itself, he explains:

> *"AM/FM controls are often found below this screen, rendering them less prominent and less accessible than in the past."*

It doesn't bode well for radio that vehicles—one of the most common places for listening to radio—are beginning to phase out this technology.

HISPANICS ARE FLEEING TV AND RADIO

Even though it's clear that TV and radio are going the way of the dinosaurs, there still seems to be a lot of confusion over whether or not these mediums work well for engaging Hispanics.

That's because it's true that this market once *loved* both. We still hear this a lot from clients who are hesitant about making the jump to social and mobile marketing. There seems to be a stubborn belief that Hispanics have somehow remained impervious to the evolution of media consumption in this country. Despite what *literally* everyone else is doing, they're remaining loyal to outdated technology because...reasons?

To be fair, Hispanics were definitely among the last markets to switch over, although not by much. We'll cover this topic more

< **28** Natalie Fragkouli & Liel Levy >

in just a moment, but advances in technology have ensured this switch is permanent. If you're hanging on to the hope that your Hispanic market will return to their old listening habits, we have a bridge to sell you.

(**Note:** We don't actually have a bridge for sale. That was a joke. We *do* offer a number of helpful marketing services for law firms, though.[22] Those *are* real. We promise.)

Anyway, as recently as 2018, *Nielsen* reported that radio was *the* leading reach vehicle for both Hispanic and Black consumers.[23]

For proponents of radio ads, this has come as welcomed news. They interpret it to mean that you can continue relying on this medium *despite* the fact that every other demographic is leaving it behind.

However, this *Nielsen* report reveals an important truth that is all-too-often ignored by those who still think radio is a great medium for engaging Hispanics:

> "Black and Hispanic consumers are leading the way when it comes to interest in and adoption of both smart speakers and streaming services."[24]

For example, here's how Hispanic adoption rates compare to those of the White population:

22 "English and Spanish Online Strategies for Law Firms," *Nanato Media*, accessed May 27, 2020, https://nanatomedia.com/legal/bilingual-digital-marketing/.

23 "Audio Today 2018: A Focus on Black and Hispanic Audiences," The Nielsen Company, Summer 2018, https://www.nielsen.com/wp-content/uploads/sites/3/2019/04/audio-today-report-july-2018.pdf.

24 "Audio Today 2018: A Focus on Black and Hispanic Audiences," The Nielsen Company, Summer 2018, https://www.nielsen.com/wp-content/uploads/sites/3/2019/04/audio-today-report-july-2018.pdf.

< Meet the US Hispanics **29** >

- Percentage with smart speakers in the home:
  - Hispanic: 21 percent.
  - White: 18 percent.

- Percentage interested in smart speakers:
  - Hispanic: 45 percent.
  - White: 40 percent.

- Percentage using audio streaming services:
  - Hispanic: 58 percent.
  - White: 36 percent.

- Percentage interested in audio streaming services:
  - Hispanic: 35 percent.
  - White: 24 percent.

As you can see, the Hispanic market loves *listening* to content, which is why radio adoption remains high compared to other demographics.

BUT it's also why the Hispanic market is leading the way when it comes to adopting new technology for listening to content and, therefore, leaving radio behind.

Even more important, US Hispanics are fleeing TV at about the same rate:

"According [to] the survey of more than 1,000 Hispanic consumers in the US, both English and Spanish-speaking, digital audio is on par with digital video in terms of Hispanics' consumption. Indeed, an equal share

< **30** Natalie Fragkouli & Liel Levy >

(42 percent) of respondents said they spend at least six hours per week listening to digital audio and watching digital video. Overall, slightly more say they listen to digital audio on a weekly basis than they watch digital video each week."[25]

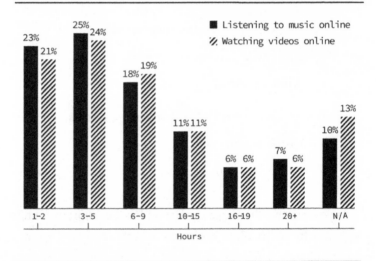

Hispanics' average time spent each week listening to music and watching videos online

■ Listening to music online

⁄, Watching videos online

Source: Marketing Charts, 2019

So, yes, Hispanics still watch TV and listen to the radio.

Many of them may still use fax machines or watch the occasional VHS. That doesn't mean either technology is worth your investment.

---

25 "US Hispanics Spend As Much Time Listening to Digital Audio as They Do Watching Digital Video," *Marketing Charts*, February 7, 2020, https://www.marketingcharts. com/demographics-and-audiences/hispanic-demographics-and-audiences-111824.

< Meet the US Hispanics **31** >

WHY DIGITAL MEDIA HAS BECOME THE BEST MEDIUM FOR MARKETING TO US HISPANICS

If you had an unlimited budget, we'd probably recommend you put some of it into TV and radio. While you're at it, you might as well pay door knockers to market your law firm. Hire one of those pilots to trail a banner with your number on it, too.

We're guessing your budget has a limit, though.

We're also guessing you'd like to make the most of it.

That's why we recommend focusing on digital media when allocating funds for marketing. This is good advice for *any* target market, but it turns out that Hispanic prospects are especially fond of digital media.

Just like we explored what *used* to work for this growing demographic, let's now look at why digital media is the present *and future* of marketing to Hispanics in the US.

HISPANICS ARE THE YOUNGEST ETHNIC GROUP IN THE COUNTRY

According to the US Census Bureau, the population of American Hispanics in 2017 was 58.9 million.[26] By 2030, that number is expected to reach 72 *million!* That's *a lot* of Americans, many of whom will someday need legal services.

But for the sake of *this* conversation, here's why those numbers are really, REALLY important to your law firm: Hispanics currently represent the youngest ethnic group in the country with a median age of just twenty-eight.[27]

---

26 "Hispanic Population to Reach 111 Million by 2060," *United States Census Bureau*, October 9, 2018, https://www.census.gov/library/visualizations/2018/comm/hispanic-projected-pop.html.

27 Mark Hugo Lopez, Jens Manuel Krogstad, and Antonio Flores, "Key Facts about Young Latinos," *Pew Research Center*, September 13, 2018, https://www.pewresearch.org/fact-tank/2018/09/13/key-facts-about-young-latinos/.

< **32** Natalie Fragkouli & Liel Levy >

Hispanic population to reach 111 million by 2060

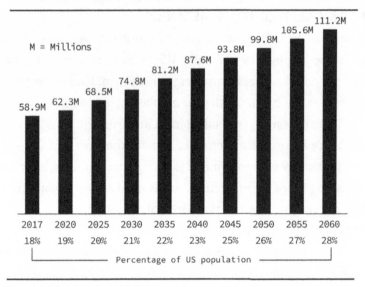

Source: US Census Bureau, 2017

About 6-in-10 Hispanics in the US are 35 or younger
% in each age group, by race/ethnicity

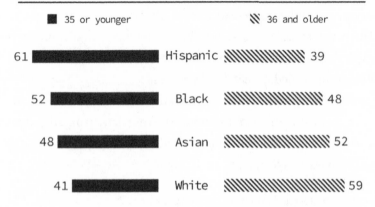

Note: Hispanics of any race. Black, Asian, and White are non-Hispanic, single race.

Source: Pew Research Center, 2016

< Meet the US Hispanics **33** >

That helps explain why this demographic has proven to be *so* comfortable adopting new technology. They're simply made up of much younger people than other ethnicities and, as we all know, young people love technology.[28]

Whereas an aging population may hurt your ability to market to other groups, that's not the case with American Hispanics as they skew so much younger. Not only is their population skyrocketing in size, but the majority of people in this group are millennials—a generation raised on Digital Age technology.

HISPANIC AMERICANS LOVE USING THE INTERNET TO FIND WHAT THEY NEED

Given the information in that last section, it should come as no surprise that Hispanic Americans are *very* comfortable going online to find the solutions they want for their problems.

eMarketer found as much when they recently did a survey that looked at the sources Hispanic internet users turn to when exploring solutions.[29] Here are the results:

- Search engines: 46 percent.

- Consumer reviews: 36 percent.

- Social networks: 32 percent.

- Product/brand sites: 28 percent.

---

28 Emily A. Vogels, "Millennials Stand out for Their Technology Use, but Older Generations Also Embrace Digital Life," *Pew Research Center*, September 9, 2019, https://www.pewresearch.org/fact-tank/2019/09/09/us-generations-technology-use/.

29 "What Sources Do US Hispanic Internet Users Use When Looking for Information About Brands, Products or Services?" *Insider Intelligence: EMarketer*, July 11, 2019, https://www.emarketer.com/chart/229970/what-sources-do-us-hispanic-internet-users -use-looking-information-about-brands-products-services-of-respondents-q1-2019.

< **34** Natalie Fragkouli & Liel Levy >

- Mobile apps: 21 percent.

- Price comparison websites: 21 percent.

- Discount voucher/coupon sites: 17 percent.

- Question & answer sites: 17 percent.

- Video sites: 16 percent.

- Forums/message boards: 13 percent.

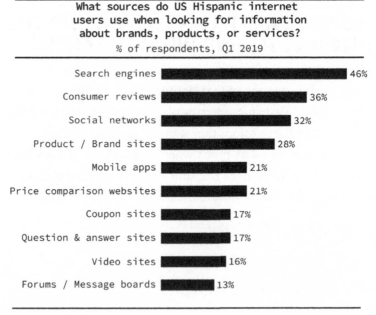

What sources do US Hispanic internet
users use when looking for information
about brands, products, or services?
% of respondents, Q1 2019

Search engines	46%
Consumer reviews	36%
Social networks	32%
Product / Brand sites	28%
Mobile apps	21%
Price comparison websites	21%
Coupon sites	17%
Question & answer sites	17%
Video sites	16%
Forums / Message boards	13%

Source: GlobalWebIndex, 2019

While search engines are still their favorite solution finders,
it's clear that Hispanic Americans are well aware of all their other
options. Some of these aren't realistic for your firm (e.g., discount
sites, forums, etc.), but this ought to serve as a reminder that

< Meet the US Hispanics **35** >

you *should* have a strategy for video marketing and social media, which we'll cover in more detail momentarily.

Furthermore, all of this information is more reason to sound the death knell for traditional media, at least as far as marketing your firm to Hispanics goes. This group has successfully transitioned to digital media, especially when it comes to searching for the solutions they need. They're not waiting for your law firm's television commercial or slowing down when they see your billboard anymore.

If they need a lawyer, they know where to look: online.

MOBILE DEVICES ARE EXTREMELY AFFORDABLE

With that being said, it's not just that Hispanics have embraced the internet and all the ways it helps them find what they want.

It's also that the *technology* required to do this has become significantly more affordable over the last ten years.

Again, not great news for traditional media. The combination of Hispanic Americans being comfortable using the internet *and* being able to afford the technology to access it means we're probably seeing the last days of television commercials and radio ads for this market.

Still, let's look at some numbers to see what has changed in recent years.

First, Hispanics use mobile devices *more* than other Americans:

"While non-Hispanics own more desktops, Hispanics have a higher rate of ownership of smartphones and tablets as opposed to non-Hispanics, according to a survey of 1,027 respondents for Specific Media and SMG Multicultural's Millward Brown survey. Three-quarters (77 percent) of the Hispanics surveyed owned a smartphone versus 70 percent of

< **36** Natalie Fragkouli & Liel Levy >

non-Hispanics, and 54 percent owned a tablet as opposed to 49 percent of non-Hispanics."[30]

Device ownership among total Hispanics

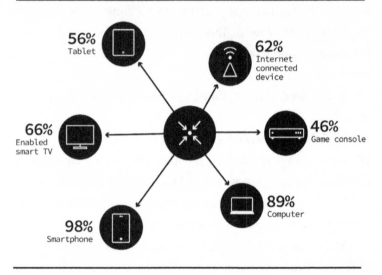

Source: Nielsen, 2020

Those are pretty significant differences, too.

With the population of Hispanic Americans growing, expect that number to continue rising in the years to come, as well.

Second, it's true that *new* smartphones have become more expensive over the past few years,[31] but it *isn't* true that these

---

30 Tanya Dua, "Hispanic Media Consumption, in 5 Charts," *Digiday*, March 16, 2015, https://digiday.com/marketing/hispanic-media-consumption-5-charts/.

31 Lisa Eadicicco, "Evidence Is Mounting That People Are Fed up with the Sky-High Cost of Smartphones, and It's Sparking a Massive Change in the Industry," *Business Insider*, December 12, 2019, https://www.businessinsider.com/ smartphone-cost-expensive-1000-apple-samsung-google-5g-change-2019- 12#smartphones-werent-always-so-expensive-1.

< Meet the US Hispanics **37** >

$1,000 phones are purchased by the majority of users. As *NPD* reported at the end of 2019:

> "...just under 10 percent of consumers are spending over $1,000 on their smartphones."[32]

As a result, manufacturers have responded by creating new mobile devices that cost less than their premium counterparts.[33] More and more people have also turned to the refurbished mobile device market for budget-friendly options.[34]

Still, this only tells half the story where Hispanic adoption rates are concerned. It's not just that there are more affordable mobile devices on the market. It's that these devices are lasting their users a lot longer, too.

Back in 2018, *NPD* released a report that showed people are keeping their smartphones longer than they used to for an average of *thirty-two months*.[35] So, when considering if they can afford

---

32 "Consumers in the Top 10 DMAs Account for More Than One-Third of $1,000+ Active Smartphones," *The NPD Group*, December 9, 2019, https://www.npd.com/wps/portal/npd/us/news/press-releases/2019/less-than-10-of-us-consumers-spend-over-1000-on-their-smartphones--according-to-npds-new-mobile-phone-tracking-service/.

33 Lisa Eadicicco, "Evidence Is Mounting That People Are Fed up with the Sky-High Cost of Smartphones, and It's Sparking a Massive Change in the Industry," *Business Insider*, December 12, 2019,https://www.businessinsider.com/smartphone-cost-expensive-1000-apple-samsung-google-5g-change-2019-12#5g-could-encourage-people-to-upgrade-but-for-a-high-price-3.

34 Joe Maring, "More People Are Buying Used/Refurbished Phones than Ever Before," *Android Central*, March 1, 2018, https://www.androidcentral.com/more-people-are-buying-usedrefurbished-phoneshttps://www.androidcentral.com/more-people-are-buying-usedrefurbished-phones-ever-ever.

35 "The Average Upgrade Cycle of a Smartphone in the US Is 32 Months, According to NPD Connected Intelligence," *The NPD Group*, July 12, 2018, https://www.npd.com/wps/portal/npd/us/news/press-releases/2018/the-average-upgrade-cycle-of-a-smartphone-in-the-u-s--is-32-months---according-to-npd-connected-intelligence/.

< **38** Natalie Fragkouli & Liel Levy >

a device—and not necessarily a new one—users are factoring in that their investment may last them nearly three years.

Finally, compare the price of owning a mobile device and a data plan to owning a TV with cable *and* the cost of in-home internet. The former option is clearly the more affordable one, which is why we're seeing such a sharp increase in Hispanic adoption while legacy media continues to wither as an effective marketing tool.

MOBILE DEVICES ALLOW FOR INDEPENDENT VIEWING

The ability to watch what they want—independent of what others around them are watching—is another key driver behind the adoption of mobile devices among Hispanic users.

The importance of cultural connection to the US Latinx

72% of Hispanics
and 75% of Hispanic households
speak Spanish at home

27% of US Hispanics
lived in multigenerational family
households in 2016

73% of US Hispanics
agree that it's important to them
that their children continue their
family's cultural traditions

73% of Hispanics
agree that their cultural-ethnic
heritage is an important part
of who they are

Source: Nielsen, 2018

< Meet the US Hispanics **39** >

That's because 27 percent of American Hispanics live in multigenerational homes.[36]

As you can imagine, different generations want to watch different things. This is only a problem, though, if the whole household is reliant on just one or two televisions.

Thanks to mobile devices, this is rarely the case anymore. Each household member can use their own mobile device to watch exactly what *they* want.

This is important because you may have two or three different Hispanic market segments under one roof, each of which may interact with your law firm on a different channel for a different reason.

It's also worth pointing out how these multigenerational environments spread technology adoption throughout the Hispanic community. It's not as though the younger generations simply sequester themselves with their devices. They're also showing the older generations how to use them. According to the *Nielsen* report we just linked to:

> "...the younger generations have much influence on older Hispanics. In fact, those fifty and older have become particularly tech-savvy, as they over-index non-Hispanic Whites by 36 percent for agreeing they like to have a lot of electronic gadgets, and by 28 percent for agreeing they often discuss their knowledge of technology or electronic products with others."[37]

---

36 "Descubrimiento Digital: The Online Lives of Latinx Consumers," The Nielsen Company, Summer 2018, https://www.nielsen.com/wp-content/uploads/sites/3/2019/04/the-online-lives-latinx-consumers.pdf.

37 "Descubrimiento Digital: The Online Lives of Latinx Consumers," The Nielsen Company, Summer 2018, https://www.nielsen.com/wp-content/uploads/sites/3/2019/04/the-online-lives-latinx-consumers.pdf, https://www.nielsen.com/wp-content/uploads/sites/3/2019/04/the-online-lives-latinx-consumers.pdf.

< **40** Natalie Fragkouli & Liel Levy >

This is just one more reason the Hispanic population in this country is fantastic for your law firm's online marketing strategy.

MOBILE DEVICES LEND THEMSELVES TO CROSS-SCREEN VIEWING

Another interesting concept that needs to be considered when exploring Hispanic media consumption is that of cross-screen viewing.[38]

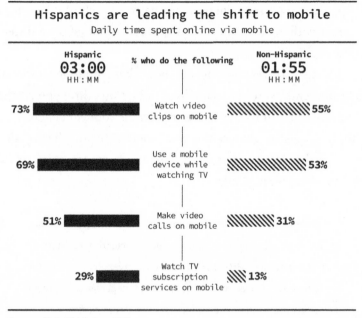

Source: GlobalWebIndex, 2018

Someone can have the TV on while still engaging with content on their mobile device. Chances are that you've done this before.

---

38 "The Media Consumption Habits of Hispanics in the USA," Global Web Index, 2018, https://ml.globenewswire.com/Resource/ Download/6ca74570-dd85-4126-b828-fcd6be0d96c0.

< Meet the US Hispanics **41** >

You might check your phone between innings, during commercials, or simply when the action on-screen slows down.

It turns out that Hispanic users are more likely to do this than the rest of the population. Sixty-nine percent of them report using a mobile device *while* they watch TV.[39] For non-Hispanic Americans, it's only 53 percent.

This might help to explain why Hispanic Americans also spend *way* more time using their mobile devices to access the internet every day (three hours) compared to everyone else (one hour, fifty-five minutes).

Thanks to cross-screen viewing, Hispanic prospects can engage with your law firm's marketing materials even if they're already watching TV.

THE RISE OF SOCIAL MEDIA

Finally, no discussion about Hispanic media consumption would be complete without touching on social media and, specifically, Facebook.

As we briefly mentioned earlier, your law firm needs a strategy for using social media to reach prospects, particularly if you plan to target the growing Hispanic market.

That's because, to put it simply, Hispanics *love* Facebook:

> "...Facebook is the number one go-to platform for US Hispanics'
>
> communication and 71 percent of respondents use Facebook to connect
>
> with loved ones every day. Nearly half (48 percent) of US Hispanics'

---

39 "The Media Consumption Habits of Hispanics in the USA," Global Web Index, 2018, https://ml.globenewswire.com/Resource/Download/6ca74570-dd85-4126-b828 -fcd6be0d96c0.

< **42**   Natalie Fragkouli & Liel Levy >

Facebook friends are family members, compared to 36 percent for the total population, the research found.

"Facebook and Facebook Messenger are also used as an alternative to calling cards to reach people both in and outside the US: 60 percent of US Hispanics use Facebook Messenger to talk with friends and family outside the US."[40]

Whereas Facebook has proven to be a fun, entertaining way for most Americans to share with their friends and family, the social media platform has functioned more as a utility for a large number of Hispanics.

Many have become internet-savvy *solely* so they can use Facebook as an affordable means of staying close with loved ones around the country or even loved ones in completely different countries.

Of course, Facebook may provide the incentive, but once Hispanics become comfortable using mobile devices to navigate the World Wide Web, it's not hard to see why TV and radio get left behind.

THE KEY TO MARKETING TO HISPANICS— REGARDLESS OF THE MEDIUM

By now, it might seem like digital media is a fail-safe option for targeting Hispanic prospects. Given the adoption rate and how enthusiastically Hispanic Americans use technology, it would be pretty difficult to waste money on digital ads, right?

Wrong.

---

40   "Digital Diversity: A Closer Look at US Hispanics," *Facebook IQ*, December 4, 2014, https://www.facebook.com/business/news/insights/ digital-diversity-a-closer-look-at-us-hispanics.

< Meet the US Hispanics **43** >

Very, *very* wrong.

The truth of the matter is that, yes, a lot of our clients come to us once they realize the well is running dry for radio and TV ads. At the same time, we hear from plenty of prospects who have invested in digital marketing but haven't seen impressive results from Hispanic prospects.

This is why understanding the Hispanic population and what makes it different from any other in the country is *crucial* to a successful ROI.

Among other things, Hispanic clients want to give their business to companies that *have proven* they understand their culture. They feel far more comfortable with these kinds of companies. You can probably assume that goes double for law firms, as comfort level is always important to people who are looking to hire an attorney.

The good news is that it's relatively easy to show Hispanic prospects that you respect their unique needs: use Spanish in your marketing materials.[41]

This is true even if you're targeting Nueva Latinas and Ambicultural Hispanics who tend to be bilingual or even favor English. Using Spanish in your marketing is seen as a sign of respect, a gesture that you're making the extra effort to single them out as a unique segment of the American population.

So, using Spanish is a great first step to winning the Hispanic market, but are you using it correctly?

Do you use the wording and expressions that the Hispanic niche in your market are using?

Do Hispanics see your ads and feel related or think that you just used Google translate?

---

41 "Why Law Firms Must Run Spanish Google Ads," *Nanato Media*, March 23, 2020.

< **44** Natalie Fragkouli & Liel Levy >

If your answers to the questions above are negative, you need help. Also, don't forget about Latinoamericana and Hispano groups. They are out there and need legal help, too. You have to make it easy for them to identify with your law firm.

Of course, many Nueva Latinas and Ambicultural Hispanics may also be looking for legal help on behalf of a family member who *only* speaks Spanish. If they see that your marketing materials aren't in Spanish or feel that their relatives would not be able to culturally relate with your law firm, they'll probably go looking for a different firm.

Neglect this distinction at your own risk.

In fact, we can almost guarantee that if you're targeting the Hispanic community and not seeing positive results, it's because you're only using English, using Spanish the wrong way, or you're not culturally identifying with this market. That's why, at Nanato Media, we don't just translate, we *trans-create* your law firm's message from one language to another.

SHOULD LAW FIRMS "CUT THE CORD" WHEN MARKETING TO US HISPANICS?

Despite everything we've just covered, we're not recommending you *completely* cut radio and television from your law firm's marketing budget.

However, if you are currently running TV and/or radio ads, we *would* highly recommend that you review the kinds of ROIs you've seen over the past few years. If you've noticed your returns are steadily dropping, it might be time to consider that it's not because you need to change up your ads. Instead, it might be time to change up your medium.

< Meet the US Hispanics **45** >

At the very least, start planning an exit strategy for putting more of your money into digital. For all the reasons we've covered here, television and radio are on their way out.

If you *aren't* currently running TV or radio ads for your law firm, we'd recommend you don't start. Unless you know that your particular segment of the Hispanic population is *especially* engaged by either medium in your local market, we don't think it's worth the investment. By the time you spend enough money to actually create ads, run them, and make any necessary modifications, you'll probably find you could have achieved the same results for a lot less by investing in digital marketing for your law firm.

Keep in mind that even if radio and television remain relevant for another ten years, they'll never be able to offer the kinds of hyper-specific targeting that social media ads do.[42] You can consistently improve your ROI by zeroing in more and more on the *exact* Hispanic buyer persona you want for your market.

OTT (over-the-top) content—the kinds that stream right to smart devices—provides similar opportunities.[43] As opposed to traditional television content, OTT allows for granular segmentation of your targeted buyers. So, if you want to continue advertising during television shows, OTT represents your best option for seeing returns.

---

42 Rebecca Riserbato, "What a Social Media Target Audience Is and How to Find It," *HubSpot Blog*, February 27, 2020, https://blog.hubspot.com/marketing/social-media-target-audience.

43 Mike Rowan, "Council Post: The State of OTT Advertising In 2020: Strong And Gaining Momentum," *Forbes*, April 21, 2020, https://www.forbes.com/sites/forbesagencycouncil/2020/04/21/the-state-of-ott-advertising-in-2020-strong-and-gaining-momentum/?sh=3fab21fe6037.

< PART 2 >

LEARN TO
PRIORITIZE

< CHAPTER 3 >

GETTING STARTED WITH YOUR HISPANIC MARKETING STRATEGY

Would it make life a lot easier if your law firm could effortlessly generate new clients on a regular basis?

(Hint: *yes*.)

Would it help profitability if you didn't have to spend so much money on acquiring these new clients?

(Again, the answer is yes.)

What if you could focus on clients who were also more than happy to market your firm to their friends and family? Would that help?

(You get the picture.)

Then, creating a marketing strategy *specifically* for your practice area's Hispanic population should be an absolute no-brainer. As marketers who specialize in these kinds of campaigns, we can assure you that if you don't make Hispanic prospects a priority, your competitors will.

That's why we've put together a comprehensive guide that will show you how to create a marketing strategy that ensures success with your local Hispanic market.

< **50** Natalie Fragkouli & Liel Levy >

THE BIGGEST MISTAKE FIRMS MAKE WHEN MARKETING TO HISPANICS

Many firms come to us after they've already struggled to engage their local Hispanic market. They don't need convincing that Hispanic clients are worth targeting with their ads. Their *real* challenge is that they simply don't know how.

Probably the biggest mistake we see these firms making is that they treat Hispanic as a highly specific label as opposed to an umbrella term.

This will absolutely doom your strategy to failure from the very beginning.

Imagine trying to target *everyone* in your market who needs a lawyer. This would include everyone who needs help setting up a will, people who have been convicted of a crime, those who are filing for divorce, and more.

It would be impossible! You simply can't use the same messaging with such a wide array of prospects.

The same holds true for the Hispanic market. There are different segments, each of which responds best to different types of ads.

In this section, we're going to cover strategies we *know* work for our partners, but it will help if you also take time to better understand the Hispanic market, so you can really key in on what *your* prospects respond to best.

< Learn to Prioritize **51** >

CHOOSING WHICH HISPANIC SEGMENTS MAKE THE MOST SENSE FOR YOUR LAW FIRM

Once you understand the five segments of the Hispanic market in the US,[44] you can start thinking about which ones make the most sense for your law firm.

Depending on where your firm practices, it might make sense to target more than one of these segments. In many cities, firms could effectively find clients among all five of them.

Whatever the case, you'll need to follow the three steps below to ensure you're putting your time and energy into strategies that will actually pay off.

1. CONSIDER WHAT YOUR BUDGET CAN REALISTICALLY SUPPORT

A big part of making sure your time and energy aren't going to waste is to first identify what your budget can actually support.

We've seen firms try to go after all five of those aforementioned segments in markets where this *could* have been realistic. The only problem was that their budgets just weren't up to tackling that big of a challenge.

That's why we are *so* adamant about starting with just one Hispanic segment. If you're practicing in New York City, Miami, Los Angeles, or another city with a large Hispanic population, you might even be able to justify two.[45]

---

44 "The 2020 Hispanic Market Report," *Claritas LLC*, September 17, 2020, https://claritas.com/resources/2020-hispanic-market-report/.

45 Jason Koebler, "11 Cities With the Most Hispanics," *US News & World Report*, December 18, 2019, https://www.usnews.com/news/slideshows/11-cities-with-the-most-hispanics.

< **52** Natalie Fragkouli & Liel Levy >

Even then, we often recommend that our partners start with just one. For many firms, successfully marketing to just one of these segments provides more than enough business. If nothing else, this simple approach will narrow your focus and improve your chances of success.

Furthermore, a *BIG* piece of successful PPC marketing is understanding how much your budget depends on the cost of your keywords.[46] If you practice in, say, New York City, you have a massive pool of Hispanic prospects.

At the same time, so do your competitors. Many of them probably focus solely on this market because of how large it is. As a result, those local keywords are going to cost more than they would in a city that doesn't have the same Hispanic population.

By starting out with just one segment, you're giving your budget the best chance of producing a profitable ROI. You can then use that added revenue to go after another segment.

Otherwise, it's just too easy for even a sizable budget to get spread too thin and limit what *could* have been fantastic returns.

2. GET CLEAR ABOUT THE ACTUAL SIZE OF YOUR PRACTICE AREA'S MARKET

This naturally leads us to our next essential step.

The reason this step comes second is because we want you to be 100 percent clear on what your law firm can really afford to spend. Once you have that hard number, you can start exploring your local Hispanic market.

Maybe you'll find that just a single segment is completely within your budget.

---

46   Erin Bell, "PPC Keyword Research Guide: How to Find the Words for Your Paid Search Campaigns," *WordStream*, April 20, 2020, https://www.wordstream.com/blog/ws/2013/11/21/ppc-keyword-research-guide.

< Learn to Prioritize **53** >

Great!

But what we want you to avoid at all costs (*literally*) is starting with assessing your local market because, if it is larger than you think, you might be tempted to increase the size of your budget beyond what is sensible.

Again, we're all about starting small and then scaling up to incredible returns.

What about the exact opposite problem?

What if you're in a practice area where there's a smaller population of Hispanic Americans?

That doesn't mean it's not worth marketing to them.

If anything, you might find that they become your best clients simply because your competitors either haven't considered them a reliable source of business or—just as likely in our experience—they simply don't know how to market to Hispanic Americans.[47]

The good news is that a PPC campaign is the fastest way to discover if your local Hispanic population is enough to justify a holistic marketing campaign for your firm.[48] Through the discovery process, you'll see just how often Hispanic Americans are looking for the kinds of services you offer.

3. COVERAGE REACH

This last step is just as important as the others, but it's one that most law firms completely overlook, even those that otherwise get the other two right.

By now, you're probably well aware of your firm's service area. You know which cities in your state you serve and which are just

---

47   "How Your Law Firm Can Get More Latino Clients," *Nanato Media*, May 30, 2019, https://nanatomedia.com/blog/three-tips-on-how-law-firms-can-get-more-latino-clients/.

48   "Why Law Firms Must Run Spanish Google Ads," *Nanato Media*, March 23, 2020, https://nanatomedia.com/blog/why-law-firms-must-run-spanish-google-ads/.

< **54** Natalie Fragkouli & Liel Levy >

too far away to generally make sense (much less *dollars and cents*).

Just like you can be tempted into straying from your budget, you might be tempted into expanding that area once you start building a PPC campaign. That's because you'll see just how far your ads could *immediately* reach. You might even find that just *a bit* outside your practice area, some of the keywords you want don't cost as much.

Granted, there are times when this might make sense (I won't make the joke again).

Maybe *just* outside your normal practice area is a sizable Hispanic population. Maybe you can also tell that they're not being actively targeted based on the costs-per-click you're seeing.[49] In other words, if you're willing to drive a few extra miles every week, you'll be sitting on your own personal goldmine.

In that case, fine. As long as it otherwise makes sense for your firm, go ahead and stretch that practice area a bit.

Another time it might pay off is if you know some of these peripheral practice areas are devoid of firms that offer *your* specialty.

Mass torts and other types of class action lawsuits are prime examples. You probably don't have a lot of competition throughout your entire state. More than likely, there are clusters of firms around the metropolitan areas that specialize in that kind of law. As such, firms in the rest of your state probably don't have an established local presence for handling these cases.

Provided you understand the intricacies of marketing to the different Hispanic segments, you could find yourself without any competitors for these valuable clients.

Roundup's many legal cases illustrate this kind of opportunity

---

49 "CPC: What Is Cost Per Click?" WordStream, accessed June 5, 2020, https://www.wordstream.com/cpc.

< Learn to Prioritize **55** >

perfectly.[50] If you have experience with Mass Torts, you could run PPC campaigns that speak to Hispanic workers who may have been affected by that company's products. You could then segment your campaign by demographics (gender, household income, etc.) to get even more specific with your ads.

Get in front of this market with these kinds of highly targeted campaigns—right at the *very top* of Google—and you can win their business before they even move down the page to where the local competitors are relegated.

With all that being said, these scenarios are the exceptions.

Usually, what you'll find is that cities outside of your normal practice area fall well within the reach of other firms. Those firms may understand those jurisdictions better—a *huge* competitive advantage, as you're probably well aware—and may have already spent years or even decades building their reputations. Even with a low CPC, targeting a Hispanic community in those cities that are otherwise out of your practice area probably isn't a winning cause.

This is another example of why it makes sense to start with a realistic PPC strategy that can get you some initial results. Once you've become the go-to law firm for Hispanics in your practice area, you can always branch out. You *might* even find that the only way to do this is by opening an entirely new branch.

---

50 Jef Feeley, Tim Loh, and Bloomberg, "Bayer May Pay $10 Billion to Settle Roundup Cancer Cases," *Fortune*, January 24, 2020, https://fortune.com/2020/01/24/bayer-pay-10-billion-roundup-cancer-cases-monsanto/.

< **56** Natalie Fragkouli & Liel Levy >

UNDERSTANDING ONE OF THE MOST IMPORTANT WAYS TO ENGAGE THE HISPANIC MARKET

Another big mistake we've seen a lot of law firms make when marketing to Hispanic populations is that they focus *solely* on their ads.

Of course, it's not bad to treat your ads as priorities. As we just covered in the last section, a lot of thought is required to see success.

And yet, Hispanic Americans—though *incredibly* active online—aren't so easily won over by standard marketing practices.[51]

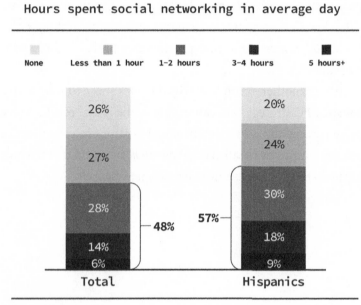

Hours spent social networking in average day

None   Less than 1 hour   1-2 hours   3-4 hours   5 hours+

Source: Nielsen, 2019

---

51   "Latinx Influencers: The Digital Community That Keeps Growing," The Nielsen Company, October 11, 2018, https://www.nielsen.com/us/en/insights/article/2018/latinx-influencers-the-digital-community-that-keeps-growing/.

< Learn to Prioritize **57** >

Instead, this is a population that places a huge emphasis on the importance of trust.[52] Obviously, as a lawyer, you know your clients have to completely trust you in order to do your job.

However, with Hispanic Americans, you have to earn that trust *long* before they become a client. You can start that process the moment they contact your law firm—which we'll cover in a moment—*but* we'd actually recommend you get started long before that point.

COMMUNITY ENGAGEMENT DOESN'T *HAVE* TO BE IN-PERSON

Recently, nationwide lockdowns were in place because of COVID-19, but we also know that many attorneys don't have enough time to regularly hold in-person events with their local Hispanic community.

Even if you think you could find time in your schedule, it may not be realistic to hold events throughout your entire practice area. If you practice in Houston, New York City, Miami, or other large metropolitan areas with equally sizable Hispanic populations, you could spend every weekend on outreach and still not get to everyone.

You may not have room in your budget for these kinds of activities, either. While the ROI of a successful event is always worth it, if funds are tight at the moment, the initial investment may be just out of your reach.

Don't worry!

Many law firms have enjoyed success without spending a single dime.

---

52 Glenn Llopis, "Earn the Trust of Hispanic Consumers and Your Brand Will Dominate," *Forbes*, April 2, 2012, https://www.forbes.com/sites/glennllopis/ 2012/04/02/earn-the-trust-of-hispanic-consumers-and-your-brand -will-dominate/?sh=4ac48dad42ad.

< **58**   Natalie Fragkouli & Liel Levy >

Instead, they set up Facebook Live events to both attract potential clients *and* build trust in the process.[53]

For example, if you're an immigration lawyer, you probably have plenty of prospects among your local Hispanic population. They may be immigrants themselves or they may be interested in helping family members emigrate to the US.

Either way, they probably also have a number of questions. What better way for them to get answers than by attending a Facebook Live event hosted by an attorney who specializes in this field?

You could give a presentation that covers the topics you know Hispanics are most curious about and then hold a Q&A session at the end.

Of course, you would also provide your contact information, should any of your participants decide they would like to move forward with a formal consultation.

It's that easy.

All you have to do is use a completely free social network, one that Hispanic people love,[54] do a short presentation on a subject that you're already an expert on, and then answer questions about that topic.

Consider, for a moment, how taking this kind of approach will position your law firm relative to the competition.

Before they ever step into your office, Hispanic prospects are able to become comfortable with you. You're not just making a quick introduction, either. Instead, you're taking the time to educate them on a legal topic of great importance *and* you're answering any questions they might have.

---

53   Margot Whitney, "The Ridiculously Awesome Guide to Facebook Live," *WordStream*, June 1, 2020, https://www.wordstream.com/blog/ws/2017/07/31/facebook-live-guide.

54   "Digital Diversity," *Facebook IQ*, December 4, 2014, https://www.facebook.com/business/news/insights/digital-diversity-a-closer-look-at-us-hispanics.

< Learn to Prioritize **59** >

There's the benefit of social proof, too.[55] As you get better and better at attracting people to your Facebook Live events, larger audiences will help instill *even more trust* in each of your Hispanic participants.

Your competitors, on the other hand, will continue to hope that Hispanic people—who value trust—will simply decide to walk into their office after just a brief phone call with their receptionist and open up to a total stranger.

...well, good luck to them.

Keep in mind there are also endless possibilities for your Facebook Live events.[56] You could team up with other professionals in the community to host regular roundtables covering topics you know are important to this population. You could also look for other community members who have their own followings and offer to join *their* events.

THREE WAYS TO BEGIN MARKETING YOUR FIRM TO HISPANIC CLIENTS

In this section, we want to pull together many of the points we've already covered into a step-by-step plan to start marketing your firm to Hispanic clients.

As we emphasized earlier, it's usually best to start small, but that *doesn't* mean you have to lower your expectations when it comes to results.

Just follow these three steps to create a powerful marketing strategy your law firm can rely on to generate Hispanic clients.

---

55 "The Ultimate Guide to Get Results With Social Proof Marketing," *AdEspresso*, October 18, 2018, https://adespresso.com/blog/how-to-create-social-proof/.

56 Leslie Green, "7 Creative Ideas for Your Next Facebook Live Event," *HubSpot*, May 6, 2020, https://blog.hubspot.com/marketing/ideas-for-facebook-live.

< **60**   Natalie Fragkouli & Liel Levy >

1. START WITH YOUR FIRM'S
CURRENT LEVEL OF EXPERIENCE

Many of you have probably had Hispanic clients before, especially if you live in cities with at least an average-sized population. Maybe they even represent a decent percentage of your firm's ongoing business.

In that case, the first step to greater success is to get exact with your efforts and really target one specific market. You'll want to review the traits that characterize each of the five unique Hispanic segments:

- Latinoamericana.
- Nueva Latino.

- Hispano.
- Ambicultural.

- Americanizado.

Focus on one that best fits your firm's current goals and start revising your marketing strategy accordingly.

If you haven't had a lot of experience serving Hispanic clients, that's okay. You just need to begin surveying the segment that's present in your practice area. Then, engage with them on their terms to build trust, as we've covered above, and develop your reputation as an authoritative lawyer who understands this community.

2. CONSIDER THE SIZE OF YOUR LOCAL MARKET

As we touched on earlier, your local market could be huge, or it might be relatively small. Either way, there's potential you shouldn't leave untapped.

You also shouldn't assume that the market is already "owned" by other firms. While it's true that other firms may already market to the Hispanic population, their attempts are probably leaving

< Learn to Prioritize **61** >

a lot of room for improvement. In our experience, most firms just don't understand American Hispanics, even if they want this market's business.

If you are in one of these larger metropolitan areas where other firms are actively targeting Hispanic prospects, you can still find success by getting even *more* specific with your campaigns. For example, if your law firm is in Houston, you could start by narrowing your campaigns to specific neighborhoods, like Denver Harbor, Magnolia Park, or Houston Heights.

Keeping it to just one neighborhood would also make it easier to hold in-person events or simply attend those being held by other groups. Add an omnichannel strategy to the mix and you have a recipe for winning over a large population of Hispanic prospects for your law firm.[57]

That's just one example.

You also need to remember that markets with large Hispanic populations could include several different backgrounds for Hispanos and Latinoamericanos. As such, you should decide to focus on just one segment and create highly relevant messages and branding for that particular community.

For instance, if you practice in Miami, there's a large population of Hispanics. Most of these people identify as Cuban. However, there is a growing Colombian community, too. You could choose this smaller market to start with and craft a message and brand more personal to them. You could invest in becoming a spokesperson to address their unique concerns.

Of course, this needs to look natural and not forced.

Whatever the case, a holistic marketing strategy that *proves*

---

57   Ted Vrountas, "How to Plan and Create the Perfect Omnichannel Marketing Strategy," *Instapage*, July 1, 2020, https://instapage.com/blog/what-is-omnichannel -marketing.

< **62** Natalie Fragkouli & Liel Levy >

you are dedicated to helping members of the Hispanic community will ensure you stand out. The vast majority of the time, they're used to seeing generic lead-generation tactics that could just as easily be aimed at any other population with a few minor tweaks. Unfortunately, this is easily recognizable and even easier to ignore.

3. LEVERAGE YOUR SPANISH-SPEAKING STAFF

Last but not least, one step we can't emphasize enough is leveraging any Spanish-speaking staff you have to make the best possible first impression with your Hispanic prospects.

In fact, we'd even recommend you prioritize bilingual candidates when hiring for lawyers, paralegals, and receptionists. That's how big a difference it can make when it comes to making your Hispanic prospects comfortable enough to become clients.

Most marketers who fail with this population do so because they fail to make this connection.

Consider the following statistics about the importance of Spanish to American Hispanics:[58]

- Eighty percent of US Hispanics don't feel they need to stop speaking Spanish to be part of the American culture.

- Eighty-six percent of respondents believe the Spanish language helps them remain connected to their culture.

- Ads targeting Hispanics in Spanish significantly increase their interest in purchasing products.

- When online, more than 80 percent of Spanish-dominant

---

58 "Is Marketing In Spanish Still Relevant To Hispanics?" *Forbes*, April 4, 2017, https://www.forbes.com/sites/onmarketing/2017/04/04/ is-marketing-in-spanish-still-relevant-to-hispanics/?sh=633fbffb7c36.

< Learn to Prioritize **63** >

Hispanics use Spanish at least half of the time when they read, write, or watch videos.

- Seventy-nine percent of Spanish-dominant, 82 percent of bilingual, and 60 percent of English-dominant Hispanics surveyed on this research think brands should reach out to consumers in both English and Spanish.

- Fifty-eight percent of Spanish-dominant Hispanics and 48 percent of bilingual Hispanics think that brands that reach out to the segment in Spanish demonstrate they value the Hispanic community.

This is why we always endorse taking a bilingual approach to ads.

It's *also* why we advise law firms to have Spanish-speaking staff members who can provide a seamless experience after prospects see those ads and then visit your office. When Spanish-speaking clients don't feel understood or struggle to communicate with their legal team, they feel an intense sense of disconnection.

That's never a good thing.

Furthermore, having bilingual team members who can communicate in Spanish with members of your local Hispanic community will help you gain valuable insights into your market, including their unique needs and concerns. Ideally, you should employ people who mirror the population you're looking to serve.

Remember, Latinos are a diverse group. There are Mexicans, Dominicans, Salvadorans, Puerto Ricans, and many, many more. If you plan to focus on one of these markets, employ people from diverse Hispanic backgrounds, too. You want your prospects to see *themselves* in every level of your staff.

< CHAPTER 4 >

WHY YOUR LAW FIRM SHOULD OPT FOR PPC BEFORE SEO

There's no question that your law firm needs online traffic. Instead, the question is, "How should you attract it?" And the answer for your law firm is PPC.

Every modern law firm needs an equally modern approach to attracting new business.

This means—unless you specialize in representing the Amish—you need to market your firm online.

Unfortunately, far too many lawyers rely solely on organic traffic to keep their schedules full. They spend countless hours and dollars on creating content that they hope will win Google's favor.

Eventually, they'll spend even more hours and dollars on trying to figure out why this proven approach didn't work.

Perhaps this sounds familiar?

Save yourself the time, money, and disappointment that goes along with trying to market your legal services solely through SEO.

Instead, invest in PPC marketing for your law firm and enjoy faster results.

< **66** Natalie Fragkouli & Liel Levy >

THE VERDICT IS IN: EIGHT REASONS PPC MARKETING FOR LAW FIRMS BEATS SEO

Don't fall for the fallacy that the frustrating path to the top of Google's organic rankings is the *only* way your firm can attract consistent business.

The truth is that the far easier way to reach that goal is by leveraging the many benefits of law firm PPC (pay-per-click) marketing.[59] Here are eight reasons successful law firms already are.

1. START SEEING RESULTS ASAP

As a lawyer, you know all about waiting around. Whether it's waiting to hear back from opposing counsel, when your court date will be, or what the judge or jury has decided, patience isn't just a virtue for attorneys. It's a requirement for the job.

Yet, if you've ever had to wait around for SEO results, you've probably felt that trait tested.

For those who are trying to choose between law firm PPC and SEO strategies, here's what a *Search Engine Journal* article had to say about how long SEO takes to work to give you some idea of what to expect:

> "You need to be prepared to invest several months to a year before seeing results from your SEO efforts, but even then, you won't be king of the hill. In fact, according to a comprehensive statistical analysis by Tim Soulo,

---

59 Daniel Gilbert, "What Is PPC & How Paid Search Marketing Works," *Search Engine Journal*, March 18, 2019, https://www.searchenginejournal.com/ppc-guide/what-is-ppc-paid-search/.

< Learn to Prioritize **67** >

only 5.7 percent of all newly published pages will get to Google's top ten within a year."[60]

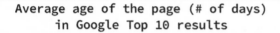

Average age of the page (# of days) in Google Top 10 results

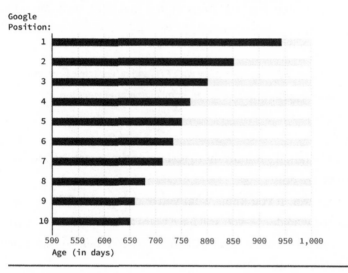

Source: Ahrefs, 2020

Eh, what's a year?

You don't mind waiting that long, right?

Or maybe even longer?

Of course, even after you begin seeing results, that doesn't mean those results will start paying for themselves. It could still be months, another year, or even longer before you *finally* see a positive ROI for your efforts.

---

60 Jeremy Knauff, "How Long Does SEO Take?" *Search Engine Journal*, June 6, 2020, https://www.searchenginejournal.com/seo-101/how-long-seo-takes/.
Tim Soulo, "How Long Does It Take to Rank in Google? (A Study by Ahrefs)," *Ahrefs*, August 6, 2020, https://ahrefs.com/blog/how-long-does-it-take-to-rank/.

< **68** Natalie Fragkouli & Liel Levy >

So, if you have a year—or *many*—to kill and you absolutely hate money, it's worth considering SEO for your law firm.

On the other hand, you could invest in the quick turnaround times of PPC.

How quick?

Here's what world-famous digital marketer, Neil Patel, had to say about the effectiveness of PPC ads:

> "If you know what you're doing with PPC and target active keywords,
> you'll see traffic increases almost immediately after you set your
> bid prices."[61]

To be fair, it's important to recognize the caveat, "if you know what you're doing."

However, if you know what you're doing with SEO—or hire someone who does—you still have years ahead of you. Work with someone who understands PPC, and you could *literally* have new clients by the next day.

2. NO LONG-TERM COMMITMENTS

Because PPC marketing for law firms doesn't take years to show results, agencies don't insist on long-term commitments. They know their clients are going to be happy and will want to secure their services again and again.

Most SEO agencies can't afford to let their clients decide on a monthly basis if it's worth it to keep working with them. Instead, they'll generally require a six-month contract—maybe longer.

---

61   Neil Patel, "How Long Does It Take to See Digital Marketing Results?" *LinkedIn*,
     September 2, 2016, https://www.linkedin.com/pulse/
     how-long-does-take-see-digital-marketing-results-neil-patel/.

< Learn to Prioritize **69** >

They know they'll need that much time to show their clients results.

One more time, here's Google's Maile Ohye explaining how long it will take an SEO agency to deliver:

> "In most cases, SEOs need four months to a year to help your business first implement improvements and then see potential benefit."[62]

So, imagine signing one of these long-term contracts only to finally realize by the *fourth month* that you're probably *not* going to make your money back.

As a lawyer, you probably don't need to be reminded about the power of contracts. You'll either need to keep paying the SEO agency—even after you've given up all hope that they'll be successful—*or* break the contract for a sizable fee.

With law firm PPC, you can stop whenever you like. If you decide to hire another PPC agency, they can start showing you results again right away. As long as you hire a PPC agency that specializes in helping law firms, they can begin targeting those high-intent users from day one. As long as the experience is there, you don't have to wait to see results.

It's not like with an SEO agency, which would need to backtrack and start over before they could build on any past results. Even those that are experienced at working with law firms can't replicate the kind of early success you'd see with a qualified PPC agency.

---

62 Google Search Central, "How to Hire an SEO," YouTube video, 01:41, February 14, 2017, https://www.youtube.com/watch?v=piSvFxV_Mo4.

< **70** Natalie Fragkouli & Liel Levy >

3. PPC ADS CAN TARGET PROSPECTS WHO
ARE READY TO BECOME CLIENTS

Another big, *BIG* problem with SEO is that it inevitably attracts a lot of tire kickers, the kinds of people who will come to your law firm's website, maybe take a look around, and then move on.

When this happens once, you hardly notice.

When it happens a dozen times a month, it becomes *extremely* annoying.

When it gets to the point that the *vast majority* of your traffic clearly never has any intention of ever becoming one of your clients, you might as well just take your money and strap it to fireworks. That will be a *much* more entertaining way of watching it go up in flames.

Unfortunately, there's not a whole lot you can do when you rely on SEO. The traditional marketing funnel is integral to the way this approach works.[63] It consists of four stages:

- Awareness of the problem.

- Interest in the potential solution.

- Consideration of *your* solution.

- Conversion into a customer.

This is *highly* effective for a lot of businesses.

Law firms *are not* one of them.

You do not want—nor can you afford—to spend money on creating content that merely makes prospects *aware* of their problem.

Your prospects—the kinds who are actively searching for a lawyer—already know what their problem is. They've been

---

< Learn to Prioritize **71** >

charged with a crime. They want a divorce. They are interested in setting up a trust. They just got into a car accident and know they need a personal injury lawyer.

What they really want is just to speak with an attorney who can help them.

The "interest" stage is equally irrelevant to law firms. Your prospects already know they need an attorney. They're past that stage the moment they turn to Google.

You want prospects who are hoping they can speak with an actual attorney *today*.

PPC marketing lets law firms catch prospects at this all-important stage. You pick the keywords related to the services you offer and that reflect buyer intent.[64] Then, you just create ads that speak *only* to those who are ready to become clients.

As we've previously shown, you can even use PPC ads to target Spanish speakers or any other demographic who falls within your market.[65]

It's this kind of hyper-focused targeting that makes the approach so powerful. Consider these statistics about the effectiveness of PPC for further proof:[66]

- PPC visitors are 50 percent more likely to buy than organic visitors.

- Sixty-five percent of all high-intent searches result in an ad click.

---

64   Dan Shewan, "Commercial Intent: How to Find Your Most Valuable Keywords," *WordStream*, August 28, 2019, https://www.wordstream.com/blog/ws/2014/06/30/commercial-intent-keywords.

65   "Why Law Firms Must Run Spanish Google Ads," *Nanato Media*, March 23, 2020, https://nanatomedia.com/blog/why-law-firms-must-run-spanish-google-ads/.

66   "SEO vs. PPC: Which Should You Focus on First?" *Quicksprout*, August 9, 2017. https://www.quicksprout.com/seo-vs-ppc-which-one-should-you-focus-on-first/.

< **72** Natalie Fragkouli & Liel Levy >

- Search ads increase brand awareness by as much as 80 percent.

- Thirty-two percent of companies use PPC to sell products directly to consumers.

- On average, businesses earn $3 for every $1.60 spent on AdWords.

That last statistic represents nearly a *2x ROI!* How many other investments can report the same thing?

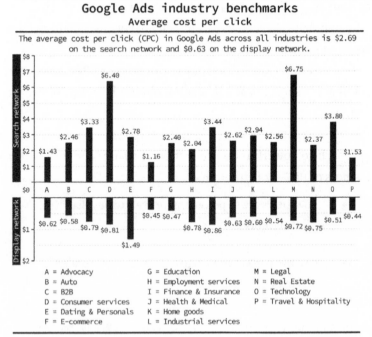

Google Ads industry benchmarks
Average cost per click

The average cost per click (CPC) in Google Ads across all industries is $2.69 on the search network and $0.63 on the display network.

A = Advocacy
B = Auto
C = B2B
D = Consumer services
E = Dating & Personals
F = E-commerce

G = Education
H = Employment services
I = Finance & Insurance
J = Health & Medical
K = Home goods
L = Industrial services

M = Legal
N = Real Estate
O = Technology
P = Travel & Hospitality

Source: WordStream, 2020

< Learn to Prioritize **73** >

4. YOU GET TO CONTROL YOUR CPA
(GOOGLE WILL ACTUALLY SHOW YOU HOW)

When *Thomson Reuters* conducted their annual State of US Small Law Firm Survey for 2019, they found that 28 percent of respondents said that *the most* significant obstacle to their success was, "Challenges acquiring new client business."[67]

However, "cost control and expense growth" clearly kept a lot of lawyers awake at night, too. Forty-five percent of respondents reported that one of the reasons they recently made a major change was to reduce costs.

With law firm PPC, you can kill both birds with one stone.

As we just covered, it's one of the absolute best ways to acquire clients. That kind of targeting, alone, will help lower your acquisition costs. No more wasting time on prospects who love free information but aren't so fond of paying for your services.

Even better is that law firm PPC makes it easy to lower your cost-per-acquisition (CPA) dramatically.[68] In fact, Google will basically reward you with lower overhead for improving your ability to effectively acquire clients.

Try to think of another channel where that's the case.

If you buy space on a billboard, bus bench, or some other public area, you might get a discount for buying in bulk, but that's about it. You're still going to significantly increase your overhead as you buy more space. *And* the vast majority of people who see those ads will never even become customers.

Remember, with PPC marketing for law firms, you *only* pay when an interested party clicks your ads.

---

67 "2019 State of US Small Law Firms Report," *Legal Executive Institute* (Thomson Reuters), accessed January 17, 2021, http://ask.legalsolutions.thomsonreuters.info/ LEI_2019_SmallLaw_State_of_Legal_Mkt_PR.

68 "What Is Cost Per Acquisition (CPA)? (Updated for 2019)," *BigCommerce*, accessed June 5, 2020, https://www.bigcommerce.com/ecommerce-answers/ what-is-cost-per-acquisition-cpa-what-is-benchmark-retailers/.

< **74** Natalie Fragkouli & Liel Levy >

The way you're able to lower your CPA with Google Ads is through its Quality Score.[69] As a smart attorney like yourself has probably already ascertained, the Quality Score is designed to measure the *quality* of your ads.

The better your ads are, the more clicks you'll get, and the more Google will make.[70] So, the better your PPC agency is at selecting keywords, homing in on ad relevancy, creating high-quality landing pages, and then revising those ads over and over, the more clicks you'll get, which means more opportunities for Google to make a buck.

Ergo, they have a *very* vested interest in your law firm's PPC ads being as successful as possible. Google will even go so far as to lower your CPC (cost-per-click), which, in turn, means a lower CPA.[71]

That kind of feedback is also a very underappreciated reason to choose PPC marketing for your law firm instead of SEO. Google doesn't give you scores where your site's SEO is concerned. It's 100 percent up to you to figure out if you're making the right changes to it. In fact, arguably the *only* feedback Google gives you is your organic ranking.

That's not very reassuring, though.

In short, Google wants you to figure out SEO on your own, through trial and very, *very* costly error. However, it's more than happy to let you know whether or not your ads will lead to lower CPAs.

---

69 "What Is Quality Score & How Does It Affect Google Ads?" WordStream, accessed June 5, 2020, https://www.wordstream.com/quality-score.

70 "Improve Your Website's Quality Score," *Google Ads*, accessed June 5, 2020, https://ads.google.com/intl/en_uk/home/resources/improve-quality-score/.

71 Larry Kim, "How to Reduce Your Cost Per Conversion by 16-80% (Sorry, Haters, Quality Score Still Matters)," *WordStream*, May 28, 2019, https://www.wordstream.com/blog/ws/2013/07/16/quality-score-cost-per-conversion.

< Learn to Prioritize **75** >

Finally, when it comes to this point, another advantage of using law firm PPC is that you'll constantly be working to improve the *same* group of ads. Unless you decide to practice a new kind of law or a completely different demographic, you'll eventually have general ad types you run over and over.

There might be a dozen of them.

There might be two dozen.

But, once you have them, they're all you need to worry about. Keep focusing on improving their quality score and watch your acquisition rates improve while your CPA drops.

With SEO, you *constantly* need to come up with new types of content. As we touched on above, there's no end to adding the content on your site. According to many content marketing experts who specialize in organic traffic, this means *multiple blog posts a week.*[72]

Aside from the time and money that will take, there's also the frustration of coming up with new types of content over and over *and over*.

Or, you know, you could just stick to the same ads, year after year, and watch new clients roll in.

That's a tough one.

5. PPC ADS GET RIGHT IN FRONT OF MOBILE USERS

Nowadays, marketing your law firm online means marketing it to mobile users.

Aside from the fact that the majority of people access the web through their mobile devices,[73] Google has been giving priority to

---

72 Kayla Carmicheal, "How Often Should You (or Your Company) Blog? [New Data],"
HubSpot, August 3, 2020, https://blog.hubspot.com/marketing/
blogging-frequency-benchmarks.

73 "Mobile Vs. Desktop Internet Usage (Latest 2020 Data)," *BroadbandSearch*, accessed
June 5, 2020, https://www.broadbandsearch.net/blog/
mobile-desktop-internet-usage-statistics.

< **76** Natalie Fragkouli & Liel Levy >

mobile-friendly sites in their search results since 2015, regardless of what the searcher is using.[74]

If that's not enough, mobile users make some of the best prospects. According to a nationwide study done by *Bloomberg* in 2018, the power of mobile marketing seems almost too good to be true:

> "When done well, mobile advertising can drive recall, clicks and
> eventually purchases. Two thirds of consumers can recall a specific
> brand they have seen advertised on mobile in the last week, 60 percent
> click on mobile ads at least weekly, and 20 percent make weekly
> purchases based off digital ads."[75]

This isn't just great for prospects who see your PPC ads when they're in need of a lawyer. Think about all the people who will see your ads and recall them later when one of their loved ones requires your help. That improved recall level could pay dividends for your law firm.

It gets even better, though.

For one thing, your paid ad will appear right at the top of a user's search results. On a mobile phone, this will take up the majority of the screen—no room for your poor competitors who are still relying solely on SEO.

But it gets *even better than that!*

With Google Ads, you can actually run call-only ads, so mobile

---

74 Winkler, Rolfe. "Google Gives Boost to Mobile-Friendly Sites." *The Wall Street Journal*, April 21, 2015, https://www.wsj.com/articles/ google-gives-boost-to-mobile-friendly-sites-1429660022.

75 "Opt-In Video Advertising Is Preferred Ad Choice for Consumers According to New Nationwide Survey; Adoption May Deter Ad," *Bloomberg*, July 26, 2018, https://www. bloomberg.com/press-releases/2018-07-26/ opt-in-video-advertising-is-preferred-ad-choice-for-consumers-according-to-new-nationwide-survey-adoption-may-deter-ad-jk2t3rsx.

< Learn to Prioritize **77** >

users just have to tap their screen to immediately start speaking with someone at your firm.[76]

That's a supercharged call-to-action that will help you get more clients *and* get them sooner. They don't have to navigate to your page to try to find your number or fill out a form. When someone needs to speak to an attorney right away, it doesn't get much better than a one-click call option right from their phone.

6. ORGANIC TRAFFIC IS *EXTREMELY* COMPETITIVE FOR LAW FIRMS

By now, we've brought up *numerous* times just how hard it is to get on the first page of Google if you don't plan to use law firm PPC.

However, it actually gets worse.

Here's what no SEO specialist wants to tell their clients: if your website doesn't show up *in the top five* search results on the first page of Google, you might as well not be on the first page at all.

Most people just don't scroll down that page past the fifth result. After you take out searchers who will simply try a new term and those who will click on our beloved ads, the first page of Google looks like this:

"On the first page alone, the first five organic results account for 67.60 percent of all the clicks and the results from six to ten account for only 3.73 percent."[77]

Ouch.

---

76 Brad Smith, "The Definitive Guide to Google's Call-Only Ads," *AdEspresso*, January 22, 2018, https://adespresso.com/blog/guide-googles-call-only-ads/.

77 Cliff Sarcona, "Organic SEO vs PPC in 2020: CTR Results & Best Practices," Zero Limit Web, March 7, 2020, https://www.zerolimitweb.com/organic-vs-ppc-2020-ctr-results-best-practices/.

< **78**   Natalie Fragkouli & Liel Levy >

So, it's not enough to work for the first page of Google. You *really* need to work to beat out *all* the competition and make it to the top five.

Detractors may try to point out that paid ads "only" get 15 percent of the total first-page traffic, *but* keep in mind that you're not paying for anyone who doesn't click. You get the benefit of being at the very top of Google—above *all* organic results—without making the same investment of time and money as those below you.

More importantly, 15 percent is *multiple times* more than most other law firms relying on SEO can ever hope to get.

And as we pointed out in the first section, you don't need to wait to start seeing results. There's no four-to-six-month timeline (if you're lucky) before you get on the first page (if you're even luckier) much less in the top five (*insanely* lucky).

All of a sudden, that 15 percent looks incredible for your business.

As you probably know, competition is one of the biggest challenges facing law firms like yours.[78] It doesn't look like that's going to change anytime soon, either.

If you're trying to fight all of those competitors in Google's organic search results, you're fighting a losing battle. Even if you're currently at the top, you'll need to keep spending more and more to stay there.

Utilize PPC marketing for your law firm and immediately start skipping the line *right to the top* of Google where prospects are clicking to become clients.

---

78   "Top 5 Challenges Facing Law Firms Today," *Legalinc*, February 15, 2019, https://legalinc.com/blog/top-5-challenges-that-firms-face-today/.

< Learn to Prioritize **79** >

7. IF YOU DON'T RUN BRAND-NAME PPC ADS, YOUR COMPETITORS WILL

How would you like to stand outside your biggest competitor's door and hand your card to all their potential clients before they step inside?

You never would, of course.

You're too busy and you're probably above that sort of thing anyway.

But it would be fun, right?

After all, you can wish their firm well without actually wishing they do better than yours.

While it's not realistic to do this kind of thing in real life—unless, of course, you have interns—Google is actually 100 percent fine with you doing it.

That's right.

You can run law firm PPC ads that focus on your competitors' brand names.[79]

For example, say the firm of "Hook & Crook" is currently winning the war for your market share. You'd definitely want to use PPC marketing for your law firm to focus on the kinds of terms your demographic searches for when they need your services.

If that's *all* you do, you should look forward to improving your client acquisition rate for all the reasons we've already covered.

But why not have a little fun with Hook & Crook?

You can target that firm's official name and any derivatives that you know their prospects often use.

Now, when those potential clients conduct their searches, your ad can show up right at the top of the page. You can address

---

79   Matt LaMontagne, "How to Run a Successful Competitor-Focused Paid Campaign," *Search Engine Watch*, June 26, 2019, https://www.searchenginewatch.com/2019/06/26/competitor-focused-paid-campaign-tips/.

< **80**   Natalie Fragkouli & Liel Levy >

the services *you know* those prospects need while also referencing what makes your firm the better choice.

In other words, you can wait right outside their virtual door and hand out your business card.

Of course, turnabout is fair play.

One or more of your competitors may be doing the exact same thing to your firm right now. That's why you also need to use law firm PPC to protect your brand. As we've advised before:

> "Set up a branding campaign on Google Ads. Don't just add your brand name to the keywords of a general campaign, as that could eat the budget of other ads targeting high-intent users. Because of relevancy, your branding campaigns should have a high clickthrough rate and therefore cost you less than they would for another law firm. Monitor the campaigns' performance and make sure you are showing up at the top of the page, and adjust your budget until you can secure that top-of-page positioning."[80]

Maybe you don't have any competitors who are getting enough traffic from Google that it would be worth using branded campaigns to market your firm to their prospects.

Fine.

However, that doesn't mean they feel the same way about you. Use PPC ads to make sure you're playing defense, so your firm's hard-earned popularity isn't putting money in a competitor's pockets.

---

80   "How to Protect Your Law Firm's Brand Name Using Google Ads," *Nanato Media*, August 6, 2019, https://nanatomedia.com/blog/how-to-protect-your-law-firms -brand-name-using-google-ads/.

< Learn to Prioritize **81** >

8. PPC ADS ARE ESSENTIAL FOR
GAINING AND GROWING YOUR TRAFFIC

And finally, our eighth reason you should be investing in PPC marketing for your law firm is that it is the best possible way to build traffic for your site.

For those of you who may have very little—or even *no*—traffic at the moment, we just covered why law firm PPC is essential for changing that. Instead of a slow, laborious, and expensive climb to the top of Mt. Google, you can enjoy an effortless ride in a cable car called PPC, one that will actually put you *above* the top organic results right away.

It's 100 percent realistic to say you could start seeing your first qualified visitors within a week—maybe even the same day.

Okay, so that's your initial traffic taken care of, but what about those of you who are already attracting visitors?

Maybe you are one of the few firms that has made it to the top five for relevant search terms.

Maybe you've successfully used social media to attract visitors.

Maybe your billboards or bus signs have brought them.

Whatever the case—no matter how much traffic you're currently attracting—PPC ads can not only increase that amount *but* improve your conversion rates, too.

This is possible through the magic of retargeting ads.[81]

Before I delve into the details, do you mind if I knock SEO *one more* time?

One more and then I'm done—promise.

Thank you.

---

81 Fahad Muhammad, "Retargeting 101: Get Started and Achieve Greater ROI," *Instapage*, July 1, 2020, https://instapage.com/blog/what-is-retargeting.

< **82** Natalie Fragkouli & Liel Levy >

When you rely on SEO for lead generation, "Approximately 96 percent of visitors that come to your website are not ready to buy."[82]

Recall how hard it was to get to the top of Google and then how little traffic you could expect from those efforts. *Now*, factor in that harrowing statistic.

Yes!

Just as a reminder from the third section: "PPC visitors are 50 percent more likely to buy than organic visitors."

Again, that's because PPC ads are so effective at targeting qualified traffic and not tire kickers who aren't even sure what they need yet.

Anyway, as I was saying, retargeting ads are a specific type of paid traffic that retarget people who have already come to your website.

This could include prospects who are among that 96 percent of visitors who come to your site but don't end up becoming clients right away.

Tracking pixels "follow" them, so when they go to other sites that support display ads in the network you're using (e.g., Google Display Network,[83] Facebook,[84] etc.), advertisements for your firm pop up.

As a result, you stay top of mind and give prospects who have already shown interest in your firm another chance to pay your site a visit. You could also have the ad bring them to a

---

82 "Website and SEO for Lead Generation," *Marketo*, accessed June 5, 2020, https://www.marketo.com/ebooks/website-and-seo-for-lead-generation/.

83 "About Display Ads and the Google Display Network," Google Ads Help, accessed June 5, 2020, https://support.google.com/google-ads/answer/2404190.

84 "Reach Existing Customers Using Facebook Ads," Facebook for Business, accessed June 5, 2020, https://www.facebook.com/business/goals/retargeting. https://support.google.com/google-ads/answer/2404190.

< Learn to Prioritize   **83** >

landing page specifically designed to convert people who may be on the fence.

Given all of these advantages, it's no surprise that website visitors who later see retargeted ads are *70 percent* more likely to convert.[85]

DRIVE, INCREASE, AND CONVERT MORE TRAFFIC FOR YOUR LAW FIRM WITH PPC

If your law firm's website doesn't receive regular traffic from prospects, it's little more than an expensive online business card.

That's not good enough.

No matter how much traffic you're currently seeing, you could be seeing a lot more by empowering your law firm with PPC ads.

---

85   "[Infographic] 7 Incredible Retargeting Ad Stats," *Wishpond*, accessed June 5, 2020, https://blog.wishpond.com/post/97225536354/infographic-7-incredible-retargeting -ad-stats.

< PART 3 >

WIN WITH PPC

< CHAPTER 5 >

WHAT LAW FIRMS NEED TO UNDERSTAND ABOUT GOOGLE ADS

There have never been more options for marketing your law firm.

You can buy space on benches, the sides of buses, billboards, and even grocery store receipts.

If you live in the twenty-first century, though, you can also invest in online marketing that is more affordable *and* reaches more prospects.

But, even then, you'll run into a multitude of options. Blog posts might work. You could start a Facebook group. Some firms even run ads on podcasts.

While there's something to be said about experimenting with different methods (provided you have *a lot* of patience and *a lot* of money), nothing has proven as powerful as Google Ads. If your firm isn't currently using them to attract prospects, especially those from your local Hispanic community, that needs to change.

Now.

Here's why.

< **88**   Natalie Fragkouli & Liel Levy >

WHAT ARE GOOGLE ADS?

Before we jump into the many, *many* specifics of Google Ads, let's start by actually defining what they are.[86]

Most people who have heard of Google Ads—formerly Google AdWords—are thinking *only* of the Google Search Network.[87]

Not you, of course.

You know better.

But just in case someone else decides to read this, it's worth pointing out that Google Ads actually cover a range of different services. Aside from the Search Network, Google Ads can also appear on specific websites, Google Shopping pages, YouTube videos, and apps. We'll delve into those options in the next section.

For now, let's briefly talk about the concept behind Google Ads.

Chances are you've seen plenty of them before, unless this is *literally* your first time using the internet (in which case, welcome!).

They're like virtual billboards that appear online. However, unlike the original version that would appear for every driver, you can decide just who gets to see your Google Ads. This is one of the biggest reasons they've become such valuable marketing assets for law firms.

For example, with Google Search Ads, you can target *only* people who are searching for the kinds of legal services you offer.[88] If you work in personal injury, you can make sure your ads appear

---

86   "Grow Your Business with Google Ads," Google Ads, https://ads.google.com/home/.

87   Dan Baum, "What are Google Display Ads? (Examples and Tips for 2020)," *Impact Plus*, October 31, 2019, https://www.impactbnd.com/blog/what-are-google -display-ads.

88   "Be Just a Google Search Away," Google Ads, https://ads.google.com/home/ campaigns/search-ads/.

< Win with PPC **89** >

when someone searches for relevant terms but *not* general ones (e.g., lawyer) or irrelevant ones (tax attorney).

You do this by defining your negative keywords for these ads, which means you can tell Google, "Don't bother showing our ads when someone searches for these terms."[89]

Maybe your personal injury firm doesn't handle medical malpractice cases. It's a waste of time and money when your marketing efforts bring you those prospects. With negative keywords, you can make sure ads for your firm *don't* show up for people who need that kind of help.

That's not all.

At *Nanato Media*, we specialize in helping firms market to every segment of the Hispanic population. So, our strategies include different ads for different segments. We know that people who identify as Latinoamericana, Hispano, Americanizado, Nueva Latino, and Ambicultural all have their own unique preferences when it comes to ads.

Thanks to Google Ads, we can get *hyper* specific about who sees our partners' ads *and* even which ads we show them.

No matter what legal services you offer or whom you want to target, you can do the exact same thing with your Google Ads. The result is a higher marketing ROI and more qualified prospects who are also more likely to become satisfied clients.

---

89 "The Role of Negative Keywords in PPC Campaigns for Law Firms," *Nanato Media,* May 30, 2020, https://nanatomedia.com/blog/the-role-of-negative-keywords-in-ppc -campaigns-for-law-firms/.

< **90**   Natalie Fragkouli & Liel Levy >

WHY GOOGLE ADS ARE *ESPECIALLY* POWERFUL FOR ATTRACTING HISPANIC PROSPECTS

Google Ads are a popular approach for all kinds of different law firms, but they're *especially* powerful for attracting Hispanic leads, which is why we always recommend them.

As Google has reported, "66 percent of US Hispanics say they pay attention to online ads—almost 20 percentage points more than the general online population."[90]

Twenty percent is a massive difference, but it's not that surprising when you consider how incredibly active Hispanics are online.[91]

As a bilingual agency, we can make Google Ads that are even *more* enticing for Hispanic prospects.

There's also the fact that Hispanics are more likely to spread the word about your legal services to their friends and family.[92] So, if one Hispanic person sees your ad, multiple people may hear about it. That's an extremely cost-effective way to increase your ROI.

---

90 Eliana Murillo, "New Research Shows How to Connect with US Hispanics Online," Think with Google, June 2015, https://www.thinkwithgoogle.com/consumer-insights/new-research-shows-how-to-connect-with-digital-hispanics-online/.

91 "Latinx Influencers: the Digital Community that Keeps Growing," *Nielsen*, October 11, 2018, https://www.nielsen.com/us/en/insights/article/2018/latinx-influencers-the-digital-community-that-keeps-growing/.

92 "Why Word-of-Mouth Should Be A Key Focus of Your Hispanic Marketing Strategy," *Marketing Charts*, October 19, 2016, https://www.marketingcharts.com/industries/media-and-entertainment-71782.

< Win with PPC **91** >

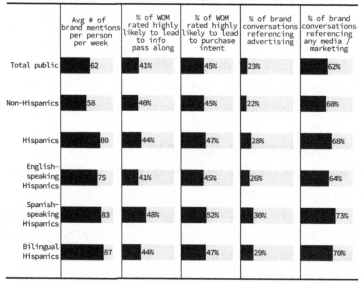

	Avg # of brand mentions per person per week	% of WOM rated highly likely to lead to info pass along	% of WOM rated highly likely to lead to purchase intent	% of brand conversations referencing advertising	% of brand conversations referencing any media / marketing
Total public	62	41%	45%	23%	62%
Non-Hispanics	58	40%	45%	22%	60%
Hispanics	80	44%	47%	28%	68%
English-speaking Hispanics	75	41%	45%	26%	64%
Spanish-speaking Hispanics	83	48%	52%	36%	73%
Bilingual Hispanics	87	44%	47%	29%	70%

Hispanics and brand word-of-mouth (WOM)
Based on an analysis of 336,126 brand mentions

Source: Marketing Charts, 2016

THREE TYPES OF GOOGLE AD CAMPAIGNS THAT ARE EFFECTIVE FOR LAW FIRMS

There are a lot of different Google Ad campaigns you can launch for your law firm.

That doesn't mean they're all equally worth it, though. We *cannot* overemphasize how important the proper allocation of your Google Ad budget will be to the success of your campaigns.[93] That might seem obvious, but many firms make the mistake of trying to spread their budgets across *every* type of Google Ad.

---

93 "6 Smart Ways to Spend Your Law Firm's Ad Credits for Google Ads," *Nanato Media,* June 3, 2020, https://nanatomedia.com/blog/six-smart-ways-to-spend-your-law -firms-ad-credits-for-google-ads/.

< **92** Natalie Fragkouli & Liel Levy >

Doing so doesn't just lower their ROI. It can completely *decimate* it because the more you run the *right* Google Ads, the better they perform. By throwing money at campaigns with no chance of succeeding, you're actually hurting the others that could.

Okay, no more doom-and-gloom (for now). Let's look at the three types of Google Ads that work well for law firms, and then we'll even briefly touch on the two you should avoid at all costs.

1. SEARCH NETWORK CAMPAIGNS

If you've ever searched for *anything*, you've seen ads from the Google Search Network.[94]

If you *haven't* searched for something before, go ahead and give it a try real quick and then cancel your *Yellow Pages* subscription. You don't need that anymore.

Alright, did you see all those ads?

That's the Google Search Network in action. These ads are fantastic because they allow you to get right to the *very top* of Google's search results ahead of all of your competitors. Getting to the top organically can easily take years, but as long as you get the setup right, you could see results from Search Ads *tomorrow*.

Also, bear in mind that Search Network campaigns target *high-intent* users.

For example, if someone had a car accident, they'd probably search for something like "car accident attorney near me" or "abogado de accidentes de auto cerca de mi."

If your law firm appears at the top of the page for this search with the right copy (or even second-to-the-top if you have the most appealing ad), you just got your new client to contact you.

---

94 "About the Google Search Network," Google Ads Help, https://support.google.com/google-ads/answer/1722047.

Your intake process was fast (hopefully) and you have a qualified lead already signed.

2. DISPLAY NETWORK CAMPAIGN

The Google Display Network (GDN) is another great option for your law firm.[95] Instead of Google's search result pages, these ads appear on more than *two million* different sites.

And yet, it's an amazing option for your law firm's marketing campaigns because it tends to be *very* underutilized compared to Search Ads.

That's not all. As HubSpot explains, the GDN offers some other incredible advantages:

> "The value for GDN boils right down to reach and affordability. Prospecting, brand awareness, and remarketing can come with a hefty price tag when pursued for traditional search ads. GDN, by comparison, bypasses a lot of costly competition from other networks. There are also endless options for customizing your audience targeting."[96]

Among other things, you can choose the sites where your ads will appear. If you've done your research—or better yet, you work with an ad agency that has (wink, wink)—you can put your ads on sites you know your market loves. For Hispanic markets, this often means putting Spanish ads on sites that are also in Spanish. You form an immediate connection with your audience *and* advertise how your firm can help.

---

95 "Display Network: Definition," Google Ads Help, https://support.google.com/google-ads/answer/117120.

96 Stephanie Hertl, "The Straightforward Guide to the Google Display Network," Hub Spot, November 10, 2020, https://blog.hubspot.com/marketing/google-display-network.

< **94** Natalie Fragkouli & Liel Levy >

3. VIDEO CAMPAIGNS

Google also supports Video Ad campaigns.[97] This includes video ads on YouTube, which Google owns.[98] Obviously, YouTube is one of the most popular sites on the planet, but another reason your firm should run video ads is that viewers have an easier time recalling video messages:[99]

> "...viewers retain 95 percent of a message when they watch it in a video compared to a mere 10 percent when reading it in text. Also, 80 percent of consumers recall a video ad they viewed in the past thirty days."[100]

Google also loves ranking videos higher in their results because, again, they own YouTube.[101]

If you're focused on the Hispanic market, you should know that Hispanics watch more videos than other markets.[102]

---

97 "About Video Ad Formats," Google Ads Help, https://support.google.com/google-ads/answer/2375464.

98 "Bring Your Story to Life with Video Ads," Google Ads, https://ads.google.com/home/campaigns/video-ads/.

99 Mike Templeman, "17 Stats And Facts Every Marketer Should Know About Video Marketing," *Forbes*, September 6, 2017, https://www.forbes.com/sites/miketempleman/2017/09/06/17-stats-about-video-marketing/?sh=182d9ceb567f.

100 Mike Templeman, "17 Stats And Facts Every Marketer Should Know About Video Marketing," *Forbes*, September 6, 2017, https://www.forbes.com/sites/miketempleman/2017/09/06/17-stats-about-video-marketing/?sh=182d9ceb567f.

101 Tracey Wallace, "How to Create Ecommerce Product Videos That Sell & Convert (Tips + Examples)," Big Commerce, https://www.bigcommerce.com/blog/ecommerce-product-videos/.

102 "Hispanic Video Content Consumption Stats," Think with Google, https://www.thinkwithgoogle.com/data/hispanic-video-content-consumption-stats/.

< Win with PPC **95** >

TWO TYPES OF GOOGLE AD CAMPAIGNS YOU CAN IGNORE

There are two other options that you'll come across when considering Google Ads for your law firm, but we generally don't recommend them to the firms we partner with on marketing campaigns.

As very few law firms have their own mobile apps, this just isn't a relevant option.

The other option is Google Shopping Ads.[103] As you're not selling a retail product, there is simply no way to leverage these types of ads for a law firm.

UNDERSTANDING HOW GOOGLE ADS WORK

Knowing which Google Ads will work best for your law firm is only the first step, though—albeit, an important one.

You still need to understand *how* to get the best possible results from these Google Ads. Otherwise, you might see an ROI, but you'll be leaving lots of money on the table.

Google Ads are like digital billboards that appear on various sites including Google's actual search results and YouTube. You can control who will see them based on keywords they're searching for, sites they visit, and YouTube videos they watch.

---

103 "Set Up Shopping Ads," Google Merchant Center Help, https://support.google.com/merchants/answer/9455869.

< **96**   Natalie Fragkouli & Liel Levy >

However, the most important factor to understand about running your ads with Google is that it works on a bidding system.[104] Here's how Google explains bidding:

> "When you select each keyword, you can choose how much you're willing to pay whenever a customer searches on that keyword and clicks your ad. This is your keyword's maximum cost-per-click, or max CPC, bid amount. Some advertisers like the control they maintain with manual bids, while others are comfortable letting the Google Ads system make bids for them."[105]

For example, if you opt for the "Maximize Clicks" automated bidding strategy, you won't define individual bid amounts for your ad groups, keywords, or placements. You'll just define your average daily budget and let Google automatically choose your maximum CPC bid amount to get you as many clicks as possible.[106] You can still set a CPC limit, though.

If you'd rather have more control, you can manually set your CPC bids for individual keywords or at the ad group level.[107] The default bid amount for an ad group will apply to *every* keyword in that campaign, but you can change that amount or any of your keywords whenever you like.

This bidding structure means your CPC will fluctuate even for the same keyword or placement. Google is actively managing

---

104 Brad Smith, "Google Ads Bidding Strategies: The Ultimate Guide," *AdEspresso*, November 3, 2020, https://adespresso.com/blog/google-ads-bidding-strategies/.

105 "About Adjusting Your Keyword Bids," Google Ads Help, https://support.google.com/google-ads/answer/2472712.

106 "Maximum CPC bid: Definition," Google Ads Help, http://support.google.com/google-ads/bin/answer.py?answer=6326.

107 "Manual CPC Bidding," Google Ads Help, https://support.google.com/google-ads/answer/2390250?hl=en.

< Win with PPC **97** >

all the other bids it's receiving, as well. That changing level of competition means some keywords may cost more one week than they did the week before. Of course, the opposite can also happen.

There's your Google Quality Score to consider, which we'll cover in just a moment.

THREE CENTRAL METRICS FOR THE SUCCESS OF YOUR LAW FIRM'S GOOGLE ADS

Before you place any bids, you have to understand three *very* important metrics, or else your foray into Google Ads is going be as short-lived as it is expensive.

1. AVERAGE LIFETIME VALUE OF YOUR CLIENTS

Even if you never intend to run a single Google Ad, you should calculate the average lifetime value of your clients.[108] Also, this section probably isn't for you, because that's *literally* all we're going to talk about here.

Once you know how much you can expect to earn from a client, you'll have a better idea of how much it's worth spending to acquire them. In turn, this will make it much easier to decide how much you should bid to earn new business.

2. IDEAL COST PER ACQUISITION

Ideally, your cost per acquisition (CPA) would be zero.[109]

Wouldn't that be nice?

---

108 "Calculate Your Customer Lifetime Value," Stitch Data, https://www.stitchdata.com/customer-lifetime-value/.

109 Clifford Chi, "The Beginner's Guide to Cost Per Acquisition (CPA)," *HubSpot*, July 12, 2019, https://blog.hubspot.com/marketing/cost-per-acquisition.

< **98** Natalie Fragkouli & Liel Levy >

It's one of the *many* reasons so many law firms focus on Hispanic clients. As we mentioned earlier, Hispanics love telling their friends and family about online ads they've seen, which means they may send you completely free referrals.

Nonetheless, it's not realistic to plan for a nonexistent CPA. The more competitive your local market is, the more your CPA will most likely be. While Google Ads are amazing for generating new leads, they're not a get-rich-quick-scheme. You have to pay for every single lead, whether they become clients or not.

For a good idea of your ideal CPA, you'll need know your:

- Average Lifetime Value of Your Clients

- Your Current CPA

- How Many Leads You Need Before You Have a New Client

Take that third amount and multiply it by your current CPA. Subtract this number from the average lifetime value of a client and you'll have your profit margin.

Knowing that, you can now decide what you want your ideal acquisition cost to be for your Google Ads.

3. YOUR AVERAGE CONVERSION RATE

You probably don't have an average conversion rate for your Google Ad campaigns *yet*, but don't worry. We have you covered.

The average conversion rate for the legal industry is 7 percent for Google Ads run on the Search Network and 1.8 percent for Display.[110]

---

110 Mark Irvine, "Google Ads Benchmarks for YOUR Industry [Updated!]," *WordStream*, October 5, 2020, https://www.wordstream.com/blog/ws/2016/02/29/google-adwords -industry-benchmarks.

< Win with PPC **99** >

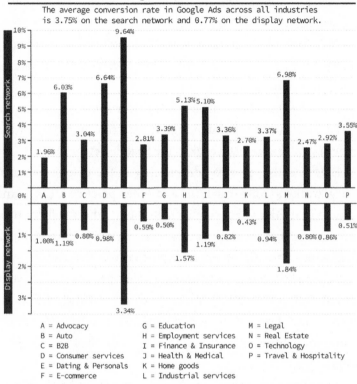

Google Ads industry benchmarks
Average conversion rate

The average conversion rate in Google Ads across all industries is 3.75% on the search network and 0.77% on the display network.

A = Advocacy
B = Auto
C = B2B
D = Consumer services
E = Dating & Personals
F = E-commerce

G = Education
H = Employment services
I = Finance & Insurance
J = Health & Medical
K = Home goods
L = Industrial services

M = Legal
N = Real Estate
O = Technology
P = Travel & Hospitality

Source: WordStream, 2020

However, if you work with an experienced agency, your conversion rate should not be below 30 percent. It could be as high as 75 percent, and depending on your market and practice area, one of every two or three calls should convert into a signed client. If anyone guarantees that every call you receive will be a signed client, you should run away. But, for someone managing Google Ads for the first time on their own, reaching the average conversion rate for the legal industry is a good place to start and optimize.

< **100**   Natalie Fragkouli & Liel Levy >

The best way to explain a Google Ads conversion is that not every click on your ad will actually convert, and not every conversion will become a signed client.

Therefore, to understand your CPA, you need to watch your conversion rate (rate in which clicks convert) and the rate at which your conversions are signed.

If it takes ten clicks on your ads before someone becomes a signed client, you have to divide your desired CPA by ten for the amount you'll bid on each click in the Search Network.

Here, we also need to address that in the case of personal injury, workers' compensation, and other practice areas, some leads will turn out to be your average client, others will not turn into signed clients at all, but every once in a while, you will land a client with a potential seven- or eight-figure settlement.

Take into account your average value per case, what your desired cost per case is (remember to be realistic), and don't forget to add those seven- or eight-figure cases that you will get from Google Ads every now and then. Include all of these in your calculations.

The point here is that your Google Ads need to be set up taking into consideration the numbers mentioned above so your advertising will be profitable for your law firm.

WHY YOU SHOULD PRIORITIZE THE SEARCH NETWORK

Speaking of the Search Network, it's our favorite option for the law firms with which we partner. For one thing, Hispanic people are very comfortable using Google to find the solutions they need.

< Win with PPC **101** >

On the Search Network, this option lets you get right at the very top of Google for your relevant keywords. There's no waiting months or even years to organically beat the competition.

MAKING THE DISPLAY NETWORK AND VIDEOS WORK FOR YOUR LAW FIRM

With that being said, we're also *big* fans of Display Networks and Video Ads. They can feature much lower CPCs and represent great opportunities to turn low-intent users into high-intent leads.

Display Ads are great for building trust with Hispanic users,[111] which is an extremely important step toward winning their business. The more they see you on sites they already trust, the more you'll earn it by proxy.

REMARKETING: A *POTENTIALLY* POWERFUL STRATEGY

Remarketing is a very popular marketing strategy. In short, it lets you *remarket* prospects who have "...previously interacted with your website or mobile app. It allows you to strategically position your ads in front of these audiences as they browse Google or its partner websites, thus helping you increase your brand awareness or remind those audiences to make a purchase."[112]

---

111 Glenn Llopis, "Earn the Trust of Hispanic Consumers and Your Brand will Dominate," April 12, 2012, https://www.forbes.com/sites/glennllopis/2012/04/02/ earn-the-trust-of-hispanic-consumers-and-your-brand-will-dominate/#bf6ee842ade7.

112 Laurence Bodine, "'Haven't We Met?' How Lawyers Use Retargeting to Attract New Business," State Bar of Wisconsin, July 20, 2018, https://www.wisbar.org/ NewsPublications/WisconsinLawyer/Pages/Article. aspx?Volume=91&Issue=7&ArticleID=26487.

< **102** Natalie Fragkouli & Liel Levy >

However, remarketing *can* backfire for some practice areas, namely those that often deal with issues of a sensitive nature.[113] For example, if you practice criminal defense, your prospect may start to worry when they begin seeing ads again and again long after their initial search. Even though it wouldn't display any of their personal information, your prospect may feel victimized. They may also not want other people who use their computer to catch on when they start seeing these ads all over.

If you do want to try remarketing, consider using Display Ads. They'll only show up on the sites you choose and will keep your firm top of mind with users who need your help.

THE GOOGLE QUALITY SCORE: YOUR KEY TO SUCCESSFUL ADS

One of the best reasons your firm should invest in Google Ads is because Google makes it *extremely* easy to improve on your results.

That might sound like a no-brainer. Why wouldn't Google want your ads to work? It ensures you'll continue to buy more ads in the future, which is great for both you and Google.

However, you don't get the same kind of feedback from other marketing initiatives. WordPress isn't going to let you know if your blogs have room for improvement. MailChimp isn't going to score your emails, so you know which ones need the most help.

These and other platforms offer you feedback, but only Google Ads gives you an actual score for every one of your initiatives. Even better, they're very clear about how you can improve your score. Again, they do this for free because they know it will help their bottom line as much as yours if your ads result in more success.

---

113 Ibid.

< Win with PPC **103** >

Best of all, the way they provide you with this feedback is extremely user-friendly: the Google Quality Score. Here's how Google describes it:

> "Quality Score is an estimate of the quality of your ads, keywords, and landing pages. Higher quality ads can lead to lower prices and better ad positions...The Quality Score is reported on a 1-1 scale and includes expected clickthrough rate, ad relevance, and landing page experience... The more relevant your ads and landing pages are to the user, the more likely it is that you'll see higher Quality Scores...Quality Score is an aggregated estimate of your overall performance in ad auctions..."[114]

Although you don't have to be a seasoned marketer to understand your Quality Score, it's literally just a number between one and ten, but it's still an incredibly powerful measurement. Your score doesn't just tell you if your ad will be relevant to your prospects, either. It will even consider your predicted CTR and how likely your landing page is to convert potential clients.

HOW TO IMPROVE YOUR GOOGLE QUALITY SCORE

That said, just looking at your score isn't going to do much to help your ads.

Instead, here are the six steps you need to take to consistently improve your law firm's Google Quality Score.

---

114 "Quality Score: Definition," Google Ads Help, https://support.google.com/google-ads/answer/140351.

< **104**   Natalie Fragkouli & Liel Levy >

1. USING HIGHLY RELEVANT KEYWORDS FOR EACH AD GROUP

One of the most common pieces of advice you'll hear about Google Ads is that your "Quality Score begins with keywords."[115]

You can check every other box, but if you don't have the right keywords for your ads, you won't get any conversions. You'll just get really, *really* frustrated.

Group similar keywords together for each of your ads, *but* only pick terms that are 100 percent relevant for your specific market.[116] If someone isn't searching for the kinds of services you offer, don't try to convince them with an irrelevant ad. No one who is looking for help with OSHA law is going to click your ad for tax mediation, even though they might be a business owner who *may* need your assistance at some point in the future.

The name of the game with keywords is *relevance*.

Choose keywords that make sense for your audience and your Quality Score will improve.

2. THE RELEVANCE OF YOUR AD COPY

Keywords aren't enough to ensure a high Google Quality Score, though. Believe it or not, people who need your help will actually *read* your ads. For some reason, a lot of firms seem to forget about this. Their ad copy is the same thing over and over again. They just switch out their keywords.

Don't do that.

Create unique, high-quality ad copy for *each* of your different segments.[117]

---

115 "How to Improve Your Google Ads Quality Score (and Earn More $$)," WordStream, https://www.wordstream.com/adwords-quality-score.

116 "Keyword Grouping: How to Group Your Keywords in Google Ads," https://www.wordstream.com/adwords-keyword-grouping.

117 Michelle Morgan, "How To Write The Best Google Ads Copy (Best Practices)," *Unbounce*, January 10, 2019, https://unbounce.com/ppc/write-best-google-ads-copy/.

< Win with PPC **105** >

Get right to the point with why *your* firm is the best option for this person's needs. For example, because our clients focus on the Hispanic market, their ad copy usually mentions that they have staff members who can speak Spanish. Even if the prospect is searching in English, this has still proven powerful because so many people are searching on behalf of family members who prefer Spanish.

Experimentation is important. Once you know which keywords are most important for your firm, try out different ways of highlighting why your firm is so great. It's worth the extra time to get more clicks and improve that all-important Quality Score.

3. *ALWAYS* PRIORITIZE IMPROVING YOUR CTR

If you're new to Google Ads or you've struggled with it in the past, it might be hard to believe that someday you might reach a CTR that feels good enough.

Again, right now, if you're not getting many—or *any*—clicks, that might be difficult to imagine, but we've seen it before. Eventually, a firm reaches a reliable CTR that regularly brings them new business, month after month. They no longer feel the need to keep improving it and focus on other goals instead.

Do not make this mistake.

Increasing the CTR of your Google Ads will mean more clicks, but it will also lead to a lower CPC, which means a *much* better ROI.[118]

---

118 "5 Hacks to Increase Clicks on Your Google AdWords Ads," *Neil Patel*, https://neilpatel.com/blog/increase-clicks-google-adwords-ads/.

< **106** Natalie Fragkouli & Liel Levy >

4. DON'T LET YOUR LANDING PAGE DROP THE BALL

Last but not least—and we really cannot stress this part enough—do not redirect users who click on your ads to your website, where they will be served with generic information and will get distracted with more CTAs.

Landing pages are built to drive traffic to a specific marketing campaign goal. The intent is to focus the visitor solely on the intent of the page, such as a free case review form submission.

No distractions.

No other options.

Simply inform and get your user to take the single action noted.

So, if you see an impressive CTR from your Google Ads, but you're not seeing conversions, and your Google Quality Score is lacking, your landing page is probably the problem.

This kind of disconnect can be jarring for potential clients. It feels like you promised them something but then didn't follow through. While some of these prospects may still contact you, that number won't be nearly as high as it would have been if you had created a landing page that was relevant to the ad.

Other smart ways to improve your landing pages include keeping load times to below five seconds, optimizing for mobile users, and including a picture of you and/or your staff.[119] Show that there are actual human beings at your firm who really do want to help.

---

119 Patrick Holmes, "The Do's and Don'ts of Creating the Best Landing Page Experience," *Instapage*, January 23, 2020, https://instapage.com/blog/adwords-landing-page-experience.

< Win with PPC **107** >

5. YOUR ACCOUNT'S HISTORICAL PERFORMANCE

As you're probably already well aware, reputation is everything for your law firm. You want to be known as a firm that gets results for your clients. You want to be known as a firm that makes your clients feel comfortable, listens to their problems, and provides empathetic responses.

Reputation is equally important for your Quality Score.

The better your ads are again and again, the better your Quality Score will be. Google will realize that your account understands how to create great ads and will reward you accordingly.

6. WORK WITH EXPERTS WHO UNDERSTAND YOUR MARKET

Finally, you probably also know how important it is to be an expert in a specific type of law. You can't be a firm that's great at family law and criminal law *and* bankruptcy law *and* environmental law.

As the old saying goes, you don't want to be a jack of all trades but a master of none.

Similarly, you probably don't have the time to master a completely different discipline. Instead, it makes more sense to work with an agency that specializes in Google Ads, especially if you're trying to generate business from a market as unique as the Hispanic population.

Let your competitors make the mistake of trying to run their own ads every week on top of the one hundred other things they need to do. Let them make the mistake of hiring an agency that claims they can succeed with *any* market.

Google's entire business model for their ads is built on serving relevant listings to their users. That's why they went to the trouble of creating the Quality Score. If you're not working with an agency that has experience creating Google Ads that are *proven*

< **108** Natalie Fragkouli & Liel Levy >

to work with the Hispanic market, you're doing the equivalent of throwing away your hard-earned money.

Highly relevant ads will *always* outperform generic versions in terms of Quality Score, CTR, and CPC. There's just no reason to *not* work with an expert (unless you hate money).

USE GOOGLE ADS TO SKYROCKET YOUR LAW FIRM'S BUSINESS

As you can see, Google Ads are the secret weapons of firms all over the country, especially those that market to the Hispanic community. There's just no better way to get in front of these prospects in an engaging way.

< CHAPTER 6 >

LAW FIRM CAMPAIGNS

GOOGLE ADS KEYWORD RESEARCH AND SEGMENTATION

Every firm should be leveraging the power of Google Ads to regularly attract new prospects. Regardless of what kind of law you practice or who your ideal client is, Google Ads has huge potential for growing your business. However, to succeed with Google Ads, you must understand two fundamentals: keyword research and segmentation.

Does your law firm need new clients on a regular basis?

No?

Alright, well, thanks for stopping by.

For everyone else, one of the easiest ways you can consistently generate new clients for your law firm is by running Google Ads. The long list of advantages includes everything from a predictable budget to the potential for instantaneous scalability.

Success with Google Ads isn't guaranteed, though. While Google has definitely gone out of their way to make their platform as user-friendly and effective as possible, we've seen a lot of law firms fall short with this powerful platform over the years.

< **110**   Natalie Fragkouli & Liel Levy >

Whether you've struggled in the past, are hoping to see better results, or have literally never heard of Google Ads until now, let's dig into the essentials you must understand to make the most of this incredible tool.

STEP 1: DEFINE THE SERVICES YOU WANT TO ADVERTISE

Advertising always begins with your audience. If you make a misstep when identifying your target market, it's going to cost you. Even a seemingly small error (e.g., missing their average age by a few years) can have huge consequences because it will impact every other facet of your marketing campaign.

For the purposes of your law firm, the audience you want to engage comes down to what kinds of services you offer and where you offer them—what is your practice area?

Hopefully, you're 100 percent clear on those. If you don't know what services you offer, you are a long way from needing Google Ads.

However, knowing your market isn't enough. To build a successful ad campaign, you'll need to understand how to use keywords and segmentation to attract these leads. To do that, you need an in-depth understanding of your law firm's buyer personas.[120]

---

120 Sam Kusinitz, "The Definition of a Buyer Persona [in Under 100 Words]," *HubSpot*,
   July 22, 2018, https://blog.hubspot.com/marketing/buyer-persona-definition-under
   -100-sr.

< Win with PPC **111** >

WHO IS MOST LIKELY TO BECOME A CLIENT?

Just about anyone *could* become one of your clients, but you can't effectively market to everyone. Instead, you want to focus your law firm's Google Ads on the kinds of prospects who are most likely to convert into clients.

This is how you increase conversions, skyrocket your ROI, and improve that all-important Google Quality Score.[121]

Again, you probably have a pretty good idea of who your ideal candidate is and the kind of market you want to engage. For example, many of our clients aim their campaigns at Hispanic prospects who need their legal services.

Whatever the case, you want to take things a step further and create concrete traits that describe your market. By doing this, you'll effectively build a portfolio of answers for all the important questions you need to ask when designing a successful marketing campaign.

In other words, you need to create accurate buyer personas for your law firm.[122]

Below, we're going to get into some of the most important ways you have to do this for optimizing your Google Search and Display Ads.

For now, let's cover a few basics you must include when creating effective buyer personas for your firm:

- **Gender:** For most firms, gender is irrelevant, but you might find that your clients tend to be overrepresented by males or females. In that case, it would be worth noting the gender of your ideal prospect.

---

121 "Quality Score: Definition," Google Ads Help,
https://support.google.com/google-ads/answer/140351.

122 Noreen Fishman, "A 9 Point Checklist to Build Buyer Personas for Legal Services," *Good 2B Social*, December 11, 2017, https://good2bsocial.com/checklist-buyer -personas-for-legal-services/.

< **112**   Natalie Fragkouli & Liel Levy >

- **Age Range:** Do your clients tend to be millennials? Gen Xers? Baby boomers? Maybe there's some overlap. When you understand the age range of your ideal clients, you'll have a much better idea of how to engage with them.

- **Ethnicity:** As a marketing agency that specializes in helping law firms attract Hispanic prospects, we know firsthand how important this trait is for success with Google Ads. For example, we've learned that understanding the cultural expectations Hispanics have for companies that want their business is central to earning their trust.[123]

- **Location:** We're going to go into a lot more detail about this one below because it has so much potential for improving your ads. Sufficed to say, as a local business that has a limited practice area—even if it's the entire state—you need to be clear about where your ideal prospects live.

- **Their Buyer's Journey:** Your law firm's prospects don't have the typical buyer's journey, but you still need to understand the events that will precede them seeing your ad.[124] Obviously, there will be a catalyst event—starting a business, deciding on divorce, getting in a car accident, etc.—but what comes next? What do they search for in Google? What device do they use? What terms are they searching for? We'll really dive into this in Step 2, so you'll have *lots* of information to include for your buyer persona.

---

123 "The Evolution of Media Consumption Amongst US Hispanics and Its Effect on Law Firm Marketing," *Nanato Media*, June 20, 2020, https://nanatomedia.com/blog/the-evolution-of-media-consumption-amongst-us-hispanics-and-its-effect-on-law-firm-marketing/.

124 Tom DiScipio, "What Is the Buyer's Journey?" *Impact*, February 5, 2016, https://www.impactbnd.com/blog/what-is-the-buyers-journey.

< Win with PPC   **113** >

BE REALISTIC ABOUT YOUR BUYER PERSONAS

Of course, it's important to be realistic where your buyer personas are concerned. Your ideal client might be someone who has millions of dollars to pay you on a regular basis. Who wouldn't want that kind of client?

But is that realistic?

Likewise, your practice area may not be big enough to accommodate a sufficient number of your ideal clients. For example, if you practice personal injury law, you might see your highest profit margins from clients who have suffered severe brain traumas. Those might be your ideal clients, but you probably won't see enough of them every year unless you live in one of the country's largest metropolitan areas.

Part of being realistic is knowing that you can't hope to generate those kinds of leads day after day. You'll need to focus on other buyer personas also.

STEP 2: IDENTIFY HOW YOUR IDEAL CLIENTS PREFER TO SEARCH FOR LAWYERS

Most firms are successful when it comes to that first step.

Again, it's a big one. Your chances of success depend on your ability to define whom you want to target and what services you want to market.

Still, it's only the *first* step. Now that you understand your buyer personas and the services they want, you need to identify how they search for those services on Google. Otherwise, all that information you just compiled in the last step won't be of much

< **114**   Natalie Fragkouli & Liel Levy >

use. You won't be able to put it into action because you won't show up where your buyer personas are looking.

SEO VS. PPC: WHICH IS BEST FOR YOUR LAW FIRM?

Since the beginning of digital marketing, the debate between SEO and PPC has been raging. Proponents of one can list a million reasons their method is superior and a million more reasons the other should be avoided at all costs.

Of course, there are also those of us who recommend both—at least for law firms. Using SEO for organic traffic can be a great way to earn "free" leads for years to come. However, you pay for those free leads upfront and generally need to wait months or even years before you start seeing any returns.

On the other hand, when done right, your PPC campaign can begin generating leads for your law firm right away.[125] We really need to stress *done right* because PPC can be challenging for novices. For those with years of experience, though, a well-designed PPC campaign can produce returns by the very next day.

That being said, there's a far more important distinction that needs to be made when deciding how to use SEO and PPC to best benefit your search term. It's one that we've seen just about every law firm miss before working with us.

The distinction is understanding the timeline a prospect is working with when they're looking to hire an attorney. Those with longer timelines will be best targeted through SEO. Those who want to speak with an attorney right away should be targeted with PPC. If you choose the wrong method, the prospects you're targeting will *never* become your clients.

---

125 "English and Spanish Pay-Per-Click (PPC) Campaign Management," Nanato Media, https://nanatomedia.com/bilingual-services/google-ads/.

< Win with PPC **115** >

Let's look at some examples to illustrate this.

If someone needs a lawyer on retainer for their business, they have a long timeline. For one thing, they probably want to educate themselves on the type of attorney their business needs, how much they have to budget, what services come with a retainer arrangement, and more. They'll earn this education through free blog posts and videos. If your firm offers these kinds of services, you'd be wise to create this type of SEO-focused content, work them through the four stages of your marketing funnel, and prove yourself to be the easy choice when they're ready to hire.[126]

To be fair, you *could* still use PPC in this situation, but you'd most likely find success by targeting keywords related to common questions (e.g., "How much does a small business attorney charge?") and then offering free e-books or case studies from your landing page. Nonetheless, you'd still want to build out an SEO-focused funnel for attracting organic traffic.

Now, imagine taking this kind of approach with a prospect who wants to sue their doctor for malpractice.

Do you think *that* type of prospect wants to spend weeks or even months researching their options?

Do you think they're interested in learning more about malpractice first?

Do you think they want to read an e-book?

Of course not!

They want to speak to you right away! They want peace of mind knowing they've consulted an expert who has answered their questions and helped them better understand their options.

Yet, countless law firms all over the country publish regular

---

126 "The Modern Digital Marketing Funnel: Explained," *Blue Corona*, July 31, 2019, https://www.bluecorona.com/blog/new-digital-marketing-funnel-strategies/.

< **116**   Natalie Fragkouli & Liel Levy >

blog posts on topics like malpractice, personal injury, criminal charges, and others that prospects don't want to read because they don't have the time. They want help this very moment!

We're not saying that keyword-optimized pages are a bad idea. Optimized pages that describe your services could earn you some free traffic, but they're also essential for explaining to prospects what it is you do and how you can help them.

It's just that you have to understand your market's timeline. If yours is a short one, they don't have the time—or probably the patience—to read page after page of content. They want to speak with you immediately, so a text ad with proper ad extensions that sends them to a relevant landing page is ideal.[127]

HOW TO IDENTIFY THE RIGHT KEYWORDS
FOR YOUR LAW FIRM'S GOOGLE ADS CAMPAIGN

Keywords are another factor that *seems* simple but can easily cause unnecessary challenges.[128] For example, if you're a personal injury attorney, you probably know that "personal injury attorney" is one of your keywords (just be sure to add your practice area in there).

But what else?

We see a lot of law firms target the kinds of questions they know prospects are likely to ask.

"Do I need a personal injury lawyer?"

"Is it worth hiring a personal injury lawyer?"

"How long does a personal injury lawsuit take?"

The problem is that these searches don't sound like they're

---

127 "Why Drive Your Law Firm's PPC Traffic to Landing Pages," *Nanato Media*, June 18, 2020, https://nanatomedia.com/blog/why-drive-your-law-firms-ppc-traffic-to-landing-pages/.

128 "What Are Keywords?" MOZ, https://moz.com/learn/seo/what-are-keywords.

< Win with PPC **117** >

being done by someone who is urgently looking to speak to an attorney, do they?

It sounds like they *might* next week or next month...*maybe.* But it doesn't sound like they're hoping to speak to someone within the hour, does it?

Again, these are the kinds of keywords we see a lot of firms target with blog posts. Unfortunately, the people who read these posts rarely become clients. It doesn't help that many of these queries aren't state specific, so your blog could rank at the very top of Google and you still wouldn't see a great ROI because most of the people who read it reside outside of your practice area.

If you're looking to simply create a fantastic online resource of free legal information that will literally never make you a dime, go right ahead. Those are fantastic queries to target. You'll get a lot of traffic and I'm sure you'll make a lot of people happy.

However, on the off chance that you have bills to pay, we *highly* recommend you prioritize high-intent keywords.[129] You want people in buying mode, not education mode.

Fortunately, you can consider your best options for free thanks to Google Keyword Planner.[130] It shows you how popular a keyword is, how much competition there is for it, and what you should plan to spend whenever you earn a click for it.

We also like to use Google's Autocomplete feature for keyword ideas.[131] Just start typing relevant keywords into the browser and let Google suggest popular options.

---

129 "Keyword Intent—The Secret to Attracting the Right Traffic," WordStream, https://www.wordstream.com/keyword-intent.

130 "Choose the right keywords," Google Ads, https://ads.google.com/home/tools/keyword-planner/.

131 Sam Hollingsworth, "Google Autocomplete: A Complete SEO Guide," *Search Engine Journal*, May 4, 2018, https://www.searchenginejournal.com/google-autocomplete-a-complete-seo-guide/251407/.

< **118**   Natalie Fragkouli & Liel Levy >

Google Trends is great, too.[132] Whereas Google Keyword Planner shows absolute search volume data, Google Trends shows the relative popularity of search terms. It even eliminates repeated searches from the same person over a short period, so the reported popularity isn't affected by small groups of people.

Google Trends shows only data for truly popular terms. So, if you are after a mass tort niche, you will probably not get much from Google Trends unless there is huge noise around the subject already.

You can also invest in any number of different paid tools for keyword research, but we suggest you start with the free ones above.[133] Get some practice finding the right terms for your firm—those with high buyer intent—and you'll have a much easier time deciding on a platform to invest in.

DON'T FORGET ABOUT YOUR
LAW FIRM'S NEGATIVE KEYWORDS

Finally, don't forget about the keywords your firm *doesn't* want to rank for. You can tell Google not to show your ads anytime a searcher enters these "negative keywords."[134]

For example, maybe you practice family law, but you don't do guardian ad litem. If your ads pop up whenever someone searches for this very common service, you'll end up paying for clicks that won't convert. Or, even worse, they'll contact your firm, take up

---

132 Nick Churick, "How to Use Google Trends for Keyword Research: 7 Effective Ways," *Ahrefs*, December 30, 2019, https://ahrefs.com/blog/ how-to-use-google-trends-for-keyword-research/.

133 Brian Dean, "15 BEST Keyword Research Tools for SEO [2021 Reviews]," *Back Linko*, January 10, 2020, https://backlinko.com/keyword-research-tools.

134 "The Role of Negative Keywords in PPC Campaigns for Law Firms," *Nanato Media*, May 30, 2020, https://nanatomedia.com/blog/the-role-of-negative-keywords -in-ppc-campaigns-for-law-firms/.

< Win with PPC **119** >

your intake team's precious time, and you'll either turn them down or just redirect them to the local bar or another attorney.

As a result, your conversion rate drops, your ROI follows, and if you are measuring conversions through Google, you are teaching the algorithm to go after the wrong type of conversions in case you consider smart bidding down the road.

Seriously, if you've been running Google Ads for your law firm but have been underwhelmed by the results, negative keywords could be all it takes to turn things around. That's how powerful they are.

STEP 3: ENTER PREDICTABILITY MODE FOR GOOGLE DISPLAY CAMPAIGNS

If you've made it this far and absorbed everything you've read, congrats. You have a very high-level understanding of what it takes to succeed with Google Ads.

Go ahead and pat yourself on the back.

Heck, we're going to do it, too. We put a lot of work into this.

Still, there's more you can do to consistently generate leads for your law firm. Specifically, you can invest in Google Display Ads.[135]

The reason we love these so much is that they can put ads in front of prospects who are about to need your services even if they're not aware of it themselves.

For example, if you help clients when they're going through divorce, you can target ads at people who are attending couples' therapy. If you handle personal injury cases, you can use ads to

---

135 "The Straightforward Guide to Google Display Ads for Law Firms," *Nanato Media*, May 23, 2020, https://nanatomedia.com/blog/the-straightforward-guide-to-google -display-ads-for-law-firms/.

< **120**   Natalie Fragkouli & Liel Levy >

target people who recently went to the emergency room or auto-body shop. Criminal defense attorneys can zero in on people who were recently in jail or in a police station.

All of these powerful options are possible thanks to content targeting, which is proven to work best for law firms.[136] You can target users by search behavior (keywords in search queries they completed in Google), locations they have visited (where the user searched for those on Google Maps), or specific websites.

You can also target prospects based on their search behavior or just the websites you know your best leads tend to visit.

Best of all, you're targeting these prospects right before they know they need your services. Literally, the next step they would take is to begin searching for an attorney, except now they won't need to because of your Google Display Ad campaigns.

HANDPICKING SPANISH SITES FOR HISPANIC CLIENTS

One great way to get your Google Display Ads in front of your prospects is by placing them on websites they like to visit. We've found this approach is especially effective with Hispanic prospects.

You can use Placement Targeting to advertise on Spanish websites or even specific web pages.[137] Make sure your ad is also written in Spanish and you'll make a great first impression with Hispanic prospects.[138]

With Google's Ad Gallery, you can customize your Display Ad

---

136 "Targeting Your Ads," Google Ads Help, https://support.google.com/google-ads/answer/1704368.

137 "About Placement Targeting," AdSense Help, https://support.google.com/adsense/answer/32856.

138 "The Value of Transcreation in Hispanic Legal Digital Marketing," *Nanato Media*, June 12, 2020, https://nanatomedia.com/blog/the-value-of-transcreation-in-hispanic-legal-digital-marketing/.

< Win with PPC **121** >

or even upload one of your own.[139] The more relevant you make yours to Hispanic prospects who need your help, the better.

STEP 4: DRILL DOWN INTO YOUR MARKET WITH SEGMENTATION

Don't stop with Display Ads, either. As powerful as they are, you can still take your firm's Google Ads campaign further.

The secret is segmentation.[140] You want to get as specific as possible with your audience, so every prospect who sees your ad feels as though it was made just for them.

Again, this is why it's worth the extra time to carefully construct detailed buyer personas.

PAY CLOSE ATTENTION TO GEOGRAPHIC LOCATION WHEN TARGETING HISPANIC PROSPECTS

Arguably *the most* important way to segment your audience is by getting clear about their geographic location. Instead of cities, focus on zip codes. These tend to be far more representative of a specific demographic.

For example, even in cities with high Hispanic populations, they tend to congregate in distinct neighborhoods.[141]

You can also add in new areas if recent developments have affected a particular area. For example, a natural disaster or

---

139 "Ad Gallery Ads in Google Ads Editor," Google Ads Editor Help, https://support.google.com/google-ads/editor/answer/1052563.

140 "What Is Market Segmentation?" *Lotame,* March 11, 2019, https://www.lotame.com/what-is-market-segmentation/.

141 James Koebler, "11 Cities With the Most Hispanics," *US News,* December 18, 2019, https://www.usnews.com/news/slideshows/11-cities-with-the-most-hispanics.

< **122** Natalie Fragkouli & Liel Levy >

large-scale accident at a factory may greatly increase the number of prospects you can market to in your service area. Just choose the right zip code to get in front of these leads. Or, if you choose to target a broader geographic location, make sure you make bid adjustments by increasing your bid percentage for zip codes with a higher Hispanic concentration.

OTHER IMPORTANT WAYS TO SEGMENT YOUR AUDIENCE

There's no end to the many ways you can effectively segment your audience. We recommend you revisit your buyer personas regularly to see if you or your team have identified any new distinctions that might be worth making for even better results from your campaigns.

Until then, here are other ways you can segment your audience to get started:

- **Income Level:** if you are an estate lawyer and are looking to target individuals who need your help because of their income level, you can choose this as a trait to target.

- **Age:** You don't want your ads to be seen by children who can't become clients (on their own, anyway), so regardless of the type of law you practice, you must use this segmentation option to keep your ads focused on adults.

- **Language:** Again, this is *very* relevant when building strategies for Hispanics, as well as campaigns that advertise immigration-related services.

Once you start seeing some results, you may find even greater success with segmenting by device.

For firms we partner with who want more Hispanic prospects, we usually focus our campaigns on mobile devices.

< Win with PPC **123** >

Hispanic people are mobile power users, so this is an easy way to improve their results right away.

STEP 5: PREPARE FOR THE INFLUX OF NEW LEADS

Believe it or not, this can be a problem.

A good problem, sure, but a problem, nonetheless, so it's something you should prepare for ahead of time.

Fortunately, it's a good problem that also has an easy solution.

You just need to make sure that you have an intake team available *when* your ads are running. Otherwise, you may see a bigger increase in missed calls than revenues.

This is especially important for those types of legal services that involve the shorter timelines we mentioned above. For example, if you're a personal injury or workers comp attorney, the vast majority of your prospects are going to be calling with a sense of urgency. They want to speak with an actual attorney ASAP. If someone doesn't answer the phone at your firm, they'll move on to the next one.

For those of you who wish to market to Hispanics, remember that they often have varying work schedules. Many of them work your typical nine-to-five jobs, but plenty also work later hours or start early. They can't necessarily call during standard hours. If you can have someone by the phone outside of nine to five and, ideally, on the weekends, you'll speak with a lot more potential clients.

< **124**   Natalie Fragkouli & Liel Levy >

DON'T WAIT TO LEVERAGE THE POWER OF GOOGLE ADS

Google Ads can reach your ideal prospects wherever they are. Whether it's at the very top of their research results, on their favorite website, or on their phone (but only when they're physically in the right location), there's no better way to advertise your legal services.

If you spend the time to master the intricacies of keyword research and segmentation, your Google Ad campaigns will pay you back every week with new prospects who are ready to become clients.

< CHAPTER 7 >

HOW TO WRITE CONVERSION COPY FOR YOUR LAW FIRM'S GOOGLE ADS CAMPAIGNS

Google Ads are often touted as *the* most cost-effective way to market your law firm. If it doesn't feel that way, it could be because you're not targeting the right keywords, or your segmentation needs work. However, most firms are completely unaware of an equally important element: high-converting copy.

You've never had more options for marketing your law firm.

You can still opt for old-school methods like bus benches, billboards, and newspaper ads.

Or if you're joining the rest of us in the twenty-first century, there are countless ways you can use online ads to put yourself in front of the exact segment you want to serve.

No matter what that segment is or how you want to serve them, there are certain fundamentals you have to master to find success.

< **126**   Natalie Fragkouli & Liel Levy >

First, you have to understand your market.[142]

Then, you have to segment them and find their keywords.[143]

These first two steps can be a lot of work, which is why so many law firms drop the ball when it comes to the third fundamental. However, if you don't nail the conversion copy it takes to get those clicks and inspire prospects to contact you, the rest of your efforts won't amount to much.

Even in today's digital realm, where you have *so much* technology for targeting your ideal prospects, one of the most important factors for success is still one of the most basic.

Until you arm your ads with copy that converts, your ROI will always suffer.

THE IMPORTANCE OF EFFECTIVE COPY IN ONLINE LAW FIRM ADS

One of the biggest challenges with writing effective copy for your law firm's ads is that it seems so simple. Compared to the other factors involved—from choosing your bidding strategy to potentially retargeting your audience—writing the messages that your prospects need to hear can feel like an afterthought.[144]

---

142 "Why Every Law Firm Must Focus on Hispanic Clients," *Nanato Media*, June 20, 2020, https://nanatomedia.com/blog/why-every-law-firm-must-focus-on-hispanic-clients/.

143 "Law Firm Campaigns: Google Ads Keyword Research and Segmentation," *Nanato Media*, June 26, 2020, https://nanatomedia.com/blog/law-firm-google-ads-keyword-research-and-segmentation/.

144 "Determine a Bid Strategy Based on Your Goals," Google Ads Help, https://support.google.com/google-ads/answer/2472725.
Brad Smith, "The Ultimate Google Ads Retargeting Guide," *AdEspresso*, July 23, 2019, https://adespresso.com/blog/google-ads-retargeting-guide/.

< Win with PPC **127** >

However, the truth is that, *without a doubt,* copy is the *most* crucial element of a successful campaign. After all, you can include incredible, professional images. You can even make high-quality videos. You can use all the different tools that Google's many platforms place at your feet.

But if the words you use to actually communicate your message don't convince your prospects that they need *your* services... who cares?

Good-looking ads don't automatically convert. On the other hand, we have seen a number of aesthetically average ads work wonders for their firms simply because the copy was so powerful.

Of course, you want both.

Our point is simply that overlooking the content of your ads would be like spending all year choosing a logo for your firm and only one day hiring the people to staff it.

EIGHT COMMON MISTAKES LAW FIRMS MAKE WITH THEIR GOOGLE ADS COPY

If your law firm plans on targeting Hispanic prospects, it's even *more* important that you prioritize your ad copy.[145]

Unfortunately, we've seen a lot of mistakes from law firms prior to partnering with us. If any of these eight examples sound familiar, it's time to reassess your copy before investing any more time and money in ads.

---

145 "Getting Started with Your Law Firm's Hispanic Marketing Strategy," *Nanato Media,* June 20, 2020, https://nanatomedia.com/blog/ getting-started-with-your-law-firms-hispanic-marketing-strategy/.

< **128**   Natalie Fragkouli & Liel Levy >

1. USING GOOGLE TRANSLATE FOR SPANISH ADS

Oh boy.

Look, Google is a very powerful tool. Obviously, we're big fans of Google Ads and all the other ways the world's most popular search engine makes it easy to market law firms to any and every segment in the country.

However, we're decidedly *not* big fans of using Google Translate to do any kind of serious translations.

Google Translate is *great* at doing very basic translations. If you want to know what a single word means, Google Translate is usually up to the task. Credit where credit's due, it can manage this task for more than *one hundred different languages*.

Not bad.

What it's *not* good at is just about any task beyond the basics. As a translator, Google lacks depth:

> "The practical utility of Google Translate and similar technologies is undeniable, and probably a good thing overall, but there is still something deeply lacking in the approach, which is conveyed by a single word: understanding. Machine translation has never focused on understanding language. Instead, the field has always tried to "decode"—to get away with not worrying about what understanding and meaning are."[146]

In other *words*—no pun intended—Google can't put together a sentence that would fool a native speaker into thinking it came from a fellow fluent speaker. It can come *close* (sometimes), but close is nowhere near good enough when you're depending on ads to keep your firm running.

---

146 Douglas Hofstadter, "The Shallowness of Google Translate," *The Atlantic*, January 30, 2018, https://www.theatlantic.com/technology/archive/2018/01/the-shallowness-of-google-translate/551570/.

< Win with PPC **129** >

People often forget how much nuance is involved with language. For example, when it comes to Spanish, the meaning of a group of words is *way* more than just the sum of its parts. It also comes down to important factors like:

- Grammar

- Culture

- Context

So, even if you were able to write an ad in perfect Spanish, it may still not bring you any new clients if you don't understand these subtle elements. At Nanato Media, we regularly improve copy for law firms by considering the country of origin of their prospects.

How you address a prospect who is from—or was raised by parents from—Mexico is going to be very different than how you would write a Spanish ad for someone from Colombia.

Or consider England and Ireland, two countries with intertwined histories that are right next to each other. If you tried using the exact same copy with both segments, you'd find that both groups ignored it. The Irish version of English is distinct in many ways from the kind their neighbors use. This is true in terms of what actual words mean, grammar, pronunciation, and general usage.

The same holds true in Spanish. Google Translate simply isn't able to address this challenge.

As a result, when firms rely on it for translations, no matter what they write, their prospects read, "No one at this firm actually speaks Spanish, so you should just keep looking."

< **130**   Natalie Fragkouli & Liel Levy >

2. WRITING THEIR COPY IN SPANGLISH

Another common mistake we've seen law firms make when marketing to Hispanic prospects is utilizing Spanglish, a hybrid version of English and Spanish.[147]

If we're being honest, sometimes, it's just lazy. They're using Google Translate for the important words (i.e., the services they provide) and then using English for everything else. They're hoping that prospects will recognize the Spanish words that matter most to them and then simply piece together the rest.

In fairness, we know that many firms choose Spanglish after a bit more thought. Spanglish is growing in popularity throughout the United States.[148] While it probably isn't anyone's *first* language, many speakers feel just as comfortable using it as Spanish or English.

So, where's the problem?

This time, the problem is that these firms don't understand how *Google* "reads."

For all its strengths, Google doesn't understand Spanglish. In fact, Spanglish isn't even listed as one of the one hundred-plus languages Google Translate can understand.

Therefore, when Google tries to understand what your ad is about, it draws a blank. Firms that take this approach force Google to come up with its own conclusions and that's never a good thing when you're trying to target markets with pinpoint accuracy.

Google doesn't like being forced to figure out your ads, either. When Google doesn't know whom you're trying to target and/or

---

147 "Spanglish," *PBS*, https://www.pbs.org/speak/seatosea/americanvarieties/spanglish/book/.

148 Vanessa Chesnut, "Love it or hate it, Spanglish is here to stay—and it's good exercise for your brain," *NBC News*, April 5, 2018, https://www.nbcnews.com/news/latino/love-it-or-hate-it-spanglish-here-stay-it-s-n859211.

< Win with PPC **131** >

what you're trying to advertise, it will drop your Quality Score.[149] After that, you'll see your cost-per-click (CPC) increase, which will have a cumulative effect on your overall budget.[150]

Of course, the worst part is that Google will all but hide your ads from potential clients. It won't want to show them to people who are otherwise searching for your services. Those ideal prospects are far more likely to click, so Google wants to show them the best ads as much as possible—not Spanglish ads it can't understand. For proof, take a look at this Spanglish ad *at the bottom of the third page*:

Ad to.do.\\\\\\\\\\\.com/faster/results ▾
Abogados De Choques - Find All You Want to Know
Search for **Abogados De Accidentes**, Discover All Useful Info You Need to Know. Find
KeyWord:**Abogados De Accidentes**, Services: Personal Injury Law, Accident Compensation,
Medical Injury Law, Work Injury Law, Family & Divorce Law, Tax Law, Probate Law.

Source: google.com, accessed June 24, 2020

That's a bad place to be for an *organic* listing. Imagine spending money for ads that end up where it's virtually *guaranteed* prospects will never see them.

Finally, it's important to note that using Spanglish in your law firm's ads can be just as ineffective with the people who regularly speak it.

Spanglish isn't considered a formal language, even among those who use it every day.[151] It's totally informal. It's also a lan-

---

149 "Quality Score: Definition," Google Ads Help, https://support.google.com/google-ads/answer/140351.

150 "Cost Per Click (CPC): Learn What Cost Per Click Means for PPC," *WordStream*, https://www.wordstream.com/cost-per-click.

151 Rachel Bierly, "Spanglish: The Validity of Spanglish as a Language," Panoramas, May 2, 2019, https://www.panoramas.pitt.edu/opinion-and-interviews/spanglish-validity-spanglish-language.

< **132**   Natalie Fragkouli & Liel Levy >

guage without any defined rules, which is why people who speak it in one city may not sound like those in a town nearby (again, think English vs. Irish).

Using this kind of very informal language to advertise something as important as legal services will almost always have the exact opposite intended effect. Prospects may know exactly what you're trying to say but may wonder why you're saying it in such an informal way. Compared to a competitor taking a much more professional approach to its copy, your firm will look amateur.

As you're probably well aware, people might look for a lot of different things in a law firm but amateur is never one of them. Your ads won't get clicked. Your Quality Score will drop. Then your ads won't even get seen.

3. WRITING IN AN INCONSISTENT TONE

Tone can be one of those vague marketing terms that are hard to hit when creating copy. However, Joanne Wiebe does a great job of describing tone in a simple but effective way:

> "Tone takes a statement and either breathes life into it...or sucks the life out of it."[152]

The tone of your ads goes beyond the actual words you're using. Either the tone makes prospects think, "This is a firm I can trust with my needs" *or* it makes them think, "While their words sound right, something is off."

Wiebe goes on to say:

---

152 Joanna Wiebe, "Tone of Voice 101: How to Write Copy That People Can Connect With," Copyhackers, https://copyhackers.com/2013/01/copywriting-tone-how-to/.

< Win with PPC **133** >

"Learning what adjective(s) your customers use most often to describe you can help you find your tone. How can that be? Because nearly every tone under the sun is simply an adjective brought to life. Your tone can be nerdy, romantic, condescending, patriotic, joyful, shocking, cool, happy, foolish, funny, formal, or flirty. Those are all, of course, adjectives. They are brought to life on the page by combining diction and syntax to create tone.

"...Your tone can be anything. Unfortunately, it is most often this one thing: BORING."[153]

Fortunately, we can narrow that down further for our purposes. With copywriting for a law firm's ads, your tone needs to be professional. "Nerdy, romantic, condescending" or any of those other options just won't fit.

We prefer professional over formal because we've seen many firms do really well with a more casual tone, albeit one that still conveys professionalism.

In fact, we regularly recommend that law firms use the more casual "tu" over the more formal "usted." Generally, we find that the former makes prospects feel more comfortable and familiar with the firm, long before they've ever actually spoken.

Still, we've partnered with some firms that have seen better results with "usted." It better fits their brand because they take this formal tone throughout their marketing assets and even when they speak with their clients.

As far as consistency goes, there is no wiggle room when it comes to grammar or punctuation. Spanglish is never a good idea for your ads.

---

153 Ibid.

That said, as far as the tone of *your* content goes, you need to pick what fits your firm best and then use it consistently across all of your ads and other marketing materials.

4. STRUCTURING AD COPY LIKE A ROBOT

Another example of law firms losing clicks because of the impression they give prospects is the robotic structuring we often see.

In short, this is what happens when law firms try to use bullet points in their ad copy.

Once again, to be fair, this may reflect the best of intentions. In the world of traditional copywriting, creating effective bullet points is considered an art form.[154] There are even copywriters who focus specifically on this one skill.

That makes sense when you consider how much sales copy relies on bullet points to draw attention and quickly communicate vital information. All you need to do is visit a single Amazon product page for proof of how important they've become. Most have two to three sets of bullet points designed to draw the eye and quickly sell the product.

Unfortunately, this kind of time-tested copywriting tactic doesn't transfer to Google Ads, where you don't have that kind of room and you're not working with nearly as much time. Prospects need to be convinced ASAP to click your ad.

Of course, Google Ads doesn't allow for the traditional bullet point list, either, which makes it all the odder that *so* many firms simply try to force a list into a short paragraph.

This is the result:

---

154 Brian Clark, "Little-Known Ways to Write Fascinating Bullet Points," *Copyblogger*, August 20, 2019, https://copyblogger.com/little-known-ways-to-write-fascinating -bullet-points/.

< Win with PPC **135** >

Source: google.com, accessed June 24, 2020

Again, you have some leeway where your tone is concerned. As long as it's professional, it can be anywhere between conversational and formal.

What it *cannot* be is robotic.

The copy above is definitely robotic. It reads like a program was tasked with taking important information off of a law firm's website and shoving it into an ad. We actually wouldn't be remotely surprised if that's exactly what happened.

Assuming that's not the case, we're all for trying to be efficient with your ad copy. You have limited space but still need to convey essential information. You just can't do it in a few words at a time. It's not just that it sounds like a robot was behind the copy—which makes it seem impersonal—it's that, ironically, these kinds of lists don't actually communicate much at all.

They're like a menu that lists the name of the dish but doesn't tell you what's in it or how it was made. Is that what customers want to see before they order?

Of course not.

Instead of providing answers, those kinds of lists only provoke more questions, which leads us to the fifth error we see so many firms make with their Google Ads.

< **136**   Natalie Fragkouli & Liel Levy >

5. POSING A QUESTION WITH YOUR ADS

Bulleted paragraphs like the ones we just described unintentionally elicit more questions than they answer.

However, it's just as bad when law firm ads intentionally pose these kinds of questions.

It's tough to know for sure, but this may be another example of well-intentioned copywriters using old-school tactics to try to grab attention. Long before the internet, one of the best ways to get a prospect to stop and take notice was with a provocative question.

That doesn't always work as well in the Digital Age. Asking questions in headers can actually plummet your conversion rates, especially when compared to a more personal approach.[155]

The big problem with using questions in Google Ads is that people don't search for questions. They search for answers. Even if they're not asking a question like, "Who is a personal injury attorney in Houston?" they still want to know, "Who is a personal injury attorney in Houston?"

This is why so many Google Ads don't get any clicks even when law firms put a lot of time and thought into creating them. They may even hire someone who has a background in copywriting. That person might think, "Need a personal injury attorney?" or "Have questions about personal injury law?" will arouse curiosity, but these kinds of headers are lackluster compared to more powerful statements.

Your header should provide the answers prospects are looking for in a confident manner. Why are you the right attorney for them? Don't leave it to them to figure out. *Tell* them. Give them that answer.

---

155 Joanna Wiebe, "The Question of Asking Questions," Copyhackers, https://copyhackers.com/2015/09/asking-questions/.

< Win with PPC **137** >

As long as you use your keywords in this header and the copy—so they stand out in the search results—you'll make it clear to prospects that your ad deserves clicking.

6. USE AS MANY CHARACTERS AS YOU CAN IN YOUR ADS

Brevity may be the soul of wit, but cutting the copy short on your ads is the soul of cutting your conversions short.

If we have a favorite mistake we see law firms make with their ad copywriting, this is probably it. We just can't wrap our heads around why this would ever be a good idea.

Sounding like a robot isn't smart, but we at least understand why some firms think throwing bullet lists in their ads is a good idea (again, it 100 percent isn't).

Using Spanglish is guaranteed to plummet your ads' Quality Scores, but we can see how a firm may think it's a really good— even respectful—idea.

However, only using half—or even less—of the space allotted to you for your Google Ad? What's the thinking there?

Maybe this is another example of traditional content creators applying their principles to a completely different medium. Lean copy works well in both blog posts and sales letters, so perhaps writers think the same will work for Google Ads?[156]

In any case, it won't.

Google has actually gone to great lengths—no pun intended *again*—to give copywriters more space for their ads. The character limit for Google Ads is now three headlines of thirty characters and two description lines of ninety characters.[157]

---

156   Ali Luke, "How to Write Short Sentences and Paragraphs the Right Way (and Why It Matters)," *ProBlogger*, January 24, 2019, https://problogger.com/short-sentences-and-paragraphs/.

157   Mark Irvine, "Google Expands Your Search Ads AGAIN! What You Need to Know," *WordStream*, September 26, 2020, https://www.wordstream.com/blog/ws/2018/08/22/new-expanded-text-ads.

< **138**   Natalie Fragkouli & Liel Levy >

That's a lot of space.

So, use it!

When we see ads like this, all we can think about is how much more the firm could have communicated with the space they left unused.

Source: google.com, accessed June 24, 2020

They could have used a lot more copy with a conversational tone to make the prospects feel more comfortable. They could have done that and boasted of their unique qualifications. They could have done both of those things and mentioned how much experience their firm had with immigration law.

One of the best things you can do with your ad copy is to remove any potential objections your prospects may have.

For example, many Hispanics are sensitive to price. If, say, you're a personal injury attorney, you could get around this objection by including that you don't charge a fee unless you win their case.

The firm in the example above didn't do any of these things with the space they were given.

And we'll bet anything their Quality Score and resulting conversions suffered because of it.

< Win with PPC **139** >

7. USING IRRELEVANT SITE LINKS

You should be very intentional about the links you choose for your law firm's ads. They shouldn't just take your prospect to your home page or a random landing page. All this will do is increase your ad spend while dropping your Quality Score and conversions.

Here's an example of what you should avoid doing.

Source: google.com, accessed June 24, 2020

These irrelevant links don't support the rest of the ad. Making matters worse, Google actually highlights them. Instead of helping the ad, they take away from it, forcing the prospect to wonder what they're doing there.

That doesn't inspire confidence, which means it won't inspire clicks.

8. USING GENERIC VALUE PROPOSITIONS AND VAGUE CTAs

Finally, do your ads make it clear why your firm is better than all the rest? Do they provide concrete value propositions?[158]

In other words, do your ads highlight why your firm is the right choice? Practicing a specific type of law is not a value proposition. Working in a certain city isn't, either. Unless your firm

---

158 Peep Laja, "How to Create a Unique Value Proposition (with Examples)," *CXL*, May 16, 2019, https://cxl.com/blog/value-proposition-examples-how-to-create/.

< **140** Natalie Fragkouli & Liel Levy >

is the only one that practices a particular form of law in a given area, those things don't make your firm stand apart.

Instead, your value proposition could be things like:

- Free consultations
- Awards

- Experience
- Board certifications

- Availability

More than likely, it will be a combination of these things. For example, you might be an award-winning firm that has been helping Hispanic people with immigration issues for more than thirty years.

Above all else, make your ads personal. That's the ultimate value proposition because no two firms are alike. As much as we preach the importance of best practices, we never recommend you try to sound like everyone else.

At Nanato Media, we don't start writing ads for the law firms we partner with until we have a deep understanding of their unique traits and what makes them different from other firms in the area.

Once you've nailed down your value proposition, you need to leverage it into a call-to-action (CTA).[159] For most firms, this would be a phone call. Let your prospects know you're waiting for their call and provide your phone number as the extension in your ad.

---

159 Billy McCaffrey, "Hook, Line, and Sinker: 7 Tips for a Killer Call-to-Action," *WordStream*, November 30, 2018, https://www.wordstream.com/blog/ws/2014/10/09/call-to-action.

< Win with PPC **141** >

DON'T SETTLE FOR LOW-PERFORMING GOOGLE AD CAMPAIGNS

Google Ad campaigns often enjoy a reputation as the most cost-effective way to advertise your law firm's services.

Unfortunately, they're often the costliest, simply because they never perform. Even worse, it's not because of the keywords. It's not because of poor segmentation. Those two factors will boost your ROI, but if you're not powering your ads with high-converting copy, there won't be any ROI.

< CHAPTER 8 >

HOW TO CREATE LANDING PAGES THAT CONVERT FOR YOUR LAW FIRM

If your law firm is like most, you've created a landing page or two that are supposed to win new clients. Unfortunately, if your firm is like most, those landing pages aren't very reliable. It's time to turn that around. In this chapter, we're going to explain the power of landing pages and then tell you the five most important factors for creating one that really wins you new business.

Having a website for your law firm isn't an option.

Either you have one or you're not going to have much of a law firm.

Of course, simply having a website isn't good enough. Your website needs the right pages, or leads won't find it. Just as bad, they might find it, but they won't find it effective at earning their business.

While different firms may need different types of web pages depending on the kinds of law they practice and the types of leads they want, every law firm's website needs landing pages.

< **144**   Natalie Fragkouli & Liel Levy >

WHAT ARE LANDING PAGES?

Before we explore what it takes to create landing pages that will actually convert prospects for your law firm, we need to establish what a landing page actually is.

Even though landing pages are extremely simple—*yet effective*—marketing assets, people still tend to define them very differently. For the most part, these definitions fall into one of two categories.

ANY PAGE CAN BE A LANDING PAGE

If you use Google Analytics to analyze your website's traffic, you may be aware of the "Landing Pages Report" (Behavior>Site Content>Landing Pages). However, this report follows a very broad definition of landing pages. *Yoast* does a good job of describing it:

> "A landing page is the first page of a session. Let's say Sarah is visiting your site. She starts her session on your site on blog post X and then reads blog post Y. In this case, blog post X is the landing page. You can translate that to the first page people land on when visiting your site. Google Analytics offers you a landing page report."[160]

Landing pages can be any page on your site, from blog posts to the home page, to anything else. As long as someone lands there, Google counts it as a landing page.

---

160 Annelieke van den Berg, "The Power of Landing Pages in Google Analytics," *Yoast*, November 7, 2018, https://yoast.com/landing-page-google-analytics/.

< Win with PPC **145** >

LANDING PAGES HAVE ONE SINGULAR GOAL

For the purposes of this post, we're going to be much more specific with our definition. After all, if pages as different as a blog post and home page can both be classified as landing pages, it's impossible to talk about how to improve them. Those distinct types of pages have completely different requirements.

Instead, landing pages are designed for *very* specific purposes. We like Unbounce's definition of a landing page:

> *"In digital marketing, a landing page is a standalone web page, created specifically for a marketing or advertising campaign. It's where a visitor "lands" after they click on a link in an email, or ads from Google, Bing, YouTube, Facebook, Instagram, Twitter, or similar places on the web.*
>
> *Unlike web pages, which typically have many goals and encourage exploration, landing pages are designed with a single focus or goal, known as a call to action (or CTA, for short)."*[161]

So, in this article, we're only talking about web pages that are designed *solely* to get your visitors to take a specific action. These landing pages typically live in subdomains and are not indexed by Google. For example, something along the lines of *help.your-lawfirm.com*. That means that the only traffic that they receive is the paid traffic of the campaign you assign to each landing page.

Your law firm may still benefit from a whole host of other types of pages—including those you want leads to land on—but you absolutely cannot afford to be without the kinds of landing pages we just described here: the kind that are designed for conversions.

---

161 "What is a Landing Page?" Unbounce, https://unbounce.com/landing-page-articles/what-is-a-landing-page/.

< **146**   Natalie Fragkouli & Liel Levy >

WHY EVERY LAW FIRM WEBSITE NEEDS LANDING PAGES

Don't worry.

We don't expect you to take our word for it.

Instead, take *hundreds* of our words for it.

We know that your law firm has countless digital assets to consider for their online campaigns, so we're going to spell out *exactly* why landing pages are one of the few you absolutely cannot be without.

LANDING PAGES ARE BETTER FOR PPC RESULTS

A website without regular traffic is worthless.

If your law firm's website doesn't regularly attract traffic, it's just an expensive business card. No one ever sees it until you tell them about it. And if you're able to do that, why not just sell them on your services right then and there?

Generally speaking, law firms can attract this traffic one of two ways: through organic traffic or paid traffic via PPC (pay-per-click) campaigns.

Organic traffic is great...if you can get it.

While many people often refer to it as "free" traffic, the problem is that it usually takes years in order to earn enough of it to gain regular leads. The only way to speed up the process is to spend money on keyword-specific pages, which really puts a damper on the whole "free" aspect so many people love.

At Nanato Media, we've talked a lot about how important it is for law firms to utilize PPC.[162] Yes, you pay for it, *but* you know

---

162 "Why PPC Is a Great Investment for Your Personal Injury Firm," *Nanato Media*, June 29, 2020, https://nanatomedia.com/blog/why-ppc-is-a-great-investment-for -your-personal-injury-firm/.

< Win with PPC **147** >

how much you're going to spend upfront, can get a much better idea of your potential ROI, and will see those results *much* faster. Those are three *huge* advantages over organic traffic.[163]

Okay, so we've established that PPC traffic is great.[164]

Unfortunately, while we often find that many law firms are on the same page when it comes to PPC traffic, they're *not* when it comes to what actual pages to send that traffic to.

We've seen a surprising number of firms that will put a lot of time and effort into their ads only to then direct them toward their home page. This isn't just bad for the reasons we brought up a moment ago (home pages don't convert well). It's bad because Google assigns a Quality Score to PPC Ads, which, in part, determines how much you'll need to pay for them.[165] One big factor that contributes to this score is the relevance of the landing page. Home pages can never be as relevant for an ad as a landing page that was specifically designed for it. In turn, they're not just dropping the ball where conversions are concerned. They're costing you more to do so.

LANDING PAGES ARE WHERE CONVERSIONS HAPPEN

In many industries, companies have to plan out a protracted marketing funnel to secure clients who find them online.[166] Generally, this involves four distinct stages, but each stage can require multiple marketing assets to finally convert clients. That's a lot of

163 "Why Your Law Firm Should Opt for PPC Before SEO," *Nanato Media*, April 9, 2020, https://nanatomedia.com/blog/why-your-law-firm-should-opt-for-ppc-before-seo/.

164 Corey Morris, "7 Powerful Benefits of Using PPC Advertising," *SEJ*, March 19, 2019, https://www.searchenginejournal.com/ppc-guide/ppc-advertising-benefits/.

165 Brad Smith, "All About AdWords Quality Score—And How to Improve It Fast," *HootSuite*, September 13, 2018, https://blog.hootsuite.com/adwords-quality-score/.

166 "The Modern Digital Marketing Funnel: Explained," *Blue Corona*, July 31, 2019, https://www.bluecorona.com/blog/new-digital-marketing-funnel-strategies/.

< **148**   Natalie Fragkouli & Liel Levy >

assets, which take a lot of time and a lot of money to put together. Then, there's the process of refining and fine-tuning them until they all work in harmony to create reliable conversions.

In other words, it's a lot of fun and extremely frustrating and expensive.

But here's the good news: law firms usually don't need those kinds of prolonged marketing funnels. As long as you're effectively taking full advantage of PPC, you can focus your efforts on qualified leads who want to speak to an attorney right away.

The same results don't happen with other pages.

For example, even if your home page looks amazing, it's still probably not going to be great for conversions. Your home page has to speak to every possible demographic you're interested in representing and, as you've probably heard before, when you're marketing to everyone, you're marketing to no one.[167]

You still need a home page. You just can't need it to deliver you new clients.

The same goes for other pages like blog posts. Most firms probably shouldn't invest in them in the first place. There are exceptions, but if your ideal lead is someone who knows they need an attorney ASAP (e.g., they were injured, they've been charged with a crime, they want to file for divorce), hoping they'll spend weeks educating themselves with your blog posts is a losing strategy.

In short, landing pages are where conversions happen. As we covered earlier, that's literally their only job. Fuel them with qualified traffic from a high-quality PPC campaign and they'll be where a lot of conversions will happen.

---

167 "To Market Successfully, Your Customer Can't Be 'Everyone' (Op-Ed)," *Business News Daily*, March 4, 2020, https://www.businessnewsdaily.com/5202-to-market-successfully-your-customer-cant-be-everyone.html.

< Win with PPC **149** >

LANDING PAGES CAN LEAD TO IMMEDIATE PHONE CALLS

This piggybacks off the last point, but it's important enough to earn its own section because most firms don't know just how powerful the right landing page can be.

In our opinion, most firms that understand the last two points still don't grasp this third one—which *really* makes all the difference.

A good landing page limits navigation.[168] There should be no links off the website or even to other pages *on* the website. Again, these pages are designed for one reason and one reason only: conversions.

Yet, most landing pages designed with this concept in mind only ever focus on getting prospects to fill out a webform or send them an email.

Those can be very effective. Live chat is another strategy that often works well, too.

However, at Nanato Media, we focus on another very important one: phone calls.

We want leads who are ready to become clients that very day. If they're willing to make a phone call after clicking on your landing page, that's a very good sign.

FIVE FACTORS THAT LEAD TO AN EFFECTIVE LANDING PAGE

You don't need to be a veteran of online marketing to understand what landing pages do. Even if you were brand new to the field,

---

168 Fahad Muhammad, "Fact: Navigation Links Kill Your Landing Page Conversion Rate," *Instapage*, June 25, 2020, https://instapage.com/blog/landing-page-conversion-rate-optimization.

< **150**   Natalie Fragkouli & Liel Levy >

you'd probably feel confident explaining the concept to someone else just based off of what you've read so far.

To some degree, that's one of the great things about landing pages. It's extremely easy to grasp what they are and, thus, why they're so valuable to your firm.

On the other hand, that can also make it seem like creating effective landing pages must be simple. After all, it's not like you need them to accomplish several things. There's just that one, simple goal: convert.

This kind of mentality is why so many law firms aren't happy with their conversion rates. It's why their Google Quality Score is so low. It's why their CPC is so high.[169]

Don't let this happen to you. Take full advantage of what landing pages have to offer your law firm by making sure yours include the following five essential factors.

1. CALL TO ACTION (CTA)

Every landing page needs a powerful call-to-action (CTA).[170] This is when you tell your prospect exactly what you want them to do. Even if you think it's obvious, you never want to leave this to chance. You should never assume your prospect will know what to do.

A perfect example of this that we see all the time is law firms that simply list their phone numbers on their landing pages. The copy on the page explains how the firm can help prospects who need specific services, so it seems safe to assume that a prospect will naturally get on the phone as soon as they're done reading.

---

169 "CPC (Cost per click)," Sprout Social, https://sproutsocial.com/glossary/cost-per-click/.

170 Megan Marrs, "17 Best Practices for Crazy-Effective Call-To-Action Buttons," *WordStream*, February 25, 2020, https://www.wordstream.com/blog/ws/2015/02/20/call-to-action-buttons.

< Win with PPC **151** >

As an attorney, you would never assume the judge or jury will side in your favor, right? You take every step possible to lead them down the path to the decision you want them to make. The same applies to landing page CTAs.

If you are trying to earn a phone call—and again we recommend that route—don't just list your number. Use a click-to-call button with the caption "Click to call now!" at the top bar of the landing page to make it even easier to earn the call. In fact, use many of them throughout the landing page. Wherever the prospect is on your page, they should be able to move their mouse to click and initiate a call. There's no law that says you can only use one CTA or that it has to come at the very bottom of the page.

Now, maybe you're not ready for handling incoming calls quite yet. Maybe you're a smaller firm—even a one-person operation—and you're worried you won't be able to handle an influx of calls throughout the day.

Whatever the case, if you decide to opt for using a webform, there are certain best practices you have to follow.

Aside from requesting the prospect's contact details, of course, the really big one is to ask the right questions on your form. You want to gain a good understanding of what your prospect's needs are and if you'll really be able to help them.

For example, if you run a mass tort ad campaign on Juul, ask whether the client smoked cigarettes before they started vaping.

Just don't overdo it.

While you want to learn as much about your prospect as possible before meeting with them, too many questions will hurt conversions. Remember, ideal prospects are the ones who want to speak with you ASAP, not fill out forms.

< **152**   Natalie Fragkouli & Liel Levy >

The right number of fields in your form is actually just three.[171] This will give you a conversion rate of at least 25 percent. Between three and five fields should still get you 20 percent, whereas including six or more will drop that to just 15 percent.

So, think long and hard about what you'd like to know before speaking with a prospect and do your best to keep those questions to a minimum. The easier it is for a prospect to get through them, the quicker you can turn them into a client.

2. ATTORNEY SHORT BIO

It should come as no surprise that before someone hires you for something as important as legal assistance, they want to know a bit about you. An effective attorney bio is helpful because:[172]

- Attorney bios rank second in terms of influence on hiring selection by general counsel. (The number one spot belongs to personal recommendations.)

- Attorney bios account for 80 percent of legal website traffic.

- Seventy-eight percent of in-house counsels rely on attorney bios when researching and hiring outside counsel.

That being said, there's a big difference between the kind of bio that might be helpful on your website and the kind you want on your actual landing page. As we just covered, your goal is to convince your prospect to contact you ASAP. Giving them your entire life story runs counter to this cause.

---

171 Syed Balkhi, "14 Form Conversion Best Practices (Backed by Research)," *WP Forms*, November 17, 2020, https://wpforms.com/research-based-tips-to-improve-contact-form-conversions/.

172 Nancy Slome, "Seven Steps to a More Authentic, Fresher Attorney Bio," Attorney at Work, https://www.attorneyatwork.com/seven-steps-authentic-fresher-attorney-bio/.

< Win with PPC **153** >

Instead, just list the most important details.

Namely, provide any credentials or experience that show you can provide the service you advertised. This isn't the place to go into your personal mission statement, why you got into law, or even where you went to school.

Put yourself in your prospect's shoes.

Will any of this matter to them quite as much as telling them how long you've been providing the services they want or how many similar cases you've handled?

Stick to those and keep the copy lean.

Then, be sure you add a professional photo of yourself. People like getting a sense for whom they'll be talking to if they follow your CTA. It reminds them that there's a real, live human being who's ready to help them with such an important matter.

3. RELEVANT INFORMATION ABOUT YOUR PRACTICE AREA

Another great way to quickly demonstrate your expertise is to talk a bit about relevant information regarding your practice area.

For example, if you run a campaign targeting leads who have recently been in auto accidents, you can add a section with a short paragraph on what the statute of limitations is in the state within which you operate.

What kind of information would be relevant to this kind of market?

Well, first you could briefly explain what their rights are and what they can realistically hope to expect by going to court. You could explain the statute of limitations in your state, as well. Obviously, you'd want to break down the benefits of securing an attorney to claim their compensation, instead of simply going at it alone (and, specifically, why you're that attorney).

By providing informative, high-quality content that is relevant

< **154**   Natalie Fragkouli & Liel Levy >

to the user, you not only add substance to your landing page, but your law firm comes across as a reliable choice. Additionally, the prospect has everything they need in terms of information about you and their case, so there's no need to keep looking. The next step is to complete the desired action: calling you.

Furthermore, when you provide this kind of relevant content that prospects find helpful, Google rewards you with a better Quality Score, which means a much lower CPC.

4. CREDENTIALS, REVIEWS, AND PROOF YOU'RE THE BEST

Don't rely solely on your bio to qualify yourself to leads. Designate a section that shows prospects why you're the best possible choice for the help they need.

This is where you'd list everything from professional awards you've received to memberships you may have in professional groups for attorneys. It's also a fantastic place to display reviews from Google or Facebook, which may actually mean a lot more to a potential client than any of your awards or memberships.

Don't forget about actual testimonials. You can pull them right from your Google My Business (GMB) Page, making it an easy way to show off just how good you are.[173]

Finally, we always tell the law firms we partner with to include any logos associated with TV or radio shows they advertise on or events they sponsor. This is especially effective if you decide to run branding campaigns.[174] This section will help reassure prospects who are specifically searching for you online that they've come to the right place.

---

173   "Engage with Customers on Google for Free," Google My Business, https://www.google.com/business/.

174   "Increase Brand Awareness," Google Ads Help, https://support.google.com/google-ads/answer/1722100.

< Win with PPC **155** >

Also, people enjoy seeing brands they know and like, so the simple inclusion of your logo is an easy way to enjoy a bit of recognition by association.

5. HEATMAPS AND OTHER BEHAVIOR ANALYSIS TOOLS

Lastly, the only thing worse than creating a landing page that doesn't convert is creating one that does but never takes extra steps to make sure it's converting as much as possible. You'd be surprised how much revenue law firms regularly leave on the table because they accept decent results, so they never bother working for extraordinary ones.

Fortunately, there are all kinds of easy ways you can track the success of your landing pages and learn how to improve them at the same time.

One of our favorites is heatmaps:

"Website heatmaps visualize the most popular (hot) and unpopular (cold) elements of a web page using colors on a scale from red to blue.

"By aggregating user behavior, heatmaps facilitate data analysis and give an at-a-glance understanding of how people interact with an individual website page—what they click on, scroll through, or ignore—which helps identify trends and optimize for further engagement."[175]

Install a heatmap tool on your landing page and you'll basically get a courtside seat at just how it's performing beyond conversions. Despite how impressive this kind of technology is, it might be even more impressive just how easy it is to understand. Heatmap refers to the visual hot and cold indicators displayed

---

175 "The Complete Guide to Website Heat Maps," Hotjar, July 30, 2020, https://www.hotjar.com/heatmaps/.

< **156**   Natalie Fragkouli & Liel Levy >

on your actual landing page. There are no technical analytics that will take practice to fully understand.

At Nanato Media, we use Crazy Egg for our heat mapping and love it.[176] As the heatmap report shows us where prospects are focusing their attention, we can use its results to easily identify and then remove any distractions that might be hurting our partners' conversions.

This is how you take a landing page from best practices and theory to actually converting at its highest possible rate among your unique market. The only other option for achieving these kinds of results is the expensive and time-consuming process of trial and error.

There are a number of other great options out there, too, when it comes to technology that will help you optimize your law firm's landing pages.

Countless behavior analytic tools exist,[177] but one type that we absolutely love is session recording platforms.[178] This software lets you virtually stand right next to the prospects visiting your landing page, so you can watch them interact with it in real-time.

Then, you can go back and watch recordings of these sessions to find out exactly what happened as different prospects interacted with your landing page. Just like with heatmaps, you don't need a high-level understanding of technical analytics to understand what you're seeing and use it to increase conversions.

---

176 "Crazy Egg Features," The Daily Egg, https://www.crazyegg.com/blog/crazy-egg-features/.

177 "14 Best Website Visitor Tracking Software Tools (By Category)," *The Daily Egg*, April 19, 2020, https://www.crazyegg.com/blog/website-visitor-tracking-software/.

178 Erin Gilliam Haije, "11 Visitor Recording and Session Replay Tools: An Overview," *Mopinion*, August 15, 2017, https://mopinion.com/11-visitor-recording-and-session-replay-tools-an-overview/.

< Win with PPC **157** >

The more often you go through these recordings, the more often you'll be able to improve your landing pages, so they secure more clients for your firm.

6. A/B TESTING

A/B testing is the act of running a simultaneous experiment between two or more variants of a landing page to see which one performs best.

You would be surprised how much you can increase conversions just by changing images or color schemes.

So, if you identify that variant A is bringing you the most conversions, pause variant B, and start trying variant C.

You can even choose the percentage of traffic you can send to each variant.

For example, send 70 percent of traffic to variant A now that you know that it works and 30 percent to variant C. The idea is to test, test, test. Don't just create a landing page and sit back.

At Nanato Media, we use Unbounce to handle A/B testing and highly recommend it.

Keep in mind that if you don't have enough traffic, A/B testing is not recommended. You generally need to have 1,000 conversions per month in order to get the right amount of data and make the most out of A/B testing.

< CHAPTER 9 >

HOW TO DOMINATE GOOGLE ADS FOR YOUR LAW FIRM

It seems like just about every law firm these days is running Google Ads, but most aren't seeing the kinds of consistent results that have made the platform so popular. Sound familiar? Are your ads barely justifying their overhead? Maybe you're not even seeing a positive ROI. If you're using Google Ads to target your local market, we're about to change that with this massive guide.

Unless you're just going to hope that word of mouth is enough to build your law firm's revenue, you need a plan for attracting new business again and again. In the twenty-first century, this means making the most of what Google has to offer. No law firm's marketing plan can afford to forget about the massive search engine.

While trying to win the organic-traffic wars is always tempting, no opportunity rivals Google Ads.

Still, it's not a tactic that guarantees results. You actually have to know what you're doing if you want to turn Google into your law firm's personal lead-generation machine.

< **160**   Natalie Fragkouli & Liel Levy >

Fortunately, we know what we're doing. Here's what it takes to dominate with Google Ads.

HOW TO SET UP A GOOGLE ADS SEARCH CAMPAIGN FOR GOOGLE ADS

After you understand which audiences and keywords to target for your Google Ads,[179] how to write ads that will convert, and have your conversion-rate-optimized landing pages developed, it's time to create your actual campaign.

The good news is that Google makes it fairly easy to set up a campaign for your firm:[180]

1. Sign in to your Google Ads account.

2. From the page menu on the left, click Campaigns.

3. To create a new ad group, click the plus button.

There it is.

That's all there is to it.

That's all it takes to start taking advantage of the most power-ful online advertising platform.

Now, that being said, if you want to see results, it's vital that you follow these tips that we've compiled from our years of experience.

---

179 "Law Firm Campaigns: Google Ads Keyword Research and Segmentation," *Nanato Media*, June 26, 2020, https://nanatomedia.com/blog/law-firm-google-ads-keyword-research-and-segmentation/.

180 "Create a Campaign," Google Ads Help, https://support.google.com/google-ads/answer/6324971.

< Win with PPC **161** >

SETTING UP YOUR AD CAMPAIGNS
BASED ON YOUR PRACTICE AREA

Without a doubt, one of the most important steps to creating effective Google Ads for your firm is making sure you're targeting prospects who live within your service area.[181] Otherwise, your ads will show to countless people who couldn't possibly hire you as an attorney, no matter how good of a fit you otherwise are for their unique needs.

Unless, because of certain circumstances like COVID-19, you decide to go statewide with bankruptcy ads, since court hearings are being done remotely, or you run a nationwide mass tort campaign, go as local as possible, especially if your budget is low. If you run campaigns in Spanish, you must know that Hispanics tend to want to visit your office to sign their cases, but then again, COVID has momentarily changed that.

Of course, your problems won't stop there. If your ads run outside of your practice area, their inability to generate clicks will dramatically drop your Google Quality Score.[182] As a result of that, you'll end up paying much higher CPCs (Cost-Per-Clicks) for having a higher CTR (clickthrough rate), which will mean an unimpressive ROI (if any at all).[183]

And, believe us, you can absolutely run campaigns outside your practice area without even wanting to. Just use generic keywords and don't have the right negative keyword list implemented,

---

181 "What Law Firms Need to Understand About Google Ads," *Nanato Media,* June 26, 2020, https://nanatomedia.com/blog/what-law-firms-need-to-understand -about-google-ads/.

182 "About Quality Score," Google Ads Help, https://support.google.com/google-ads/ answer/7050591.

183 "CPC (Cost per Click)," Sprout Social, https://sproutsocial.com/glossary/ cost-per-click/. "Clickthrough Rate (CTR): Definition," Google Ads Help, https://support.google.com/google-ads/answer/2615875.

< **162**   Natalie Fragkouli & Liel Levy >

and your budget can go to waste in the early morning hours. Or have numerous impressions from people who will never click on your ad since it is not relevant to their search.

This might seem obvious, but it can't be overemphasized. Some firms try to go outside their practice areas just to see if it's possible to increase their pool of prospects.

To be fair, Google Ads can be extremely effective at reaching prospects you'd otherwise never reach. And if you have a large budget and large intake team, we recommend you try this approach. But if not, sit tight and be specific. Every cent counts.

However, we still recommend you wait until after you've seen success with your current practice area. For one thing, keeping the location you target consistent will make it easier for you to judge the effectiveness of your campaigns. Deviating from the area you usually market to will naturally make it harder for you to distribute your budget (more on that in a moment).

For example, if you are a personal injury attorney with one legal office, and you want to advertise in just one city for car accidents, truck accidents, and motorcycle accidents, you will most likely have to set up a single campaign with three different ad groups as you probably don't have an unlimited budget.

This advice is in line with Google's own recommendations about ad groups:

> "Every ad group should have at least three quality ads. That way,
> the system can optimize your performance, and you can check your
> performance data to learn what message resonates best with your
> audience."[184]

---

184 "Create Specific Ad Groups with at Least 3 Ads," Google Ads Help,
https://support.google.com/google-ads/answer/7510328.

< Win with PPC **163** >

Even if you literally only offer one legal service, you should create three different ads around this ad group for best results. However, at Nanato Media, we typically craft five ads per ad group (sometimes more) to make sure we test enough copy options and allow for optimizations that will yield excellent results from your PPC campaigns.

CONSIDER YOUR BUDGET WHEN PRIORITIZING YOUR PRACTICE AREAS

As a business owner, you're already well aware of how important your budget is to your firm's success. You need to consider it every time you make a business decision.

That being said, the budget for your Google Ads campaigns will play an especially crucial role in their success—or lack thereof.[185]

Remember, you pay for every click—*not* every conversion. Therefore, you need to be smart about which keywords you use to target which prospects (including their locations). You also need to keep in mind that these keywords cost different amounts (especially if you decide to bid manually, more on that later)— yet another reason to keep your budget front-and-center when designing your law firm's Google Ads campaigns.

Going back to our previous example, let's say your personal-injury practice focuses on three main types of automobile accidents: those involving cars, trucks, and motorcycles.

Ideally, you could run one campaign and three ad groups, one for each of these types of accidents. Based on the advice we offered a moment ago, you would also create five ads for each ad

185 Allen Finn, "The Complete, Digestible Guide to Google Ads Budgets," *WordStream*, August 28, 2019, https://www.wordstream.com/blog/ws/2016/09/14/adwords-budget-guide.

< **164**   Natalie Fragkouli & Liel Levy >

group. So, at the very least, your law firm would be running fif-teen ads throughout the week.

By running a campaign with an ad group dedicated to each practice area, you basically make sure that the user is served a relevant ad to their search. It is very likely that they will click the ad, and your budget is divided between those ads.

For example, if there is more demand one day for motorcycle accidents, Google will allow for these clicks to come in, but when your daily budget is finished, the rest of your ad groups won't have the opportunity to show up on Google.

You can only set your budget at the campaign level. At Nanato Media, we always recommend to the firms we partner with that they run PPC ads targeting Hispanic prospects.[186]

To make these types of ads as effective as possible, these firms also need to invest in Spanish versions. Relying solely on English copy means disregarding prospects who only speak Spanish. Many Hispanic prospects who speak English will also ignore English ads, though, because they see them as a sign that the firm doesn't understand their culture.

If you advertise to your local Hispanic market, you will have to create another campaign in Spanish with the same ad groups and set the campaign's language settings in Spanish. You can include English language settings to reach Nueva Latina y Ambicultural Hispanics who might be searching for legal help in Spanish but use their browsers in English.

In short, when setting up your initial Google Ads groups, be sure you think long and hard about your budget and your cam-paign's goals. One of the many reasons to love PPC is that it's so easy to scale up your efforts. While it's important that you invest enough to see returns, you can still start small.

---

186 "Why Law Firms Must Run Spanish Google Ads," *Nanato Media*, March 23, 2020, https://nanatomedia.com/blog/why-law-firms-must-run-spanish-google-ads/.

< Win with PPC **165** >

Consider focusing on your more desired practice area that brings the highest ROI for your law firm, the right service area, and the right demographic. Typically, Spanish clicks tend to cost less than English clicks on Google, so keep that in mind. Once you begin seeing returns, you can reinvest the profits into growing your campaigns to include more prospects.

UNDERSTANDING KEYWORD MATCH TYPES AND AD TYPES

If you've made it this far into learning about Google Ad Search Campaigns, chances are that you're already well aware of the role keywords play.[187] In fact, you've probably already chosen the ones you think will be most important for your firm's campaigns.

That's all well and good, but there's another aspect of choosing keywords that not enough business owners seem to know about. In our experience, people who own their own law firms are definitely no exception. Unfortunately, overlooking this simple step is an extremely costly mistake. This oversight can even be enough to convince some people that PPC simply doesn't work.

What we're talking about is the powerful concept of keyword matching. As Google describes it:

"Keyword match types help control which searches on Google can trigger your ad. So you could use broad match to show your ad to a wide audience or you could use exact match to hone in on specific groups of customers."[188]

---

187 "Keywords: What Are Keywords & Why Do They Matter for PPC?" WordStream, https://www.wordstream.com/keyword.

188 "About Keyboard Matching Options," Google Ads Help, https://support.google.com/google-ads/answer/7478529.

< **166**   Natalie Fragkouli & Liel Levy >

THE CONSEQUENCES OF BROAD MATCH KEYWORDS

Business owners who are new to using Google Ads usually opt for Broad Match keywords.[189] This is an option that will show your ad for a specific keyword, as well as variations of it and related keywords. For example, you may pick the keyword "car accident" for one of your ads. If you choose the Broad Match option, Google may also show your ad for keywords like "auto accident" and "truck accident." It might get even broader and show your ad to people who searched for "traffic accident," "traffic accident laws," "traffic accident report," "traffic accident prevention," etc.

A tip here: don't ever target such a term. You will waste your clicks from people who are searching for car accidents in the local news. Be specific. You are an attorney. You want people who are looking for an attorney and are ready to convert to find you.

Again, this seems ideal to many business owners—at first. It seems to them as though this is a great way to put one of the most important aspects of their campaigns on autopilot. You don't need years and years of experience if Google will take care of matching your keywords with relevant prospects, right?

However, the broader your keywords are, the more you need to optimize to get the most out of each click you earn. Even then, the broad nature of your keywords means that the problem of unwanted clicks is unavoidable. Those unwanted clicks aren't just annoying. They're not just a waste of money, either. They'll hurt your Google Quality Score and every other aspect of your campaigns.

Perhaps worst of all, it's very difficult to improve your ad quality when you're not able to attract qualified prospects.[190] Relying

---

189 "Broad Match: Definition," Google Ads Help, https://support.google.com/google-ads/answer/2407779.

190 "Improve Your Ad Quality," Google Ads Help, https://support.google.com/google-ads/answer/2404196.

< Win with PPC **167** >

too heavily on broadly matched keywords means you'll have a harder time identifying which options give you the best ROI.

THE THREE OTHER MATCH TYPES YOU MUST LEVERAGE WITH YOUR AD CAMPAIGNS

Make sure you use broad match modifier, exact match, and phrase match types and monitor them daily at the very minimum. They can be a great way to quickly and effectively explore all of your law firm's options for keywords and place the unwanted terms in your negative keyword list. Here's what each keyword match type we suggest you use means:

- **Modified Broad Match**—This is a step between Broad Match and the more specific options below. With a Modified Broad Match, you can lock certain words or even phrases into place using the "+" parameter.[191] By doing this, you can still keep a relatively broad audience while increasing the control you have over who sees your ads.

- **Phrase Match**—For even more control, Phrase Match is a great option.[192] It will ensure your ads appear only when prospects search for your key phrase using the keywords you want in the exact order you determined. Queries can still include other words before or after your specified phrases.

- **Exact Match**—As the name suggests, this is the most restrictive option. For years, if you chose Exact Match, Google would show only your ad to users who had typed the exact keywords or

---

191 Lisa Wilkinson, "'What Do Those Plus Signs Mean?' Modified Broad Match for Beginners," *WordStream*, February 25, 2020, https://www.wordstream.com/blog/ws/2013/03/22/modified-broad-match-for-beginners.

192 "Phrase Match: Definition," Google Ads Help, https://support.google.com/google-ads/answer/2407784.

< **168** Natalie Fragkouli & Liel Levy >

phrases you specified.[193] That recently changed, so that Google may still show your ads if the searcher uses synonyms, similar variations, or the plural version of your specific keywords.

By investing in all three options, you'll get a holistic view of all the keywords and phrases that will work best for each of your law firm's individual ads. Then, all you need to do is pay attention to which of these bring you signed cases, and you'll be well on your way to consistently reliable campaigns.

Just remember to always give your campaigns enough time for Google to gather and deliver data on them. You'll also need to pair this information with sufficient data from your CRM (Customer Relationship Management) platform.[194] If you're not already using one, now would be the time to get started.

In the meantime, survey your team to see if they have information you can utilize to make even better use of the data Google is giving you about your keyword options.

If you're new to running Google Ads, it might be very tempting to stuff keywords into every ad group, even those that don't necessarily seem relevant.[195] Generally speaking, you'll only be allowed to use eighteen per ad group.

That said, we highly recommend that you keep your keyword list nice and short. It's much easier to manage something that becomes progressively more important as you increase the number of your law firm's campaigns or ad groups within the same campaign.

---

193 "Exact Match Keywords: Everything You Need to Know," WordStream, https://www.wordstream.com/exact-match.

194 "What is a CRM?" HubSpot, https://www.hubspot.com/growth-stack/what-is-crm.

195 "Irrelevant Keywords," Google Search Central, January 12, 2021, https://support.google.com/webmasters/answer/66358.

< Win with PPC **169** >

Furthermore, the more targeted your list is, the easier it is to achieve a high Quality Score with Google. You should be checking this score regularly, of course, but you'll find it's much easier to improve it—and maintain those improvements—when you can easily manage your keyword list.[196]

THE FIVE AD EXTENSIONS YOUR LAW FIRM NEEDS

These last two sections are of vital importance. Yet they're two that we often find law firms completely miss. Most owners who contact us to partner on Google Ads haven't even heard of these two incredibly important concepts.

The first one we're going to explore is the five extensions for your Google Ads that no firm should be without.[197]

1. THE POWER OF CALL EXTENSIONS

For law firms, the absolute most important extension is the Call Extension[198] (not to be confused with call-only ads[199]). The great thing about these extensions is that they make it incredibly easy for prospects to contact you and speak with you right away. They don't even have to visit your law firm's landing page or fill anything out beforehand. If your prospects have an urgent need to talk with a lawyer ASAP, this extension is a necessity.

---

196 "Check Your Quality Score," Google Ads Help, https://support.google.com/google-ads/answer/2454010.

197 "Select Extensions to Use," Google Ads Help, https://support.google.com/google-ads/answer/7332837.

198 "Use Call Extensions," Google Ads Help, https://support.google.com/google-ads/answer/2404182.

199 "10 Ways to Succeed with Google Call-Only Campaigns," *WordStream*, August 28, 2019, https://www.wordstream.com/blog/ws/2015/11/11/call-only-campaigns.

< **170**   Natalie Fragkouli & Liel Levy   >

Every firm should take advantage of this incredible extension, but we are especially adamant when we recommend it to firms that want business from Spanish-speaking prospects. Most don't want to put as much time into researching your firm or going through your Facebook accounts as their English-speaking counterparts do. They just want to speak with a law firm they believe can help them. If you make this easy with the call extension—and you have the right Spanish copy to engage with them—you'll find it's easy to attract these kinds of prospects.

2. LOCATION EXTENSIONS

Next, Location Extensions are another one we can't recommend enough to law firms.[200]

First, they'll make it as easy as possible for prospects to find your office so they can come in and speak with you in person. All they have to do is click on the extension and directions will pop right up.

Second, and more importantly, location extensions will immediately prove to your prospects that your law office is a legitimate, local firm. Competitors who lack this kind of validation may appear to prospects as though they're not authentic.

Including this extension will also give your firm the potential for a second ad impression on the local pack. It will also make your office visible at the top of the page even if your bid otherwise isn't enough to win your ad a spot with the others up there. So, you could still receive the click without spending the same kind of money as other firms.

---

200 "About Location Extensions," Google Ads Help, https://support.google.com/
google-ads/answer/2404182.

< Win with PPC **171** >

3. CALLOUT EXTENSIONS

As a law firm, one of the most critical steps you can take to win new business is to show how your firm stands out from all the rest. This isn't always easy, though, especially when it comes to winning that kind of competition when you're being directly compared to all of the companies using Google Ads.

That's why we love Callout Extensions.[201] They let you specify the unique advantages your firm offers prospects who choose them when they need legal help.

For example, say you have forty years of experience, you have won billions of dollars for your clients, you offer twenty-four-seven service—all of this can be displayed with a Callout Extension to tell the prospect why your firm is the superior choice.

Aside from the fact that this extension will win your Google Ads more interest, we also know it's a fantastic way of finding out exactly what your prospects care about most. For instance, you might discover that mentioning your years of experience doesn't get you as many clicks as talking about all the cases you've won or the total amount you've earned for your past clients.

You can then take these insights and do a better job of calling attention to them on your landing pages and throughout your website to earn even more business.

4. SITELINK EXTENSIONS

Sitelink Extensions really help make your ad much more prominent by making it bigger.[202] Again, this is a huge advantage when you consider how important it is for your firm to stand out from the competition.

---

201 "About Callout Extensions," Google Ads Help, https://support.google.com/google-ads/answer/6079510.

202 "About Sitelink Extensions," Google Ads Help, https://support.google.com/google-ads/answer/2375416.

< **172** Natalie Fragkouli & Liel Levy >

That's not the only reason we love Sitelink Extensions, though. We also love how they can showcase more specific info about your firm and provide links to other landing pages you have built for a specific campaign.[203] This way, you can target different segments within a campaign with different landing pages, ensuring everyone gets the kind of information they require to convert from a prospect to a client.

Just remember not to link to generic pages on your website with Sitelink Extensions. Doing so will make it much harder to monitor the performance of your campaign. Trying to court specific segments with general copy is always a losing plan, too.

5. STRUCTURED SNIPPET EXTENSIONS

Finally, you'll be doing your campaigns a huge favor if you add Structured Snippet Extensions to them.[204] These extensions let you highlight the kinds of legal services your firm offers, so there's no mistaking what you do.

For example, if you're an immigration attorney, you could list services like handling family-based visas, employment-based visas, and more.

Honestly, after that, we wouldn't recommend any other extensions for your law firm campaigns. There are plenty of others you could choose to include, but they won't offer the same kinds of ROI and, instead, will just give you more to manage. As long as you leverage the five we just described, you'll see plenty of impressive results.

---

203 "Why Drive Your Law Firm's PPC Traffic to Landing Pages," *Nanato Media*, June 18, 2020, https://nanatomedia.com/blog/why-drive-your-law-firms-ppc-traffic -to-landing-pages/.

204 "About Structured Snippet Extensions," Google Ads Help, https://support.google.com/google-ads/answer/6280012.

< Win with PPC **173** >

DON'T FORGET ABOUT THE IMPORTANCE OF AN EFFECTIVE AD SCHEDULE

Once you check all the other boxes for your law firm's Google Ad campaign, it's easy to overlook the importance of this final step. If you get everything else right, but don't nail this one, at the very least, you'll be leaving a lot of business for your competitors. At worst, all of your efforts will fail to produce the kind of positive ROI you need for your law firm.

And yet, we're talking about a really simple concept: when to schedule your Google Ads.[205]

When you're just starting out, it might actually make sense to just run them indiscriminately: twenty-four hours a day, seven days a week. Otherwise, you risk making an assumption based on when you think it would be best to run your ads. If that assumption is even slightly off, you might be doing your competitors a huge favor.

As with so many things related to Google Ads, treat this initial approach as a test. Analyze the results so you can get a better idea of what times will actually get you the most leads. Then, reschedule your ads accordingly.

As we touched on in the last section, we're huge fans of outfitting your ads with Call Extensions, so prospects can get ahold of you ASAP. If you plan to go that route, we can't stress enough that you should only schedule your call extension to show up on your ads during days and times when your intake team is available to answer the phone. Ideally, you want your intake team to answer

---

205 Alison Glazer, "The Best Time to Run Google Ads: How to Optimize Your Ad Campaigns for Time of Day," Whole Whale, https://www.wholewhale.com/tips/best-time-to-run-google-ads/.

< **174**   Natalie Fragkouli & Liel Levy >

these calls within just one or two rings. Remember, if your prospects are clicking the option to call you from an ad, they urgently want to speak with you.

Here's one last insider tip, especially if you plan to run personal injury campaigns or any others that have high CPCs: run your ads *after* hours.

That's right. As opposed to the advice we just gave you about phone calls, we actually recommend you run your ads starting at five o'clock in the evening. You can turn them off anytime between midnight and six o'clock in the morning. Run them during the weekends, too.

Then, take Monday off. This is when bidders with the biggest budgets think it's a good idea to bid as high as they can afford. They want to capture anyone who needs to speak with an attorney because of something that happened over the weekend (e.g., they were injured, arrested, etc.).

By taking this approach, you'll steer clear of bloated CPCs but still capture plenty of leads.

< CHAPTER 10 >

SIX ADVANCED GOOGLE ADS STRATEGIES FOR YOUR LAW FIRM

Before you spend more on your Google Ads campaigns, make sure you're not leaving some of their potential on the table. With the six advanced strategies we list in this chapter, you're about to see how you can take your campaigns to another level and quickly secure more qualified leads than ever before.

It should go without saying that Google Ads are the best possible way for law firms to secure new leads.

If it doesn't, well...that's a problem.

Law firms all over the country rely on Google Ads for new business.

However, even firms that have successfully utilized Google Ads for years often come up short. Even worse, they usually don't realize how much potential business they're leaving on the table.

At Nanato Media, we're proud of the fact that one of the many ways we stand out from the crowd is that we know Google Ads inside and out. When we create campaigns for our partners, we don't stop with the basics.

< **176**   Natalie Fragkouli & Liel Levy   >

Instead, we love using these six advanced strategies to ensure our Google Ads campaigns always go above and beyond.

1. CREATING A CUSTOMIZED BID STRATEGY FOR YOUR UNIQUE ADVERTISING GOALS

Often, when a law firm contacts us to partner on their marketing efforts, one of the first things they'll do is tell us that they already tried PPC and "it doesn't work."

Of course, that comes as a real shock to us, seeing as how PPC is *fantastic* for law firms and we have years of experience to prove it.[206]

What we usually discover they really meant is that PPC didn't work well for them.

Interestingly, many of these firms were successful at navigating many of the initial challenges associated with successful PPC campaigns: setting up an account, choosing keywords, writing copy, etc.

Instead, what ultimately sank these firms' PPC campaigns was that they didn't have an effective bidding strategy in place. The right bidding strategy for Google Ads is about so much more than just protecting your budget. Although that's important, it's just as much about making sure your ads are able to perform.

The first step to launching a successful Google Ads campaign for your law firm is to consider your unique advertising goals. Obviously, the end goal is to generate more leads, so you sign more clients, so you can make more money.

---

206 "Why PPC Is a Great Investment for Your Personal Injury Firm," *Nanato Media*, June 29, 2020, https://nanatomedia.com/blog/why-ppc-is-a-great-investment-for-your -personal-injury-firm/.

< Win with PPC **177** >

What we're talking about is specific to Google Ads, though. The bidding strategy for your campaign will need to focus on one of the following metrics:

- Clicks

- Impressions

- Conversions

Only after you choose one of these targets can you then choose an effective bidding strategy for hitting it again and again and again.

CONSIDERING YOUR OPTIONS
FOR BIDDING ON GOOGLE ADS

When it comes to bidding, Google Ads gives you two main options:

- **Manual Bidding:** As the name suggests, with this bidding method, you set your own maximum cost-per-click (CPC) and set a bid for each keyword you are targeting.[207]

- **Automated Bidding:** As Google likes to put it, this strategy, "Takes the heavy lifting and guesswork out of setting bids to meet your performance goals."[208] You choose your goals and Google automates the bidding based on your choice of strategy: Maximize Clicks, Target Impression Share, Target CPA, Target ROAS, Maximize Conversions, and Maximize Conversions Value.

---

207 "Manual CPC Bidding," Google Ads Help, https://support.google.com/google-ads/answer/2390250.
"Cost Per Click (CPC): Learn What Cost Per Click Means for PPC," WordStream, https://www.wordstream.com/cost-per-click.

208 "About Automated Bidding," Google Ads Help, https://support.google.com/google-ads/answer/2979071.

< **178**   Natalie Fragkouli & Liel Levy >

- **Smart Bidding:** Google considers Smart Bidding Strategies to be, "A subset of automated bid strategies that optimize for conversions or conversion value."[209] This advanced bidding strategy even uses machine learning to optimize your bids so they maximize both your law firm's "conversions and conversion value across your campaign or bidding portfolio."[210] This strategy also includes four subsets of its own:

  - Target CPA[211]

  - Target ROAS[212]

  - Maximize Conversions[213]

  - Maximize Conversion Value[214]

As you can see, Google Ads aren't lacking for options when it comes to bidding strategies.

Nonetheless, for many firms, this is more of a problem than a benefit. They simply don't know which of these strategies to pick and, while they're all extremely impressive, the wrong decision can still be a costly one.

---

209 "Smart Bidding: Definition," Google Ads Help, https://support.google.com/google-ads/answer/7066642.

210 "About Target CPA Bidding," Google Ads Help, https://support.google.com/google-ads/answer/7066642.

211 "About Target CPA Bidding," Google Ads Help, https://support.google.com/google-ads/answer/6268632.

212 "About Target ROAS Bidding," Google Ads Help, https://support.google.com/google-ads/answer/6268637.

213 "About Maximize Conversions Bidding," Google Ads Help, https://support.google.com/google-ads/answer/7381968.

214 "About Maximize Conversion Value Bidding," Google Ads Help, https://support.google.com/google-ads/answer/7684216.

< Win with PPC **179** >

WHICH STRATEGY IS RIGHT FOR YOUR LAW FIRM?

While it makes sense that many firms eventually give up on Google Ads because they get lost trying to determine the right bidding strategy, that's not going to happen to you.

You have us.

And we have years of experience helping law firms leverage the full power of Google Ads.

The surprising answer most of our partners don't expect is that we recommend they use a manual bidding strategy for their Google Ads.

Really?

Look, we know it doesn't come across as impressive as your other options. Anything that involves machine learning has to be the absolute best, right?

Well, no, not always in this case (we'll cover an exception a bit later).

If you are completely and absolutely brand new to Google Ads and you don't have years to change that, then, yes, it's probably best you choose one of the bidding strategies that gives Google a chance to help you.

However, the tradeoff for that choice is that you won't see a dependable ROI. Even with the help of machine learning, Google can't possibly know as much about your market as you do. As powerful as its algorithms are, they're still going to make mistakes when bidding on the right keywords, and even these minor mistakes have costs that will accumulate.

For law firms, this kind of approach just isn't realistic. You need new leads on a regular basis. You need them to be qualified leads, too, so they actually turn into clients. You can't risk "getting your feet wet" with Google Ads by choosing a strategy that doesn't let you control the most important factors.

< **180** Natalie Fragkouli & Liel Levy >

That's why we recommend manual bidding strategies to our partners.

The more control you have, the easier it will be to lower your cost-per-acquisition (CPA).[215] Instead of casting a wide net with automated bidding, you can practically handpick the types of leads who will see your ads. This doesn't just drop your CPC over time. It improves your ROI, and most importantly, it ensures you can sleep at night knowing your firm isn't going to run low on new cases.

All this is possible because a Manual Bidding Strategy lets you choose the maximum amount you would like to pay per click for any given keyword. Again, Google can try to do this and even has some very impressive technology for doing so. It's why so many inexperienced attorneys try doing PPC on their own. Google makes it seem easy.

However, the truth is that your knowledge of your market is a competitive advantage that even Google can't beat. You can consider keywords for your campaigns that may convert at a much higher rate than others. This includes the kind of keywords that are more likely to attract qualified prospects who bring you cases that you can sign.

Don't give up this advantage or your Google Ads campaigns will absolutely suffer.

WHY MANUAL BIDDING STRATEGIES ARE ESSENTIAL FOR TACKLING HIGH-CPC KEYWORDS

Another reason many law firms try other bidding strategies is that they hear how effective they've been for other companies.

---

215 "What is Cost Per Acquisition (CPA)? (Updated for 2019)," Big Commerce, https://www.bigcommerce.com/ecommerce-answers/ what-is-cost-per-acquisition-cpa-what-is-benchmark-retailers/.

< Win with PPC **181** >

The problem is that those companies are in completely different industries or particular legal verticals. Those industries may see miniscule CPCs. In that case, bloated overhead may not seem like that big of a deal.

This isn't ever the case with law firms, especially when it comes to PPC for personal injury or workers comp firms that operate in competitive markets.[216]

If you work in one of these two legal fields, then you already know that their markets are extremely competitive. As a result, the corresponding CPCs tend to be extremely high. This is when it's absolutely essential that you use a manual strategy that gives you full control over your bids. Otherwise, you're practically gambling, and the stakes are exceedingly high.

Let's look at an example to drive home this important point.

Say you run a personal injury firm, so your goal is to target high-intent users by winning positions at the top of Google's result pages for keywords that are relevant to this market. Better still, you can use that positioning to utilize Call Extensions, so prospects can literally talk to you right away.[217]

While you could target all kinds of keywords, you'd probably agree that an especially valuable one would be, "car accident lawyer near me." In that case, the prospect clearly needs your services at that very moment.

As such, you'd want to take advantage of the Manual Bidding Strategy to raise your bids on that particular keyword. You could keep doing so until you finally see your ad in the top spot on Google for that very valuable search term.

---

216 "7 Ways to Improve ROI on Personal Injury PPC," *Nanato Media*, July 19, 2020, https://nanatomedia.com/blog/seven-ways-to-improve-roi-on-personal-injury-ppc/.

217 "Use Call Extensions," Google Ads Help, https://support.google.com/google-ads/answer/7159346.

< **182**   Natalie Fragkouli & Liel Levy >

We always tell our partners to use Google's very helpful Ad Preview and Diagnosis Tool, which, among other things:

> "...shows a preview of a Google search result page for a specific term. This helps you see which ads and extensions are appearing for your keyword. Once you enter a search term and other criteria like language and location, the tool will tell you whether your ad is eligible to appear in that situation."[218]

In other words, the Ad Preview and Diagnosis Tool acts like a crystal ball, so you have a better idea of what to expect from your investment. This is just one more way you can supercharge your firm's Manual Bidding Strategy.

It's also worth pointing out that sometimes you can still see impressive ROIs even if you only make the second or third place at the top of Google's results page. However, this is only true if you can write exceptional Google Ad copy that can reliably win those clicks.[219]

Otherwise, don't settle for anything other than the top spot. Manually raise your bids until you're able to win it for the keywords you know hold the most value in your market.

We always tell our partners that it is far better to spend their entire day's budget to win just one click if it will convert into a client than to spend it on a million clicks that won't yield them a single conversion. This might seem obvious, but it's easy to be tempted to play the numbers game instead of zeroing in on the most valuable keywords.

---

218 "Ad Preview and Diagnosis Tool," Google Ads Help, https://support.google.com/google-ads/answer/148778.

219 Brad Smith, "6 Adwords Copywriting Tips That Will Grab Anyone's Attention," *AdEspresso,* January 29, 2018, https://adespresso.com/blog/adwords-copywriting-tips/.

< Win with PPC **183** >

Before we move on to the next section, we want to leave you with one very important piece of advice for marketing to Hispanic prospects—something we recommend all firms do.[220]

It's vital to keep in mind that Hispanics—especially those who predominantly speak Spanish—will usually call you the moment they see your ad online. They want to speak to someone right away, which is why it's a good idea to use call extensions whenever you're targeting Hispanics with your Google Ads.[221]

Even with the help of call extensions, though, your goal still needs to be reaching the top of Google. In the end, a combination of great copywriting, the right ad extension, a high Quality Score, and the right bid is all it takes to consistently generate qualified leads for your firm.[222]

TARGETING HIGH-VOLUME, LOW-CPC CAMPAIGNS

Maybe you work in a legal field where the keywords you need to target come with much lower CPCs. In that case, you can afford to launch high-volume Google Ads campaigns. Two examples where we see this a lot with law firms is PPC campaigns for immigration and family law.[223]

As we mentioned earlier, in a high-volume, low-CPC situation, we understand why many firms opt for automated bid strategies.

---

220 "Why Every Law Firm Must Focus on Hispanic Clients," *Nanato Media*, June 20, 2020, https://nanatomedia.com/blog/why-every-law-firm-must-focus-on-hispanic -clients/.

221 Greg Swan, "Google Call Extensions: How to Set Up and Track," *Tinuiti*, June 22, 2020, https://tinuiti.com/blog/paid-search/google-call-extensions/.

222 "About Quality Score," Google Ads Help, https://support.google.com/google-ads/ answer/7050591.

223 "SEO vs PPC for Immigration Law Firms: Which To Use and How," *Nanato Media*, July 27, 2020, https://nanatomedia.com/blog/seo-vs-ppc-for-immigration-law-firms -which-to-use-and-how/.

< **184**   Natalie Fragkouli & Liel Levy >

Just be sure to set the maximum cost-per-click bid limit, so it's well within your budget.[224] Otherwise, you are going to learn a very expensive lesson.

Okay, but what does this mean for your firm's bidding strategy?

It still depends on your ultimate goals. Even though you're automating your bids and leaving much of your campaign up to Google, that doesn't change. The line of business may be the same, but some accounts will behave differently than others.

In the past, we've tried Target CPA for partners who were personal injury attorneys and saw very impressive results. However, we've also seen Target CPA completely miss the mark for other partners.

If you don't mind budgeting for some experimenting, it might be worth trying Target CPA to see what your results are.

You could also make sure that conversion tracking is set up for your account and then get started with a Maximize Clicks Strategy.[225] This would help give your campaign some initial momentum and then you could switch over to Maximize Conversions.

In the end, there is not just one Google Ads strategy that always works best for every single law firm. There are just too many variables involved—from competition to the local market and more.

The vast majority of the time if you partner with experts, manual bidding is going to be best. Otherwise, prepare for a lot of experimentation to find the right strategy for your unique firm.

---

224 "Maximum CPC Bid: Definition," Google Ads Help, https://support.google.com/google-ads/answer/6326.

225 "Set Up Conversion Tracking for Your Website," Google Ads Help, https://support.google.com/google-ads/answer/6095821.

< Win with PPC **185** >

2. KEEPING TRACK OF YOUR CONVERSIONS

In a previous section, we briefly touched on a very important component to succeeding with Google Ads: tracking conversions.[226] We recommend you set this up even if you're planning to use a Manual Bidding Strategy for your campaigns.

For one thing, it's extremely easy to do.

More importantly, though, conversion tracking will show you what a prospect does after they interact with your ad. Ideally, they'll call your firm to speak with an attorney right away. At the very least, you hope they'll fill out a form, so you can contact them about their case.

If you don't track your prospects, you'll never be sure how they interact with your landing page, which will rob you of the opportunity to improve it. Conversion tracking will also give you insights into other important factors like:

- Keywords

- Ads

- Ad Groups

Use all of this information to constantly improve your Google Ads campaigns and you'll realize massive increases to your profits.

If you plan to utilize Smart Bidding Strategies like Maximize Conversions, then it's essential you take the time to set up conversion tracking.[227] Otherwise, you can't expect your campaign to be

---

226 "Different Ways to Track Conversions," Google Ads Help, https://support.google. com/google-ads/answer/1722054.

227 "About Conversion Tracking," Google Ads Help, https://support.google.com/ google-ads/answer/1722022.

< **186**   Natalie Fragkouli & Liel Levy >

very effective because it's based on conversions that are reported in your Google Ads account.

To see even better results from your campaigns, we also recommend you use Google's conversion metrics in tandem with others that are important to your law firm. For example, you should compare them with how many prospects actually become clients.

By keeping a close eye on your conversions, you'll be able to see how many prospects interact with your Google Ads on one device or browser before converting on another.

This way, no conversion goes untracked and, no matter where they happen, you'll have the data to learn how to go out and repeat the process.

3. MANAGE YOUR CAMPAIGNS WITH BIDDING SCRIPTS

As you've probably noticed by now, bidding strategies can be fairly complicated, even if you decide to outsource much of the heavy lifting to Google.

It's worth mentioning here that one potential solution to a lot of this complexity is using Bidding Scripts. In short, these scripts let you automate the bidding process while still maintaining a great deal of control and flexibility. By automatically integrating helpful third-party datasets, you can increase available data, too. The result can be better, more effective bidding and Google Ads campaigns that produce greater ROIs.

Like many of the other tips we've mentioned, finding the right Google Ads bidding scripts for your firm will probably take

< Win with PPC **187** >

some experimentation.[228] At Nanato Media, we use Google Apps Script to automate Google Ads management.[229]

4. UTILIZE HOURLY DAYPARTING TO MAKE THE BEST USE OF YOUR TIME (AND BIDS)

Dayparting is one of our absolute favorite PPC tactics.[230] We utilize it to schedule our partners' ads for certain times of the day and/or certain days of the week depending on when we know they're most likely to convert target audiences.

Every firm is different, but we almost always use dayparting to automate hourly optimizations. In our experience, just about every single local market has a peak time or specific day when searches, impressions, and clicks spike. It only makes sense to capitalize on these incredible opportunities.

How do we do so for the law firms that rely on us?

It's actually quite simple.

We do everything we can to make their ads as visible as possible during those times and days.

Okay, but how do you know when the best times and days are for your firm?

It's fairly simple.

The first thing you need to do is run your Google Ads for at least a few months. That's because we don't want to rely on

---

228 "5 AdWords Scripts for Smarter Bidding," *WordStream*, July 31, 2019, https://www.wordstream.com/blog/ws/2018/01/05/adwords-bidding-scripts.

229 "Many Google Apps, One Platform in the Cloud," Google Apps Script, https://developers.google.com/apps-script.

230 "Dayparting: What Is Dayparting?" WordStream, https://www.wordstream.com/dayparting.

< **188**   Natalie Fragkouli & Liel Levy >

guesswork for such an important decision. Instead, we want to know exactly when your market is most active. The only way to do that is to actually run a campaign that will garner impressions and clicks.

After you have at least three months of data, it's time to dive in for insights.

Go to your Google Ads account and navigate to the Dimensions Tab, analyze the reports, and set your bids accordingly.[231]

If you opt for a Manual Bidding Strategy, you can use hourly campaign-level dayparting scripts that will let you set hourly bid adjustments for every campaign in Google Ads.[232] This is the same approach we usually take with our partners.

By automatically running this script every single hour, you will always have your desired bid adjustments ready for the next couple of hours.

Pretty cool, huh?

The one catch is that to effectively execute this kind of strategy, you need advanced knowledge and years of experience with Google Ads.

If you don't have that, hopefully you can find someone who does (hint, hint).[233]

---

231 Tom Demers, "Google AdWords Reporting Guide: AdWords Dimensions Tab Tips & Tutorials," *WordStream*, June 11, 2020, https://www.wordstream.com/blog/ws/2011/10/11/google-adwords-dimensions-tab-guide.

232 Frederick Vallaeys, "Hourly Campaign-Level Dayparting for AdWords," Optmyzr AdWords Scripts, https://www.optmyzr.com/scripts/hourly-campaign-level-dayparting-for-adwords/.

233 "About Us," Nanato Media, https://nanatomedia.com/about-us/.

< Win with PPC **189** >

5. USE BUDGET SCRIPTS TO OPTIMIZE YOUR SPEND

Speaking of the power of scripts, let's touch on another one we're big fans of at Nanato Media: Budget Scripts.[234]

These scripts automatically check if an item (e.g., keyword, ad, ad group, campaign, or account) exceeds your law firm's budget.

This is particularly useful if you have allocated different amounts to each of your campaigns and want the peace of mind that comes from knowing none of them will overspend.

Another reason to love Budget Scripts is because they'll let you bid on keywords within specific ad groups of your campaigns that produce inconsistent results without overspending. We recommend this when a keyword has converted for you before, comes with a cheap CPC but is also very hit-or-miss. This applies to generic, short-tail keywords, the kinds that usually consist only of two words.

Instead of giving up on it altogether, you can set a specific budget script just for this keyword. That way, the script can pause further spending on this fickle keyword the moment you hit your budget for it. Once this happens, you'll have more budget left for the other keywords you want to target that month.

One more budget script we really love for our partners is "Reach Target Monthly Spend." You can set that monthly spend in your script and decide at what time each day it should change your budget. Typically, this happens after hours to ensure you spend your entire budget.

With this approach, you might run your ads with a $100 budget one day and a $400 budget the next. It all depends on the budget you have available.

---

234 Matilde Mualim, "About: Flexible Budgets," https://nanatomedia.com/about-us/.

< **190**   Natalie Fragkouli & Liel Levy >

That said, all of these benefits are only available to those who choose a Manual Bidding Strategy.

6. RUIN YOUR COMPETITORS' FUN WITH FRAUD PREVENTION SOFTWARE

Finally, we need to talk about the importance of fraud prevention for your Google Ads campaigns.

This piece is crucial.

As you've been busy reading this section, there's a good chance that one of your competitors has been busy clicking your ad.

No, it's not because they need representation and have conceded you're superior.

Instead, it's because they take great pleasure in wasting your money.

They click your ad.

You get charged.

They leave your landing page.

They deplete your budget, so your ads no longer show that day.

They laugh hysterically at your expense.

Their ad shows up the next time a user searches for an attorney because they knocked you out from the auction.

What can you do?

We're not going to sugarcoat this: if you're not partnering with us, not a whole lot.

Nothing is stopping your competitors from driving up your overhead while driving down your conversions.

Why can't we stop this from happening?

< Win with PPC **191** >

Because, at Nanato Media, we use sophisticated fraud prevention software to make sure you don't pay for those clicks.

You read that right.

HOW OUR FRAUD PREVENTION SOFTWARE WORKS

To keep our partners' competitors from ruining their campaigns, we use software that blocks the IP address of any user after their first click. How long we block it for depends. For example, we usually block an IP address for three months for our partners with personal injury firms.

After all, it is very unlikely that someone will get in a car accident, click the ad, not convert, get in another accident within three months, click on the same ad, and this time convert.

We also make sure to exclude IP ranges when too many clicks are made by different IP addresses from the same range. This is another way we keep competitors from hurting your law firm's ad campaigns.

TURNING GOOGLE ADS INTO A RELIABLE RESOURCE FOR CONSISTENT LEADS

Google Ads campaigns have too much potential to be taken lightly.

If you're not already utilizing the six strategies we listed above, that's exactly what you're doing. You're allowing one of the best ways to secure new clients for your firm to fall short.

< CHAPTER 11 >

WHY ADVERTISING WITH GOOGLE DISPLAY ADS IS A MUST FOR LAW FIRMS

What if we told you that one of the most effective ways to market your law firm was also one of the most underutilized? Sound too good to be true? It's not. Google display ads are extremely powerful for marketing and remarketing to your most valued prospects, and yet most firms aren't running them. Change that and you'll enjoy one incredible competitive advantage.

Thanks to the internet, there have never been more ways to market your law firm.

Of course, all of those options can often feel overwhelming. Running a law firm is hard enough without having to learn about a million different ways to acquire new clients.

It's why most attorneys familiarize themselves with SEO and PPC, and that's about it.

While those are both powerful strategies—and two we regularly help firms with—you're making a costly mistake if you ignore the incredible potential of Google display ads.

< **194**   Natalie Fragkouli & Liel Levy >

Aside from the fact that most of your competitors probably aren't using them, Google display ads offer a host of other unique advantages. Learn to leverage them and you could soon have a massive pool of prospects all to yourself.

WHAT ARE GOOGLE DISPLAY ADS?

As the name suggests, Google display ads are advertisements that are displayed all over the internet, from blog posts to YouTube videos and even to mobile apps.[235] This is thanks to the absolutely massive Google Display Network, which comprises more than two million websites.

That reach is why you have undoubtedly seen Google display ads before. In fact, you've probably seen them today—even numerous times.

Before we get into the reasons we love Google display ads and how to use them so that you love them too, let's quickly talk about what they are.

Like Google Search and Google Ads, Google display ads run on intent. They're not showing up randomly. There's a reason why you see ads on sites for products or services you recently showed interest in elsewhere.

While Google Search and Ad campaigns are limited to Search Engine Results Pages (SERPs), Google display ads can show up on any Google property or site within the Google Display network. Google uses cookies and data from its users to track what they search for and what websites they visit. It then uses this information to decide which ads to show users and where to show them.

---

235 "Reach More People in More Places Online," Google Ads, https://ads.google.com/home/campaigns/display-ads/.

< Win with PPC **195** >

WHY WE LOVE GOOGLE DISPLAY ADS FOR LAW FIRMS

Here's how Google explains the reach of their display ads:

"The Google Display Network reaches 90 percent of internet users worldwide, across millions of websites, news pages, blogs, and Google sites like Gmail and YouTube."

Ninety percent!

That's one reason we absolutely love Google display ads for law firms.[236] While other networks are great, none of them can boast anything even remotely close to this kind of reach.

Here are two more reasons we recommend them to every firm we partner with:

- **Branding:** Display ads let you visually display what differentiates your firm from the competition. Showing prospects how professional, friendly, and diverse your firm is will give you a huge advantage over competitors who rely solely on the text from their *PPC ads* to get users to their landing pages.[237]

- **Staying Top-of-Mind:** Ideally, you'd love to appear in front of a prospect the moment they need a law firm. That's why we still love PPC ads for our partners. However, running display ads is how you can always stay top of mind with your market, so

---

236 "The Straightforward Guide to Google Display Ads for Law Firms," *Nanato Media,* May 23, 2020, https://nanatomedia.com/blog/the-straightforward-guide-to-google-display-ads-for-law-firms/.

237 "Why PPC Is a Great Investment for Your Personal Injury Firm," *Nanato Media,* June 29, 2020, https://nanatomedia.com/blog/why-ppc-is-a-great-investment-for-your-personal-injury-firm/.

< **196**   Natalie Fragkouli & Liel Levy >

they think of you the moment they—or someone they know—needs legal help. In this way, you lock in their business before they even search for it in Google.

In short, Google display ads are the ultimate asset for building awareness with your market before your competitors can through SEO or PPC.

At the same time, with a variety of bidding options, ad formats, and reporting, Google display ads don't force you into casting a wide net. Display campaigns allow you to set how, when, and where your ads are shown.

THE TWO TYPES OF GOOGLE DISPLAY AD CAMPAIGNS

That said, most of the law firms we've worked with who had previously tried Google display ads came up short. In some cases, they came up very short. Even though the Google Ad Network gives them access to more than two million sites, these firms lost a lot of money trying to make the most of it.

Aside from the fact that these attorneys obviously aren't professional marketers, we'd say that one of the biggest reasons for their underwhelming results was that they didn't understand the two different campaign options.

SMART DISPLAY CAMPAIGNS

Smart Display campaigns offer full automation.[238] For this kind of campaign, you provide a handful of inputs:

---

238 "About Smart Display Campaigns," Google Ads Help, https://support.google.com/google-ads/answer/7020281.

< Win with PPC **197** >

- What Your Ads Will Say
- Images You Want to Use
- Daily Budget

- Cost-Per-Acquisition (CPA)
- Performance Targets

Once you provide them, Google will mix and match your ads at scale.

However, you won't be eligible to run Smart Display campaigns until you have gotten at least fifty conversions with Display campaigns. We'll cover those next. Otherwise, you need to earn at least one hundred conversions on Search in the last thirty days. Either way, you'll also have to configure conversion tracking in your Google Ads account to track this metric and qualify.[239]

So, while this level of automation may seem like an invaluable feature, it's hard to recommend Smart Display campaigns to anyone other than those who run large law firms. If you don't run ads nationwide—or at least in a few different states—you'll be far better off investing in our next option.

STANDARD DISPLAY CAMPAIGNS

Standard display ad campaigns certainly don't sound nearly as effective as their "smarter" counterparts, but they're actually the version we recommend to the law firms that partner with us.[240]

---

239 "Set Up Conversion Tracking for Your Website," Google Ads Help, https://support.google.com/google-ads/answer/6095821.

240 "Standard Display Ads," Google Ads Help, https://support.google.com/displayspecs/answer/187449.

< **198**   Natalie Fragkouli & Liel Levy >

That's because they give you *full* control over every aspect of your Google display ad campaign. You can manually choose the targeting, bidding, and ad formats for your firm.

At Nanato Media, we're all about customizing campaigns for law firms. Automation sounds great, but you'll never reach your best possible ROI if you don't control, test, and refine its most influential factors.

Fortunately, that's exactly what we're going to show you how to do with the rest of this article.

CHOOSING WHO TO TARGET AND HOW WITH YOUR GOOGLE DISPLAY ADS

Before you can start seeing impressive returns from your Google display ads, you have to know how to target your ideal prospects.[241] Otherwise, you'll suffer the same fate that so many law firms have before contacting us: lots of time and money spent with no new clients to show for it.

This is another reason we generally don't recommend Smart Display campaigns. Effective targeting is so important that we don't even trust Google to get it right. You're much better off taking the time to understand how it works and then putting in more time at mastering it.

Making this extra effort is even more important if you do have competitors who are running display ads. Chances are they stopped short of becoming proficient at targeting. They might've assumed Google can take care of it for them. Let their mistake become your advantage.

---

241 "Targeting Settings on the Display Network," Google Ads Help, https://support.
google.com/google-ads/answer/1209882.

< Win with PPC **199** >

When determining which one of your ads will display for which of your target markets, you need to pay special attention to your total ad reach.[242] This is the number of people you'll be targeting with these ads. You also have to keep an eye on whom you'll be targeting.

That first metric may look impressive, showing you the thousands of people who could potentially learn all about your firm.

But if those people don't stand a good chance of becoming paying clients someday, what's the point? You might as well just throw that money away (Note: don't actually do that; we'll show you how to target the right people).

Reviewing who will see your display ads will also tell you whether or not you need more than one ad group within your campaign or if a second campaign is needed. Deciding on a new ad group or campaign could make all the difference for your display ad ROI.

For example, many of the firms we partner with want to market to Hispanic prospects among others.[243] They come to us because, unfortunately, they're not having a lot of success.

Whenever we hear this, we're almost always right in assuming that the problem is they're trying to target all of their prospects with the same campaign. This, despite the fact that many of their Hispanic prospects will either speak Spanish or at least favor ads in Spanish for cultural reasons.

While there are a number of different ways we can help this kind of client, simply choosing the right language for their campaign is usually enough to start turning their results around.

242 "About Ad Reach," Google Ads Help, https://support.google.com/google-ads/answer/1722045.

243 "Getting Started with Your Law Firm's Hispanic Marketing Strategy," *Nanato Media*, June 20, 2020, https://nanatomedia.com/blog/getting-started-with-your-law-firms-hispanic-marketing-strategy/.

< **200**   Natalie Fragkouli & Liel Levy >

Now that you have a better understanding of how Google lets you target potential clients with display ads, let's look at the three most important options for law firms.

KEYWORD TARGETING ASSOCIATED WITH PAGES, APPS, AND VIDEOS

Targeting keywords is the most common form for law firms using Google display ads.[244]

However, targeting keywords for display ads is different than the way it works for PPC and SEO. Again, that's because you're showing your ads to users based on the sites, apps, or videos they visit. They're not being displayed based directly on the keywords they're entering into Google's search engine.

Instead, you choose keywords you want to target, and then Google searches its network for sites, apps, and videos that it associates with them. In this way, the outcome is still very similar—your ad shows up in front of relevant groups—even though Google takes a different approach to getting there.

Let's look at a quick example to see what this might look like.

Say you're a divorce attorney who wants to market your firm to people who are actively looking for help filing for divorce. In that case, you would probably want to target keyword phrases like, "how to file for a divorce" as, presumably, that's what your ideal prospect would be searching for in Google.

Once you decide to target that keyword, Google will look for those users and then show your display ads to them whenever they visit a site on their network.

Another thing to love about Google display ads is that you'll actually do better by targeting keywords with high impressions.

---

244 "Choose Keywords for Display Network Campaigns," Google Ads Help, https://support.google.com/google-ads/answer/2453986.

< Win with PPC **201** >

These are the keywords that will make sure you reach the most users possible, but they also tend to have very low CPCs.

Furthermore, you can use them to reach prospects who are still in the very early stages of the marketing funnel. In the above example, they might not be ready to meet with an attorney today, but because they're actively researching how to file for divorce, there's a good chance that will change soon.

Plus, you can use a remarketing campaign to show up in front of them again and again as they progress closer to needing representation. We'll cover remarketing in just a moment.

UNDERSTANDING AUDIENCE VS. CONTENT KEYWORDS

When targeting keywords for your law firm's campaigns, it's important that you understand your two options: Audience (the default) and Content.[245]

If you choose Audience, you're telling Google to show your display ads to anyone who may be interested in your targeted keywords, whether or not they're on a relevant site.

If you select Content, your ads will display only on sites, apps, and videos that Google knows are contextually relevant to your campaign's targeted keywords.

We usually recommend you target your keywords based on Content. Otherwise, your ads will show to users who aren't in the right mindset to contact an attorney at that very moment.

For example, say you're a personal injury attorney and you run a car accident campaign. By choosing Audience, prospects may see your ad even though they're just checking the local news. Sure, they need your help, but at that moment they just want to know the weather before they head to work.

---

245 "Choose Keywords for Display Network Campaigns," Google Ads Help, https://support.google.com/google-ads/answer/2453986.

< **202**   Natalie Fragkouli & Liel Levy >

Now, compare that to showing your ad to someone who's on an auto body shop's website. The chances are now much better that they will want to talk to a personal injury attorney.

It's not that the Audience keyword setting is never a good idea, though. It can be a good place to start if you have a low advertising budget and just want to drive brand awareness.

In this last example, you could always create an auto body shop ad group and then set up keyword targeting for auto body shop brand names in your service area or search terms related to auto body shops.

NEGATIVE KEYWORDS

Negative keywords are just as important for display ads as they are in PPC.[246] If you don't include them in your campaigns, they're bound to show up on irrelevant sites.

That said, negative keywords work a bit differently with display ads.

Depending on the other keywords or targeting methods you're using for an ad group, some places where your ad appears may occasionally contain your negative keywords.

On the other hand, you can avoid targeting unrelated sites by implementing content exclusions and site category options.[247]

DEMOGRAPHIC TARGETING

Finally, you can also target prospects based on demographics.[248]

---

246 "About Content Exclusions and Site Category Options," Google Ads Help, https://support.google.com/google-ads/answer/3306596.

247 "Set Content Exclusions and Site Category Options," Google Ads Help, https://support.google.com/google-ads/answer/7444288.

248 "About Demographic Targeting," Google Ads Help, https://support.google.com/google-ads/answer/2580383.https://support.google.com/google-ads/answer/7444288

< Win with PPC **203** >

This can include age, gender, parental status, and household income.

That last one has proven to be especially helpful for our law-firm partners who focus on workers' compensation cases.

For a Spanish workers' compensation campaign, they can select Spanish for the language and then exclude the household income options from "Top 10 percent," "11–20 percent," and "21–30 percent" and more. By doing so, they can make sure they are reaching only blue-collar workers.

You can also use a combination of demographic targeting, like excluding certain age groups (e.g., users who are older than sixty-five).

CHOOSING THE BEST FORMAT FOR YOUR LAW FIRM'S DISPLAY ADS

You have two options for formatting your Google display ads: either create responsive ads or upload your own image ads.

Responsive ads automatically adjust their size, appearance, and format to fit available ad spaces.[249] So, the same responsive ad may appear as a small text ad in one place and a large image ad in another.

To create this kind of ad, you need to enter its assets (i.e., headlines, descriptions, images, and logos).

At Nanato Media, we are all about control, so when deciding on the display ad format for your ad, we recommend you go with the second option: designing and uploading your own image ads. This is one of the many times a design team like

---

249 "Create a Responsive Display Ad," Google Ads Help, https://support.google.com/google-ads/answer/7005917.

< **204**   Natalie Fragkouli & Liel Levy >

ours can help. We can design the images for your ads to make sure your message is consistent, on-brand, and completely in line with your website.

As we touched on earlier, whenever you automate your ads, you lose some measure of control. If you are all about your brand image, you probably won't be happy with how responsive ads show as text ads on Display Network websites. Unfortunately, there's no option to remove text ads. So, uploading your own ads is best for controlling your brand experience.

ONE BIG MISTAKE YOU HAVE TO AVOID AT ALL COSTS

One big mistake you must avoid at all costs is opting to run your Search campaigns' text ads in both the Search and Display Network.

Running text ads in the Display Network not only won't work but, even worse, you'll basically authorize Google to use as much of your central strategy budget (Search Network) for display campaigns. This will directly impact your search campaign performance. For your display campaigns, run them separately using the tips provided in this section.

Here's the really important thing you have to remember: Google Ads make it really easy to walk right into this mistake when you're setting up your search campaigns. It's set that way by default, so you need to uncheck this option in the network settings.

< Win with PPC **205** >

REFINING PLACEMENT TARGETING

While we have a lot of really great things to say about the Google Display Network, you can't take full advantage of it with a set-it-and-forget-it strategy. That kind of approach is actually a really good way to waste a lot of money.

For the same reasons automation doesn't work, you need to pay close attention to your campaigns or they'll quickly result in disappointment.

The placement of your display ads is a perfect example of what we're talking about. You need to make sure that you're always checking in on your Google display ad campaigns to see where, exactly, your ads are being shown. As powerful as Google is, it can still make mistakes. Worse, it can compound those mistakes over and over—charging you each time—if you don't step in and stop it.

So, if you discover that an ad placement isn't helping your firm attract qualified prospects, you need to refine that campaign to put a stop to it and help Google better understand where your ads have the best chance for success.

We always recommend to the law firms we partner with to use placement targeting to check on where their display ads are actually being shown.[250]

By doing so, they can decide to increase their bids accordingly to improve exposure where it helps most and/or block placements where they know they're not seeing any results. Either way, they'll improve the ROI of their marketing budget.

---

250 "Targeting Settings on the Display Network," Google Ads Help,
https://support.google.com/google-ads/answer/1209882.

< **206**   Natalie Fragkouli & Liel Levy >

USING REMARKETING TO SKYROCKET YOUR DISPLAY ADS' ROI

Speaking of simple—but effective—ways you can increase the returns you get on your ad spend, nothing compares to the power of remarketing.[251]

For those who may be unfamiliar with the practice, remarketing—sometimes called retargeting—is pretty much what it sounds like. It's a strategy that allows you to continue marketing to a current prospect.

However, the real strength of this strategy is that you're marketing only to prospects who have already shown interest in your legal services. One of the most common versions is showing your ads to a prospect who has already visited your law firm's website.

Even better, you can remarket to them across completely different campaign types.

For example, at Nanato Media, we always make sure that visitors who go from our partners' search campaigns to their Google ads landing pages are also being served their display ads.[252]

When done successfully, remarketing *will dramatically* increase your campaigns' conversion rates and ROIs. That's because past site visitors who are already familiar with your brand and what your law firm has to offer are much more likely to become customers.

After all, they've already shown they're considering hiring your firm. For whatever reason, they haven't hired you yet, but you

---

251 "How Does Google Remarketing Work?" WordStream, https://www.wordstream.com/google-remarketing.

252 "Why Drive Your Law Firm's PPC Traffic to Landing Pages," *Nanato Media,* June 18, 2020, https://nanatomedia.com/blog/why-drive-your-law-firms-ppc-traffic -to-landing-pages/.

< Win with PPC **207** >

stand a good chance of changing that if you continue reminding them of why they visited your website in the first place.

Compare that to simply advertising to prospects who have shown no interest in your site. Sure, they may do so eventually, but until then, you can't be sure if they're actually a prospect.

LEAD FORMS FOR DISPLAY ADS

Google has announced that by the end of the year (2021), it will start offering lead forms for display ads.[253]

This will be very powerful for converting leads who have shown some level of intent but don't want to stop what they're doing when they see your ad. With these new lead forms, they can still convert by effortlessly sending you their contact information.

These forms will allow you to request your prospect's:

- Name

- Email

- Phone Number

- Postal Code

- City

- State

- County

- Business Name

- Job Title

- Work Email

- Work Phone

You can also include present questions based on the legal service's vertical.

---

253 Kim Spalding, "Tap into Intent to Generate Leads," *Google Ads & Commerce Blog*, August 5, 2020, https://blog.google/products/ads-commerce/generate-leads/.

< **208**   Natalie Fragkouli & Liel Levy >

This is huge news for companies that advertise with Google as lead forms are something it's been testing since as far back as 2010. Companies have been requesting this improvement for even longer. It will make a big difference for securing qualified prospects who would have otherwise ignored a display ad, even though they need legal help.

It's one more very big reason to start leveraging Google display ads for your law firm ASAP.

USE GOOGLE DISPLAY ADS FOR THE ULTIMATE COMPETITIVE ADVANTAGE

We know that Google display ads can seem intimidating. They involve a lot of moving parts, and most attorneys aren't as familiar with them as they are with PPC and SEO. Many aren't familiar with them at all.

But that's why they're such a competitive advantage.

Despite the fact that they're affordable, have an almost unlimited reach, can catch prospects before they even know they'll need you, and are completely customizable, most firms are trying to get by without them.

Don't make the same mistake.

< CHAPTER 12 >

THE ULTIMATE GUIDE TO FACEBOOK ADS FOR LAW FIRMS

If you're not currently marketing your law firm on Facebook, you better hope your competitors are making the same mistake. Seriously. Facebook represents one of the most cost-effective ways to market your firm and allows you to learn more about your firm's market. Our ultimate guide will take you through everything you need to know to start running successful Facebook ads right away.

If you thought Facebook was only good for stalking old flames and getting into political arguments with your relatives...

Well, you were close.

However, as it turns out, Facebook is also absolutely amazing for marketing your law firm to new leads. If you're not already using it for that, might we suggest you start ASAP?

< **210** Natalie Fragkouli & Liel Levy >

WHY FACEBOOK ADS HAVE BECOME MANDATORY FOR LAW FIRMS

Facebook introduced its Ads platform more than a decade ago.[254]

Since then, it's becoming the marketing darling of countless companies across practically every industry.

And yet, we still hear from law firm owners all the time who have never run a single Facebook Ad.

Before we show you how our digital marketing agency has used Facebook for years to consistently generate leads for law firms, let's briefly discuss why this is such a powerhouse platform for marketing.

FACEBOOK IS KING OF SOCIAL MEDIA

A whopping 71 percent of American adults use Facebook.[255]

That's not just a lot.

That's the highest penetration of any traditional social media network—by a lot. We wouldn't consider YouTube a traditional social media network, but it still beats out Facebook for users with 74 percent of Americans.

On the other hand, compared to actual social media platforms, Facebook is far more popular. Only 38 percent of American adults use Instagram, which is still a lot more than Twitter accounts at just 23 percent.

Put another way, if you combine Instagram and Twitter's penetration into the American market, Facebook is still ahead by 20 percent.

---

254 "Facebook Unveils Facebook Ads," *Facebook Newsroom*, November 6, 2007, https://about.fb.com/news/2007/11/facebook-unveils-facebook-ads/.

255 "Social Media Sites as Pathways to News," *Pew Research Center*, September 16, 2019, https://www.journalism.org/2019/10/02/americans-are-wary-of-the-role-social-media-sites-play-in-delivering-the-news/pj_2019-09-25_social-media -and-news_0-08/.

< Win with PPC **211** >

Those numbers alone would be reason enough for us to advocate running Facebook ads for law firms.

But it actually gets better.

WHY FACEBOOK IS FANTASTIC FOR MARKETING TO HISPANIC PROSPECTS

At Nanato Media, we're here to show you how your law firm can reach your local Hispanic prospects.[256] After all, we are the leading Hispanic marketing agency for law firms in the nation. So, who better than us to give you insights?

It's us.

Just us.

According to a study done by the Pew Research Center's Internet Project, 80 percent of the country's Hispanic adults use social media. That's significantly more than the 72 percent average for the rest of the country.

Furthermore, Hispanic social media users in the US are more likely to follow brands on platforms like Facebook.

In another study done by Unilever, researchers found that Hispanic consumers are twice as likely as the rest of US consumers to share content on social media and click content shared by others.

That's not all, either.

Hispanic consumers share five times more often on social media than non-Hispanic users. Content shared by Hispanics is also 35 percent more likely to earn clicks than content shared by others.

---

256 "Why Every Law Firm Must Focus on Hispanic Clients," *Nanato Media,* June 20, 2020, https://nanatomedia.com/blog/why-every-law-firm-must-focus-on-hispanic -clients/.

< **212**   Natalie Fragkouli & Liel Levy >

FACEBOOK VS. GOOGLE ADS

One of the most common questions we get about Facebook ads is, "What if I'm already running Google Ads for my law firm? Do I still need to run Facebook ads, too?"

The answer is yes.

Look, we love Google Ads for law firms and have spent years refining a process that ensures ours are as effective as they can possibly be.[257]

So, we're definitely not telling anyone to give up Google Ads for Facebook. There is no better advertising than targeting high-intent users who have already decided that they need a lawyer. But Facebook can be surprisingly beneficial, too.

What we are saying is that you should use both to generate sufficient leads while protecting your budget.

That's because Facebook ads are *much* cheaper than the prices you have to pay on Google for keywords related to your practice area.[258] This is especially true for law firms where it's not uncommon to pay hundreds of dollars for a single click—one which might not even convert!

Sure, this means casting a much wider net, but given the savings you'll enjoy, most law firm owners are perfectly happy with the tradeoff.

Still, we know that many owners remain wary about the prospect. To them, a wide net is analogous with mixed results. When they think of Facebook, they think of people who have come to

---

257 "What Law Firms Need to Understand About Google Ads," *Nanato Media*, June 26, 2020, https://nanatomedia.com/blog/what-law-firms-need-to-understand-about-google-ads/.https://nanatomedia.com/blog/why-every-law-firm-must-focus-on-hispanic-clients/

258 Rebecca Bowden, "Google Ads vs. Facebook Ads: Which is the Best Choice for Your Business?" Agency Analytics, https://agencyanalytics.com/blog/google-ads-vs-facebook-ads.

< Win with PPC **213** >

peruse their friends' photos or leave updates about their day.

In short, they believe that Facebook is largely an entertainment site. They find it hard to believe that anyone—much less law firms—can use it as a major channel for reliable leads.

Fortunately, this just makes Facebook that much more powerful for those firms that do invest in its ads. If you want to join their ranks and start seeing more leads in your funnel, then it's time to learn how to actually run successful Facebook ads.

NINE ESSENTIAL STEPS TO RUNNING SUCCESSFUL FACEBOOK ADS FOR YOUR FIRM

With all that being said, yours wouldn't be the first law firm to run Facebook ads but be disappointed by the results. You may have tried numerous times. Maybe you even modified your approach each of those times, hoping the new attempt would be the one that finally works.

Again, if this sounds familiar, you're not alone. Over the years, we've worked with a number of law firms that had given up on the idea of running Facebook ads.

As a digital agency that specializes in Facebook ads, take it from us: they work. They actually work quite well for law firms. It's no exaggeration to say that Facebook could become your law firm's most successful channel for new leads.

However, as you already know, it's not that easy. The reason we've been so effective at using Facebook ads for our law-firm partners is because we always take advantage of these eight essential steps.

< **214**   Natalie Fragkouli & Liel Levy >

1. BOOSTING YOUR LAW FIRM'S ORGANIC POSTS

Perhaps the easiest step to increasing your exposure through Facebook ads is through utilizing Facebook posts. By doing so, you increase the chances that it will reach your ideal audience. In this way, you greatly reduce the size of your aforementioned net.

As long as you have a business page, Facebook will let you boost your posts.[259]

Another aspect that makes it both user-friendly and effective is that you don't need to understand Facebook Ad Manager to boost your ads.[260] It's a great way to get started generating new leads even if you've never run any type of ads before.

Literally, all you need to do is pick posts from your law firm's business page that you want to promote. Then, just click the "Boost Post" button and, as the command implies, it will be pushed out in front of more people. By boosting it, you will enjoy more reactions, comments, and shares. Of course, that means your post may reach lots of new people who then decide to follow your law firm's page.

Boosting is something you should get in the habit of doing even for your regular content that you post to engage your community and followers. Again, boosting your posts is fairly affordable, so it's a cost-effective way to continue building your Facebook audience.

That being said, we're not telling you to boost every post. That's a great way to quickly overwhelm your budget.

Instead, boost only those posts that are targeted at potential leads. The posts should give prospects a clear reason why they ought to become a client. Give them a clear call to action

---

259 "About Facebook Pages," Facebook for Business, https://www.facebook.com/business/help/461775097570076.

260 "Ads Manager," Facebook for Business.

< Win with PPC **215** >

and redirect them to a specific landing page with high-converting ad copy.

Also, while generating leads is always the end goal, it helps a lot if you use Facebook to build your brand.[261] Not every post needs to be about the services you offer. They definitely don't all need a call to action, either.

These efforts will be particularly helpful if you plan to market to Hispanic prospects.[262] They like to see proof that your firm understands their culture. For even better results, experiment with Facebook posts in Spanish, which is another way to prove you understand how important their culture is to them.[263]

2. HOW FACEBOOK BOOSTED POSTS DIFFER FROM FACEBOOK ADS

It might sound like Boosted Posts and Facebook ads are basically the same thing, but there are definitely some important differences you need to understand before proceeding.

Boosted Posts target two objectives:

- Engagement
- Website visits

The aim is to improve your Facebook posts' visibility and engagement (i.e., likes, comments, and shares). It's a quick and inexpensive practice for staying on top of your prospects' minds

261 Omar Jenblat, "Build Your Brand With Facebook Business Marketing," *Forbes*, October 31, 2017, https://www.forbes.com/sites/forbesagencycouncil/2017/10/31/build-your-brand-with-facebook-business-marketing/#4c0380943aca.

262 "Getting Started with Your Law Firm's Hispanic Marketing Strategy," *Nanato Media*, June 20, 2020, https://nanatomedia.com/blog/getting-started-with-your-law -firms-hispanic-marketing-strategy/.

263 "Bilingual Facebook Ads," Nanato Media, https://nanatomedia.com/bilingual -services/facebook-ads/.

< **216**   Natalie Fragkouli & Liel Levy >

by appearing in front of them again and again. That way, when they *do* need a lawyer, they know exactly whom to contact.

With Facebook ads, you may target the following objectives:[264]

- Awareness
- Consideration
- Conversions

Broken down further, you can pursue these objectives by creating ads specific to any of these goals:

- Brand awareness
- Reach
- Traffic
- Engagement
- App installs
- Video views
- Lead generation
- Messages
- Conversions
- Catalog sales
- Store traffic

Facebook Ad Manager will also let you further customize your ads depending on which goals you choose. For example, you could decide to add a call-to-action button to your ad or use language and behavior targeting to drill down into your demographic even more.[265]

---

264 "Choose the Right Objective," Facebook for Business, https://www.facebook.com/business/help/1438417719786914.

265 "About Call-to-Action Ads," Facebook for Business, https://www.facebook.com/business/help/465446147173921.
"Ad Targeting," Facebook for Business, https://www.facebook.com/business/ads/ad-targeting.

< Win with PPC **217** >

3. LEVERAGING THE POWER OF FACEBOOK LEAD ADS

One of our favorite ways to quickly produce impressive results for the law firms we partner with is through Facebook Lead Ads.[266]

They're yet another way that Facebook makes it easy for firms to generate leads and begin the process of converting them—even for those who have no prior experience using this platform.

With a Facebook Lead Ad, when a qualified prospect sees it, they just tap on it and a form will immediately pop up. Better still, this form arrives prepopulated with their contact information—taken directly from their Facebook profile.

Now, you may be wondering, "What if the information is outdated or just incorrect?"

Good question!

The way we get around this potential problem when helping firms is to add a "preferred phone number" prompt to the form. Facebook lets you customize these forms and by including this simple prompt, it draws the attention of your lead, so they'll notice if there's another number they should provide. This section has to be typed in manually.

We also highly recommend that you add a screening question to your Facebook Lead Ads.[267] This allows you to immediately check the answer provided to decide if a lead is truly qualified or not.

Otherwise, you risk taking the time to call one of these prospects only to learn that they misunderstood the service you provide.

Usually, these questions can be something really simple that

---

266 "Lead Ads," Facebook for Business, https://www.facebook.com/business/ads/lead-ads.

267 "Add Custom Questions to Your Instant Form," Facebook for Business, https://www.facebook.com/business/help/774623835981457.

< **218**   Natalie Fragkouli & Liel Levy   >

asks the prospect to summarize what they need. For example, if you are a personal injury lawyer, you could ask, "What type of accident were you in?" That's all it takes to make sure they're really someone who needs your business.

Another option we recommend is adding an Appointment Request to your form to get a better idea of how serious a prospect is about scheduling a consultation with you and when they'd be available to do it.[268]

Then, consider adding a Completion section.[269] This feature is fantastic for keeping prospects engaged after they've submitted their information. You can add one of the following call-to-action buttons to your form:

- **View website:** This will take your new lead to your website or a specific landing page.

- **Download:** Allow leads to download content related to the service they need—a great way to build trust with your soon-to-be client.

- **Call business:** This is the CTA we recommend as it makes it easy for users to convert then and there, eliminating additional steps.

With Facebook Lead Ads, you can turn interest into engagement and turn that engagement into new business.

---

268 "Use Appointment Request in Your Instant Form," Facebook for Business, https://www.facebook.com/business/help/374052383033400.

269 "Add a Completion Section to Your Instant Form," Facebook for Business, https://www.facebook.com/business/help/314132612401196.

< Win with PPC **219** >

4. USING FACEBOOK PIXELS FOR EASY RETARGETING

Retargeting is one of those marketing practices that really separate law firms that do alright and law firms that need to open another office.[270]

That's because most prospects won't convert the first time they interact with one of your marketing assets (e.g., when they initially visit your website). By utilizing cookies, though, you can continue to advertise to these prospects—prospects who showed genuine interest in your firm—even as they travel elsewhere on the internet.

If this sounds complicated, don't worry. Facebook offers what is probably one of the easiest ways to start retargeting your prospects.

All you need to do is add the Facebook pixel to your website.[271]

This small piece of code allows you to track people who visit your website from Facebook ads. As a result, you can run retargeting campaigns that help you earn their business even after they've left your site.

You can even use it to create custom audiences for your marketing campaigns based on specific actions visitors have taken once they've made it to your website.[272] By doing so, you can build even more specific campaigns that speak directly to a custom audience's unique needs.

---

270 Fahad Muhammad, "Retargeting 101: Everything You Need to Achieve Greater ROI," *Instapage,* July 1, 2020, https://instapage.com/blog/what-is-retargeting.

271 "The Facebook Pixel," Facebook for Business, https://www.facebook.com/business/learn/facebook-ads-pixel.

272 "Custom Audiences," Facebook for Business, https://www.facebook.com/business/m/custom-audience.

< **220**   Natalie Fragkouli & Liel Levy >

5. CREATING LOOKALIKE AUDIENCES
TO FIND MORE HIGH-VALUE PROSPECTS

That's not the only thing this powerful little piece of code can do, though.

With retargeting, you can continuously advertise to prospects who managed to somehow find your site first.

That's great, but what about all those other leads who may need your help but haven't, for whatever reason, found your website yet?

Well, your trusty Facebook pixel can help there, too.

They allow you to create Lookalike Audiences.[273] As you may have guessed, this is an audience you create based on what you're already marketing to successfully.

To create this kind of powerful marketing tool, just pick a Source Audience.[274] This is one of those aforementioned Custom Audiences made with information you pulled from your pixel.

Facebook will analyze this Source Audience and identify common qualities among its members.

Then, it will go looking for similar (lookalike) Facebook users the next time you run an ad.

For example, let's say you installed the Facebook pixel on your law firm's website. After enough time, you discover that your highest-converting leads are women between the ages of forty to forty-five who live in your city, have children, and work full-time jobs.

You could then create a Lookalike Audience to find even more of these women, say by running the ads in another city or even state.

---

273 "About Lookalike Audiences," Facebook for Business, https://www.facebook.com/business/help/164749007013531.

274 "Source Audience," Facebook for Business, https://www.facebook.com/business/help/475669712534537.

< Win with PPC **221** >

6. UNDERSTANDING ACCURATE AUDIENCE TARGETING

If all of these powerful Facebook ads tools weren't enough, we're only halfway done with our favorite methods for getting the most from this incredible opportunity.

As we've mentioned, we believe the Hispanic community in America is a truly underappreciated market for law firms and, at the same time, they are a big opportunity for those law firms who decide to reach the Hispanic community.

One thing we love about investing in Facebook ads is how you can improve your ROI through advanced audience targeting methods.

For example, we can create ads that target Facebook users based on specific affinities or the languages they speak.[275] A very common segment we use is targeting users who speak Spanish and are part of the Hispanic Multicultural Affinity.

One really helpful feature when taking advantage of this tool is that Facebook will respond to your designations by telling you what kind of reach you can expect. If your reach is too low, just remove one of your audience's characteristics and try again.

Of course, to make the most out of this powerful feature, you need to understand your local Hispanic market. The better you know their preferences (e.g., English or Spanish), what kinds of services they're interested in, and what culture they celebrate, the better you'll be at winning their business.

---

275 "For US Hispanic Marketers, New Language-Based Targeting Segments," *Facebook for Business*, April 14, 2014, https://www.facebook.com/business/news/ New-Language-Based-Targeting-Segments.

< **222**   Natalie Fragkouli & Liel Levy   >

7. BUILD ENGAGEMENT CUSTOM
AUDIENCES TO CAPITALIZE ON INTENT

One of the most frustrating aspects of marketing is acknowledging that you got this close to converting a prospect only to lose them during the final step.

Unfortunately, this is extremely common.

In e-commerce, an incredible *69.57 percent* of online shoppers will go through a company's entire buying process only to abandon their shopping carts.[276]

So, it should come as no surprise that you could be losing some of your prospects just before they become clients.

The way to combat this is with Engagement Custom Audiences.[277] This specific type of custom audience targets users who have interacted with your law firm's content through one of Facebook's services or apps.

This type of engagement includes anything from opening up one of your firm's lead forms to spending time watching one of its promotional videos.

You can even use Engagement Custom Audiences to create the kinds of Lookalike Audiences we described earlier. The advantage of that kind of Lookalike Audience would be that you know the market you're using as a reference came so close to becoming clients for your firm.

Facebook gives you five different engagement types for creating this kind of Custom Audience:

---

276 "44 Cart Abandonment Rate Statistics," Baymard Institute, https://www.baymard.com/lists/cart-abandonment-rate.

277 "About Engagement Custom Audiences," Facebook for Business, https://www.facebook.com/business/help/1090330204367211.

< Win with PPC **223** >

- Canvas/Collection[278]
- Event[279]
- Facebook Page[280]
- Instagram

- Business Profile[281]
- Lead Form[282]
- Video[283]

You can even specify how far back you want Facebook to go when collecting users who engaged to ensure you're using the best possible audience.

8. ALWAYS KEEP YOUR FACEBOOK ADS FRESH AND INTERESTING

Ad fatigue is a very real thing for companies marketing on Facebook.[284]

You really have to prioritize rotating your ads and uploading new ones regularly. At Nanato Media, we generally recommend four to five ads within each of your law firm's campaign Ad Sets.

---

278 "Create an Instant Experience Engagement Custom Audience," Facebook for Business, https://www.facebook.com/help/1056178197835021.

279 "About Custom Audiences for Event Ads," Facebook for Business, https://www.facebook.com/help/325746814515381.

280 "Create a Custom Audience from Page Engagements," Facebook for Business, https://www.facebook.com/help/221146184973131.

281 "Create an Instagram Account Custom Audience," Facebook for Business, https://www.facebook.com/help/214981095688584https://www.facebook.com/help/214981095688584.

282 "Create a Lead Form Custom Audience," Facebook for Business, https://www.facebook.com/help/900802126698360.

283 "Create an Engagement Custom Audience from Video Views," Facebook for Business, https://www.facebook.com/help/1099865760056389.

284 Charlie Lawrance, "How to Recognize and Overcome Facebook Ad Fatigue," *Social Media Examiner*, July 23, 2018, https://www.socialmediaexaminer.com/recognize-overcome-facebook-ad-fatigue/.

< **224**   Natalie Fragkouli & Liel Levy >

If you can incorporate video, so much the better.

The great thing about using videos on social is that no one really expects them to look professional. It's true. You can get away with just using your phone to record one of your client's testimonials. Having them record themselves and send the video to you works, as well. Then, just add compelling copy to it with a relevant call to action and you're on your way to attracting new leads.

If that seems a bit complicated for you right now, no worries. You can also use a single image or an image carousel. Use relevant photos or a custom creative. The only hard-and-fast rules are that the visuals must be relevant, communicate exactly what it is you do, and how that benefits clients. For that last part, incorporate your client's pain points.[285]

For example, say you're running a workers' compensation campaign. You'd want your ad to make it clear that your prospects' employers cannot fire them because they exercised their rights to file a case with you.

Add an image that will grab their attention long enough that they quit scrolling, and you'll have yourself a winning ad.

9. RUN YOUR LEAD ADS ON FACEBOOK AND INSTAGRAM

Finally, we recommend that you use Automatic Placements to run ads on Facebook and Instagram.[286] Facebook is still king of the hill when it comes to social media—by a long shot.

You can very easily repurpose ads that work well on Facebook so they're perfect for Instagram, too.

---

285 Dan Shewan, "Pain Points: A Guide to Finding & Solving Your Customers' Problems," *WordStream*, May 1, 2020, https://www.wordstream.com/blog/ws/2018/02/28/pain-points.

286 "Why We Recommend Automatic Placements," Facebook for Business, https://www.facebook.com/business/help/196554084569964.

< Win with PPC **225** >

All you have to do is leverage Automatic Placements. Targeting works the same on both platforms, so you don't have to worry about taking on a new learning curve. Just bring the ads that are working for you on Facebook to another social media platform with plenty of potential.

THE ABSOLUTE BIGGEST MISTAKES LAW FIRMS MAKE WITH FACEBOOK ADS

By now, you have all the information you need to consistently run successful Facebook ads for your firm no matter what kind of law you practice.

Congrats!

But hang on just one moment.

We've seen firms go through this kind of training and still fail to produce impressive results.

How?

They try taking a "set-it-and-forget-it" approach.

They want to just post an ad and then sit back and listen to their receptionist's phone ring.

If they heard that's how it works, it wasn't from us. We're actual experts with Facebook marketing, which means we have real-life experience.

As such, we are adamant that there's a little more work to be done if you want Facebook to deliver you a lot of leads.

This means you need to monitor the performance of your post or Lead Ad to gauge if you're seeing enough of an ROI to justify the spend. Facebook analytics will help a lot with this,

< **226** Natalie Fragkouli & Liel Levy >

making it fairly easy to determine what's working and what's not in real-time.[287]

For every single ad you run on Facebook, you can view valuable insights by going to Ad Manager. Some of these insights include:

- The number of people who see your ad.

- The number of people who click on your ad.

- The amount you spend on your ad.

You still need to take it just one step further, though.

Once you have this information, cross-reference it with the results you're actually seeing with your firm. This will provide a great foundation for optimizing your Facebook ads even further.

THE EASIEST WAY TO TURN FACEBOOK INTO YOUR FIRM'S REFERRAL MACHINE

You now have the blueprint for utilizing Facebook to reach out, engage with, and attract qualified prospects to your law firm's website and landing pages.

With practice and dedication, it shouldn't take too long to start seeing results.

---

287 "People-first Analytics for an Omni-channel World," Facebook Analytics, https://analytics.facebook.com/.

< PART 4 >

MEASURING RESULTS

< CHAPTER 13 >

HOW TO MEASURE THE RESULTS OF YOUR LAW FIRM'S PPC CAMPAIGNS

Before you can improve your law firm's PPC campaigns, you need to know where they really stand. Instead of wading through a sea of different metrics, let us show you which ones are most important for Google and Facebook ads. Understand what to measure and you'll know where to improve.

Although PPC ads are easily the best investment you can make in marketing your law firm, there's no doubt that they can be challenging.[288]

And thank goodness for that or we wouldn't have jobs.

But still, we get it.

If you've tried leveraging PPC ads in the past or you actually started investing in them before you gave up, we 100 percent understand.

---

288 "Why PPC Is a Great Investment for Your Personal Injury Firm," *Nanato Media,* June 29, 2020, https://nanatomedia.com/blog/why-ppc-is-a-great-investment-for-your-personal-injury-firm/.

< **230**   Natalie Fragkouli & Liel Levy >

They're definitely not as user-friendly as simply paying someone to put your picture and phone number on a bus, park bench, or billboard.

Of course, that's also part of the reason they offer such a better ROI. While successful PPC campaigns require more knowledge, their successes are also worth a lot more.

That's why we're going to use our years of experience in PPC marketing to explain one of the most important—but overlooked—aspects of successful campaigns: measuring results.

THE SECRET WEAPON FOR ACHIEVING THE BEST POSSIBLE RESULT FOR YOUR LAW FIRM'S ONLINE CAMPAIGNS

You'd think that measuring the results of a PPC campaign would be something that every business owner loves learning about. After all, this step is when you get to relish just how well your firm has done.

Most of us don't like dieting or working out, but it feels incredible to step on a scale and see how much weight you've lost or, even better, buy those pants with the smaller waist size.

And yet, in our experience, measuring PPC results is often a neglected step.

What's worse is that a lot of firms that come to us for help were actually doing okay with their PPC campaigns. They were seeing some results. The reason they weren't seeing more of them, though, is because they didn't know how to properly assess them for opportunities to do even better.

Imagine losing that weight but not knowing what new activities or habits were responsible. You'd have a hard time

< Measuring Results **231** >

maintaining that success, and even though you might feel great, you'd probably give up.

Don't let this happen to your firm.

The metrics you use for measuring the results of your law firm's PPC campaigns are just as important as any other you'd use for improving business. You wouldn't ignore billable hours, would you?

At the same time, many law firms we've partnered with were struggling before they came to us not because they weren't monitoring their metrics but because they were monitoring the wrong ones.

To use our weight loss example, imagine tracking your results by constantly checking your shoe size or the length of your hair instead of your actual weight, waist size, BMI, blood pressure, or simply how good you felt about yourself.

It would be impossible to reach anything resembling an ambitious goal.

The same goes for your law firm's campaigns. If you don't know which metrics matter most, we can assure you that it's very easy to monitor the wrong ones and waste a lot of money in the process.

GET CLEAR ABOUT WHAT YOUR
UNIQUE MARKETING OBJECTIVES ARE

At Nanato Media, we're very proud of regularly publishing blog posts that offer detailed advice about law firm PPC best practices.

That said, we're even more proud of the fact that we have *never* positioned this advice as plug-and-play. It's definitely tempting. We're well aware that many people would prefer to hear that they could dramatically improve their law firm's revenue just by copying one simple strategy that works for everyone.

< **232**   Natalie Fragkouli & Liel Levy >

Not surprisingly, that just isn't the case.

In fact, your unique firm doesn't just need its own unique strategy. You also need to constantly stay on top of things, so you're able to evolve that strategy as necessary—first to adjust for your local market as you learn more about it and then to optimize for the best possible results.

Every campaign is different.

Every market is different.

In short, there are no magic rules that will make your campaigns successful. The key to success is to use the best information you have available to create campaigns, know the right metrics to track your results, and then optimize, optimize, optimize.

For us, that means optimizing hourly.

WHAT OBJECTIVES ARE YOU AFTER?

Before we cover the most important metrics to monitor for Google and Facebook ads, there's one essential step you have to take before you launch a campaign on either platform.

You must understand what your objectives are.

When we say every campaign is different, we literally mean every aspect. Objectives are no exception.

For most law firms, the goal is to generate new online leads and sign them as clients who will turn a profit.

That's not everyone, though.

If that's your objective, great, but if it's also the only one you've ever had, you might want to consider other potential goals you could have for your PPC campaigns.

For example, it's not uncommon for law firms to come to us because they want to use PPC campaigns to build awareness about themselves. We see this a lot from law firms that specialize in handling mass torts. Other firms have been advertising for

< Measuring Results **233** >

years on TV and radio, and now they want to protect their brand from their competitors, so they put a premium on protecting their brand. Therefore, they are more focused on impression share and how often their ads show up at the very top when a user searches for their brand name on Google.[289]

FIVE METRICS YOU ABSOLUTELY HAVE TO MEASURE WHEN RUNNING GOOGLE ADS FOR YOUR LAW FIRM

Alright, let's get to the good stuff.

Assuming you promise to take everything we just talked about seriously, let's finally dive into the fun part that will really make a difference to your law firm's Google Ads ROI.

These are the five PPC KPIs that we advise you track every day.

1. WHERE IT ALL STARTS: CLICKS

We'll start with what hopefully seems a bit obvious, but keep reading because we're going to go into a lot of helpful details here.

Regardless of the type of campaign you're running or the exact type of result you want, every single conversion begins with a click. That's why, not surprisingly, clicks are the earliest indicator of a PPC campaign's success. You obviously can't call it effective if it can't even hit the first necessary milestone of just earning that initial click.

As such, we recommend that you keep a close eye on the clicks for your campaigns. At the very least, this means checking in on this metric every single day.

---

289 "How to Protect Your Law Firm's Brand Name Using Google Ad," *Nanato Media,* August 6, 2019, https://nanatomedia.com/blog/how-to-protect-your-law-firms -brand-name-using-google-ads/.

< **234** Natalie Fragkouli & Liel Levy >

Again, we don't even wait longer than an hour before checking in. So, if possible, we'd say you should review the kinds of clicks your ad is getting as often as you can.

Why?

Because if you have ads that aren't generating clicks, what's the point of keeping them active? Assuming the ad is getting impressions, this means that for whatever reason, prospects aren't convinced it's worth clicking.

That's not going to change by simply letting the ad run longer.

2. HOW MUCH THOSE CLICKS
ARE COSTING YOU: COST-PER-CLICK

The second absolutely essential Google Ads metric you must pay close and constant attention to is your campaign's cost-per-click (CPC).[290] As you probably guessed, this refers to how much you're spending on average when a prospect clicks one of your ads.

What you need to avoid at all costs (literally) is having a CPC that represents a loss. We'll cover this in more detail next, but you can't be sure you're actually making a profit until you know what the CPC on your campaign is.

If you're new to PPC, don't be surprised if you think you did everything right only to quickly realize—once you've actually launched your campaign—that your CPC needs adjusting.

For example, you may have set your budget and bids too high in the beginning and then find out that in your unique market and/or your firm's specific practice area, you are getting charged for a fraction of your bid for each of your keywords.

Okay, that definitely wouldn't be a bad thing. That would actually be a really good thing.

---

290 "Cost-per-Click (CPC): Definition," Google Ads Help, https://support.google.com/google-ads/answer/116495.

< Measuring Results **235** >

But you'd want to make adjustments accordingly to take full advantage of that really good thing.

Unfortunately, a much more common scenario is when a law firm sees limited results from their PPC campaigns because their CPCs are so high. The firm's budget simply isn't up to the task of taking on such a competitive market where those kinds of lofty CPCs are perhaps the norm.

Most of the time, we recommend that firms facing this kind of challenge increase their budget. By spending more, they can afford the kinds of CPCs that may be necessary to enjoy impressive results.

That's not the only solution to this problem, though. There's another one that's far less obvious and does a good job of exemplifying why you can't just take a cookie-cutter approach to PPC. For many firms, increasing their budget is the best solution to the problem of high CPCs.

However, for others, the right thing to do—as odd as this will sound—is to actually lower your bids. By doing so, you might find that your firm is able to secure more clicks in a given day without having to increase the amount you spend. That's a real win-win situation!

Will this clever strategy always be the right move?

No.

Again, this is why we're going to keep hammering on the point that you need to check in on these metrics regularly for best results.

In this case, the major risk is that your position might be lower than you were hoping for. Recall that, for many companies, the goal for their PPC campaigns is brand awareness, so landing anywhere but at the top of the page is out of the question. They'd view that as an abject failure.

< **236**   Natalie Fragkouli & Liel Levy >

On the other hand, if your objective is to secure new leads and turn them into paying clients, you shouldn't care where your ad ends up as long as it's achieving that goal for you. Your campaigns may be marked as having a limited budget, but what do you care? They're still successful.

In the end, it's all about trial and error, which is why experience is such a massive advantage in PPC.

If you're new and years away from gaining that kind of experience with running PPC campaigns for law firms, here's an important piece of advice: when you start out, always bid manually.[291] This will build a cache of historical data you can leverage later, but it will also give you that valuable experience.

Finally, remember one thing: if it's not broken, don't fix it. When a PPC campaign is getting your law firm results, the worst thing you can do is overthink or overoptimize.

3. WHERE YOUR MONEY GOES: CONVERSION RATE AND COST PER CONVERSION

If you haven't already, be sure to set up conversion tracking within your Google Ads.[292]

One of the reasons we always advise our law firm partners to do this is because it makes it possible—and *easy*—to cross-reference your clicks with your conversions.

Why do you want to do that?

Simple.

Because you want to make sure that the clicks you're working so hard for actually convert.

---

291 Adam Proehl, "What You Need to Know About PPC Budgets & Bidding," *Search Engine Journal*, March 28, 2019, https://www.searchenginejournal.com/ppc-guide/budgets-bidding/.

292 "Add a Conversion Tracking Tag to Your Website," Google Ads Help, https://support.google.com/google-ads/answer/6331314.

< Measuring Results **237** >

Not just that, either.

You need to know at what rate those conversions are happening.

You can determine your conversion rate in Google Ads by dividing the number of conversions your ad has received by the total number of clicks it earned.[293]

It couldn't be simpler.

It's imperative that you know what your cost-per-conversion is in Google Ads as a reference. But remember this is not your real CPA, since you most likely want to calculate this number based on signed cases.

Don't worry. We will look at that next.

DON'T FORGET ABOUT YOUR KEYWORDS

Before we move on to our fourth important metric that you must monitor for PPC success, there's another category related to CPC that we have to cover: keywords.

Put simply, you have to check what keywords actually convert. Then, just like we advised earlier, you should pause bids on any keywords that are underperforming. At the very least, decrease them until you figure out what kinds of adjustments are necessary.

Otherwise, you'll continue spending a lot of money on keywords that just don't covert. Those are budget eaters you need to identify ASAP (hence, daily checks), so you can eliminate them before they come to represent massive overhead.

---

293 "Conversion Rate: Definition," Google Ads Help, https://support.google.com/google-ads/answer/2684489.

< **238** Natalie Fragkouli & Liel Levy >

4. HOW MUCH GOOGLE LIKES YOUR EFFORTS: KEYWORD QUALITY SCORES

Speaking of keywords, you don't need to spend years gaining experience with PPC to appreciate that some are simply better than others. Treat all of the keywords related to your service the same, and your budget will soon pay a hefty price.

However, what often takes people years to appreciate is just how important the Google Quality Score is to the success of their campaigns.[294] This is definitely one that you ignore at your own risk.

We have talked a lot about how Quality Score affects your Google Ads because there's just no underestimating the role it plays whether your campaigns help your business or help you go out of business.[295]

Quality Score shows you an estimate of how relevant your ads, keywords, and landing pages are to people who see your ad. Your current Quality Score and its component scores can be seen with four Quality Score status columns:

- Quality Score

- Landing Page Experience

- Ad Relevance

- Expected Clickthrough Rate (CTR)

Therefore, with a Quality Score, Google intends to give you a general sense of the quality of your ads.

---

294 "About Quality Score," Google Ads Help, https://support.google.com/google-ads/answer/7050591.

295 "What Law Firms Need to Understand About Google Ads," *Nanato Media*, June 26, 2020, https://nanatomedia.com/blog/what-law-firms-need-to-understand-about-google-ads/.

< Measuring Results **239** >

The one to ten Quality Score reported for each keyword in your account is an estimate of the quality of your ads and their corresponding landing pages.

From an advertiser's viewpoint, Quality Score is extremely important for many reasons. This metric determines whether a keyword is even eligible to enter an auction in the first place and whether or not your ad will show for a user's query on the Google Search Network.

Additionally, Quality Score, along with CPC bid, determines ad rank, which is very important, especially for advertisers with a limited budget. The ad rank formula for the Google Search Network is as follows:

Ad Rank = CPC bid x Quality Score

Overall, Quality Score has a larger overall impact on campaign performance. If you have strongly and consistently integrated Quality Scores throughout your account, you're likely to see a strong conversion experience for your searchers, pricing discounts, and a well-organized campaign.

WHAT TO DO ABOUT LOW QUALITY SCORES

If you see you're earning a three out of ten or five out of ten, you definitely need to rethink your campaign and ad group organization. Split your keywords into smaller ad groups and then rewrite your ads to address the specific keywords you are bidding on for each.

What if the problem is your landing page?

If your landing page still shows as below average even after you've adjusted your keywords, then you should probably have it reviewed by experts like us.

< **240**   Natalie Fragkouli & Liel Levy >

What your landing page needs is conversion rate optimization (CRO).[296] You have to invest in relevant copy that corresponds to each specific ad group in your campaign.

If you use your website pages as landing pages, it's time to change that.

If your Quality Scores are six out of ten, split test new ad copy that's entirely different from anything you've ever tried before and see if you can get that CTR up.[297]

Monitor them carefully and cut losing ads when you have enough data to make the call.

5. ALL THE NECESSARY DETAILS: AUCTION INSIGHTS

The Auction insights report tells you your:[298]

- Impression Share
- Top of Page Rate
- Overlap Rate
- Absolute Top of Page Rate
- Position Above Rate
- Outranking Share

The report will show you these metrics for the date range you choose. This makes it easy to compare your performance with your direct competitor law firms who are taking part in the same auctions.

You can generate a report for one or more keywords, ad groups, or campaigns (as long as they meet a minimum threshold of activity for the time period selected), and then segment your results by time and device.

---

296 "Conversion Rate Optimization," MOZ, https://moz.com/learn/seo/conversion-rate-optimization

297 Allen Finn, "10X Your A/B Testing with Google Ads Variations," *WordStream*, July 17, 2020, https://www.wordstream.com/blog/ws/2018/02/13/adwords-ad-variations.

298 "Use Auction Insights to Compare Performance," Google Ads Help, https://support.google.com/google-ads/answer/2579754.

< Measuring Results **241** >

Impression share, top of page rate, and absolute top of page rate are the most important auction site statistics.

Therefore, let's take a quick look at what each means.

IMPRESSION SHARE

Impression share is the number of impressions your ad receives divided by the estimated number of impressions you were eligible to receive.[299]

Eligibility is based on your current ads' targeting settings, approval statuses, and Quality Scores. Impression share is a powerful way to understand whether or not your law firm's ads might reach more people if you increased your bid or budget.

TOP OF PAGE RATE

Top of page rate is how often your ad (or the ad of another participant, depending on which row you're viewing) was shown at the top of the page, above the organic search results.

To increase your top of the page rate, you'll need to increase your Ad Rank.[300] Since Ad Rank is what determines your ad's position in the auction, and ad rank depends on your bids and quality scores, you have two factors to focus on:

- Increasing your max CPC bids

- Improving your quality score

The goal here is to get this rate as close as possible to 100 percent so your law firm ads are competitive enough to get clicks and conversions.

---

299 "About Impression Share," Google Ads Help, https://support.google.com/google-ads/answer/2497703.

300 "About Ad Position and Ad Rank," Google Ads Help, https://support.google.com/google-ads/answer/1722122.

< **242**   Natalie Fragkouli & Liel Levy >

ABSOLUTE TOP OF THE PAGE RATE

Now, absolute top of the page rate tells you how often your ad was shown as the very first ad above the organic search results, or at the absolute top.

This is always a great metric to aim for, but it's particularly important for Brand Protection campaigns in Spanish campaigns as Hispanics often prefer to initiate a call.[301] Therefore, the higher your ads show up, the better your chances will be to get that desired click.

Note that Top of Page Rate and Absolute Top of Page Rate are available only in the Search Network.

HOW TO SUCCESSFULLY MEASURE THE RESULTS OF YOUR FACEBOOK ADS

While Google Ads are an essential marketing asset for every modern law firm—and one that you now know how to optimize—you can't ignore Facebook ads.[302] This is especially true if, like so many of our partners, you want to market to Hispanics.[303]

1. THE MOST IMPORTANT KPI FOR FACEBOOK MARKETING

This probably won't come as too much of a surprise, but if you're running Facebook ads, the most important KPI for your firm is leads.

---

301 "Why Your Law Firm Needs a Brand Protection Google Ad Campaign," *Nanato Media*, August 19, 2020, https://nanatomedia.com/blog/ why-your-law-firm-needs-a-brand-protection-google-ad-campaign/.

302 "An Introduction to Facebook Ads for Personal Injury Law Firms," *Nanato Media*, July 14, 2020, https://nanatomedia.com/blog/ an-introduction-to-facebook-ads-for-personal-injury-law-firms/.

303 "Digital Diversity: A Closer Look at US Hispanics," *Facebook for Business*, December 5, 2014, https://www.facebook.com/business/news/insights/ digital-diversity-a-closer-look-at-us-hispanics.

< Measuring Results **243** >

To see how well you're doing, go to the Facebook Results page for advertisers. This page will tell you how many leads you've been able to generate through your law firm's Facebook ads.

However, just because leads are your most important KPI, that certainly doesn't make them your only KPI. While many advertisers stop at leads, we encourage you to pay close attention to these four others.

2. HOW MANY PEOPLE SEE YOUR AD

Although this metric may sound a lot like impressions, reach is actually different. Reach will tell you how many people have seen your ad at least once.[304] On the other hand, impressions will include multiple views of your ads, even though they came from the same person.[305]

Reach is a great KPI, especially when you first turn on a new campaign and want to quickly see how visible it is to your audience.

3. HOW MUCH IT COSTS FOR YOUR AD TO CONVERT

Cost per result will basically tell you how much each lead is costing you, similar to cost per conversion in Google Ads.[306]

You can use cost per result to compare performances among different campaigns and identify areas of opportunity. This metric can also help you determine your bid for future ad sets.

A number of different factors can affect this metric, including your:

---

304 "Unique Metrics," Facebook for Business, https://www.facebook.com/help/283579896000936.

305 "Impressions," Facebook for Business, https://www.facebook.com/help/675615482516035.

306 "Cost per Result," Facebook for Business, https://www.facebook.com/business/help/762109693832964.

< **244**   Natalie Fragkouli & Liel Levy >

- Auction Bid

- Target Audience

- Optimization Type

- Ad Creative and Messaging

- Schedule

Your cost per result is calculated by the total amount spent divided by the number of results.[307]

4. WHERE YOUR AD SHOWS UP

When advertising on Facebook, your ad placement has a massive impact on advertising costs.[308]

So, after you've identified your top-performing ad placements, go ahead and optimize your campaigns accordingly by increasing your bids on the top-performing ad placements and/or removing ad sets if their placements perform below all expectations.

307 "Amount Spent," Facebook for Business, https://www.facebook.com/business/help/1406571646230212.
"Results," Facebook for Business, https://www.facebook.com/business/help/611432918970668.

308 "About Placements in Ads Manager," Facebook for Business, https://www.facebook.com/business/help/407108559393196.

< Measuring Results **245** >

5. HOW OFTEN FACEBOOK USERS SEE YOUR AD

Check frequency to see how many times each Facebook user sees your ads.[309]

Obviously, you want to make sure people are seeing them enough to attract adequate clicks, but it's just as important that you defend against ad fatigue.[310] After all, the more people see your ads, the more bored they'll get. That's bad enough, but it will also make your cost per result increase.

You can overcome this common problem by creating several ad variations with different designs and/or set up an ad campaign with multiple ad sets that have different ads. Then schedule each of them to be active on a different weekday.

This way, people will see a different ad every day and your ads won't become repetitive.

---

309 "Frequency," Facebook for Business, https://www.facebook.com/business/ help/1546570362238584.

310 Charlie Lawrance, "How to Recognize and Overcome Facebook Ad Fatigue," *Social Media Examiner,* July 23, 2018, https://www.socialmediaexaminer.com/ recognize-overcome-facebook-ad-fatigue/.

< CHAPTER 14 >

HOW TO MAKE THE MOST FROM YOUR LAW FIRM'S BUSINESS METRICS

If you're not already measuring the business metrics for your law firm, that's something you should start doing immediately. However, keeping track of them isn't enough. This powerful data should be actively informing the decisions you make about your law firm's marketing campaigns, so you regularly increase the number of qualified leads you generate each month.

Running a successful law firm means running successful marketing campaigns.

Unless you have an age-old reputation that's able to passively generate constant leads, your firm's success depends on campaigns that bring in new clients.

Even a sparkling reputation that goes back decades is no longer enough to count on. In the Digital Age, new upstarts with the right marketing campaigns could quickly even the score.

Chances are, you already know all of this.

You may not be running the most effective campaigns, but you must know that digital marketing is essential if you're going

< **248**   Natalie Fragkouli & Liel Levy >

to keep leads coming in the door without needlessly spending dollars in the opposite direction.

In our experience, what most law firms don't know is that achieving results just isn't enough for continuously running successful marketing campaigns.

They're a good start, but the most successful law firms know that the secret to getting even more from those results is by actually tracking them.

WHY THE RIGHT BUSINESS METRICS ARE CENTRAL TO YOUR LAW FIRM'S DIGITAL MARKETING STRATEGY

One of the oldest sayings in business goes something like this, "If you can't measure it, you can't improve it."

Most law firm owners understand it's important to track their campaigns. How else will they know if they're effective or not?

But that's as far as they go with their tracking.

As long as they see that "money in" is less than the amount of "money out," they consider their campaign a success.

That is not how you measure success!

In our opinion, you're not properly measuring for success if your efforts don't show you how you can get more of it. The typical "money-in/money-out" paradigm doesn't meet this essential requirement.

Consequently, if your firm is relying on this simple measure, it is 100 percent, without-a-doubt leaving money on the table.

And, in our experience, it's a lot of money.

The better you understand what's working to generate leads, the more of them you can generate.

< Measuring Results **249** >

Finally, if that's not enough reason to rethink how you assess your lead-generation success, think about this: every lead you fail to generate is one more you're handing to a competitor.

If you won't take business metrics seriously to help your firm, consider doing it to annoy another.

WHAT IS A QUALIFIED LEAD FOR YOUR FIRM?

These discussions about lead generation bring up a very important question: What exactly is a qualified lead?[311]

Simply put, a qualified lead is someone who matches one of your buyer personas and is currently in need of an attorney.[312] In the case of many Hispanic Americans, this could also refer to a family member who is helping them secure legal services—one more reason to run English and Spanish ads.[313]

That being said, we can already hear some of you declaring, "My leads don't always need representation right away" (you're very loud).

For example, many of the law firms we partner with are immigration attorneys. To them, a qualified lead is anyone who contacts them for an initial consultation, since that's something they would normally bill for.

The legal field is a vast one, so if the definition we gave above for a qualified lead doesn't fit yours like a glove, you won't hurt our feelings. Adjust it accordingly for how your firm bills.

---

311 AJ Traver, "Qualified Versus Unqualified Leads," *SugarCRM*, March 21, 2020, https://www.sugarcrm.com/blog/qualified-versus-unqualified-leads/.

312 "How to Create Your Law Firm's Buyer Persona," *Nanato Media*, September 13, 2020, https://nanatomedia.com/blog/how-to-create-your-law-firms-buyer-persona/.

313 "Getting Started with Your Law Firm's Hispanic Marketing Strategy," *Nanato Media*, June 20, 2020, https://nanatomedia.com/blog/getting-started-with-your-law-firms-hispanic-marketing-strategy/.

< **250**   Natalie Fragkouli & Liel Levy >

TECHNOLOGY IS CENTRAL FOR SUCCESSFULLY TRACKING YOUR BUSINESS METRICS

What absolutely will hurt our feelings, though, is if you let your firm's bottom line suffer because you're not properly tracking your leads using relevant business metrics.

Want to make it worse?

If you really want to get under our skin, try tracking the metrics that matter to your firm most without using technology.

That's like trying to mentally keep track of how much gas is left in your car.

Is it possible?

Maybe.

Is it necessary?

Absolutely not.

Should you even bother when there is such an obvious and cost-effective alternative?

No.

One hundred percent no.

Nonetheless, we've been in the helping-law-firms-generate-lots-of-leads game for a very long time. If you're new to monitoring your lead-generation metrics, we know it may be a bit overwhelming trying to decide which technology to actually use.

There's no lack of options. Unfortunately, that includes a lot of bad ones.

But don't worry.

We're here to help!

< Measuring Results **251** >

DON'T JUST TAKE PHONE CALLS—TRACK THEM

To begin our list of ways your firm can dramatically increase its leads by tracking them with technology, we'll start with one of the most basic, and yet, most important.

1. CALL TRACKING

According to a study done by Google and FindLaw on law firm marketing,[314] 74 percent of prospective clients research attorneys online first before actually calling them. Furthermore, another 69 percent of prospects conduct this search with a smartphone.

What does this mean for your law firm?

Well, first, you better have a website that is mobile friendly.[315] Not only do the vast majority of your prospects probably use smartphones to look up your site, but Google prefers mobile-friendly sites, too.[316] So, if you want to show up in search, you better show up in phones.

To track those important phone calls effectively, you need to utilize call-tracking technology.[317] These solutions make it easy for your law firm to measure the effectiveness of your digital marketing efforts. As the term suggests, call tracking will actually track

---

314 Halden Ingwersen, "The Top 15 Legal Marketing Statistics for 2017," *Capterra*, February 14, 2017, http://blog.capterra.com/the-top-15-legal-marketing -statistics-for-2017/.

315 Kristen McCormick, "5 Reasons to Have a Mobile-Friendly Business Website," *Thrive Hive*, April 9, 2018, https://thrivehive.com/mobile-friendly-website-benefits/.

316 Adam Uzialko, "Why Your Website Needs to Be Google Mobile-Friendly," *Business News Daily*, January 5, 2020, https://www.businessnewsdaily.com/7808-google -search-ranking-mobile.html.

317 Derek Andersen, "What is Call Tracking and How Does it Work?" *Dailog Tech*, June 4, 2020, https://www.dialogtech.com/blog/what-is-call-tracking.

< **252**   Natalie Fragkouli & Liel Levy   >

your firm's incoming calls, so you know which of your marketing assets is behind them.

Wouldn't that be helpful?

After all, it's unlikely that every one of your marketing assets is equally contributing to those phone calls. That means one or two might be leading the pack. If that difference is significant, it should change how you invest in your marketing.

In fact, if you aren't currently tracking your law firm's incoming calls, it's possible that you don't know where 80 *percent* of your conversions come from.

Think about that for a moment.

If you're just assuming that you know what marketing channels are driving the phone calls your firm relies on for new business, there's a good chance you're misallocating a large amount of your budget—maybe even the majority of it.

Imagine if you could increase the number of phone calls your firm receives from qualified leads without increasing your marketing budget.

That's what many firms end up doing when they invest in call tracking.

You may even discover that one or more of your current channels aren't contributing at all, which means you were basically throwing your money away. Why not recycle it instead by putting that money toward an effective channel, so you can reuse it again in the future?

2. DYNAMIC NUMBER INSERTION

Are you sold on tracking calls?

Then, let's talk about the best possible way to do that.

The method we've always recommended to the law firms we

< Measuring Results   **253** >

partner with is called dynamic number insertion.[318]

It's a simple concept that derives powerful results for law firms.

The way it works is that your leads will see a different phone number to call depending on what channel they're using to find it and where they're located when they do it.

Of course, all of these numbers lead to the same place: your firm. Whether they get the number through Facebook or Google, whether they're calling from the state capital or a city over, your leads have the exact same experience.

Starting to see how this works so well for tracking leads?

Even though your leads can't tell the difference, you've effectively established two important insights:

- Their geographic location

- How they found your number

Could this help you make better use of your budget?

MAKING THE TRANSITION AN EASY ONE

If you're like a lot of the firms we partner with, this sounds like an incredible idea, but there's just one problem:

Transitioning to this new method.

This can seem especially daunting if you run a personal injury firm. For probably the last thirty years or so, you've most likely followed a best practice that has largely gone unquestioned: always use a single, branded phone number across all of your ad channels.

Fortunately, there is a very easy way to abide by the principle behind this practice while still leveraging the full potential of call tracking.

---

318 "Dynamic Number Insertion (DNI)," Twilio Docs, https://www.twilio.com/docs/glossary/what-is-dynamic-number-insertion.

< **254**   Natalie Fragkouli & Liel Levy >

All you need to do is show your firm's vanity number as an image on your landing page, but when someone clicks it, it dials the corresponding tracking number.

Again, nothing changes for your lead.

Now, to be fair, there is only so much you can do about using your vanity number with call tracking, as call extensions or call-only ads will always display change tracking numbers.[319]

3. KEYWORD-LEVEL TRACKING

As you can see, we're big fans of tracking.

With keyword-level tracking, you'll enjoy all kinds of useful data about how your leads got your contact information:[320]

- Referring URL
- Landing Page of Origin
- Search Terms

How does this tactic work?

Again, it's simple (another thing we're big fans of).

When a visitor arrives on your landing page by following an online search, they will be assigned a unique phone number for the entirety of their stay. That specific number sticks with them for as long as they're on your landing page. They're the only ones who can see that specific number while they are online with you.

Therefore, when they call, you'll know:

- What keywords they used to get to your landing page

- What landing page they landed on

---

319 "Create Google Ads Call-only Ads," Search Ads 360 Help, https://support.google.com/searchads/answer/6306066.

320 "Capture Full Session Details for Callers with Visitor-level Call Tracking," CallRail, https://www.callrail.com/call-tracking/reporting/keyword-level-tracking/.

< Measuring Results **255** >

Then, you can take that information to optimize those landing pages, prioritize winning keywords, adjust your bidding strategy, and most importantly wield a powerful competitive edge.

4. CALL RECORDING

This next one is fairly self-explanatory and self-evident in terms of why it's so helpful.

By utilizing call recordings for both your inbound and outbound calls, you can easily go back and reference every second of every call with every lead.[321]

You'll be glad you invested in this helpful tool the next time you can't remember an important detail, or your receptionist forgot to write something down.

However, for the purposes of marketing, nothing beats call recordings for quantifying the reasons people call your firm. Specifically, you can assess if these reasons align with the campaigns that brought them to you.

That's not all.

Call recordings allow you to evaluate your intake quality, too, including how fast your intake team is able to answer the phone. That might sound like a small detail, but if your team is constantly late to picking up, many of the leads you're working so hard to generate may be heading to the competition.

Of course, it's just as important to ensure that your intake team is friendly, respectful, and helpful when people call.

In short, don't leave anything to chance where your actual calls are concerned. Record them. Listen to them. Improve every aspect of them.

---

321 "Review Calls at Any Time with Call Recording," CallRail, https://www.callrail.com/call-tracking/manage/call-recording/.

< **256** Natalie Fragkouli & Liel Levy >

5. MULTICHANNEL ATTRIBUTION

We can't stress enough how important it is to invest in the power of multichannel attribution.[322] This one decision will show you every single touchpoint that led your lead to making a phone call.

Think of how much that could teach you about how to optimize this pathway.

For example, say a visitor arrives at your landing page through a Google Ad.

But it's not until two days later that they remember visiting your website and decide to return for more information.

So, what do they do?

Well, they don't have your ad up anymore, so they get to your site by doing a Google search. Once they have the information they wanted, they leave.

Fast forward five days and one of your retargeting ads grabs their attention.[323]

As the tracking code from that ad will remember the original channel for that visitor, they will see the same phone number each time they interact with your online presence.

Once they finally convert from leads to clients, you'll have a breakdown of every interaction they had with your site and which marketing channels were responsible, so you're able to make data-backed decisions about how to proceed.

---

322 "See a Full History of Every Interaction a Caller Has with Your Business," CallRail, https://www.callrail.com/call-tracking/reporting/multichannel-lead-attribution/.

323 Fahad Muhammad, "Retargeting 101: Everything You Need to Achieve Greater ROI," *Instapage*, July 1, 2020, https://instapage.com/blog/what-is-retargeting.

< Measuring Results **257** >

THE KEY TO MAKING THE MOST
OUT OF YOUR LEADS: SCORE THEM!

If all you do is take the above advice and use technology to track your leads, you will generate and convert more of them in a very short period of time.

Unfortunately, doing so is going to create a new problem for your firm:

Too many leads.

I know. I know. We're sorry. There's very little you can do. When you combine the potential of tracking your leads with the power of modern technology, it's inevitable that you're going to end up with more leads than ever before.

However, if you can forgive us, we'd like to propose a solution: lead scoring.[324]

The way to do this is by making sure your intake team members always mark incoming calls and form submissions as either qualified or non-qualified leads. Have them include any other relevant notes that may be helpful, too.

This will give you an aggregate of helpful information that you can pull from to better understand what kinds of leads your marketing assets are generating and the ROI you're seeing from each one.

The call-tracking platforms we mentioned earlier will automatically handle much of this valuable process for you. They utilize machine-learning models like conversation intelligence features, transcripts, and keyword spotting to efficiently provide you with valuable data.

While there is a large number of call-tracking platforms out there, we firmly stand behind CallRail as our recommendation.[325]

---

324 Debra Mitchell, "How to Qualify Marketing Leaders," *CallRail*, January 31, 2020, https://www.callrail.com/blog/how-to-qualify-marketing-leads/.

325 "Call Tracking & Marketing Analytics Software," CallRail, https://www.callrail.com/.

< **258**   Natalie Fragkouli & Liel Levy >

At Nanato Media, we have been proud CallRail partners for a while now and we couldn't be happier with the insights it gives us for optimizing law firm PPC campaigns based on *real* business metrics.

That said, if you decide to explore your options, we have another recommendation: ask them whether or not they do form and text tracking. You want to track all conversion types—not just phone calls.

STREAMLINING YOUR LEAD GENERATION PROCESS WITH A CRM

Customer Relationship Management (CRM) solutions are another example of one that has become fundamental to effective lead generation for modern law firms.[326] They work by storing all the relevant information you record about a prospect in one easily accessible place while also reducing the number of redundant processes your team would otherwise have to perform.

Your CRM begins recording this information the first time you interact with a qualified lead and then continues doing so until your very last meeting.

At their most basic level, a simple CRM will allow you to set meetings and manage the contact information for all your potential clients.

However, if you use them well, CRMs will allow you to effectively extract data so that you can analyze your workflows, relationships, and success rate with new and current clients.

Remember, if you can measure something, you can improve it.

---

326 "Client Intake, CRM, & Marketing Automation Software," Lawyerist, https://lawyerist.com/reviews/intake-crm/.

< Measuring Results **259** >

After years of working closely with a number of law firms, we can tell you that the most successful ones store their clients' contact information (including legal needs), notes from previous interactions, and even relevant biographical data. This wouldn't be possible if they didn't utilize CRMs.

By tracking previous interactions with your clients, you can engage on a more personal level, rather than playing catch-up for the first few minutes of every meeting. This will be a much better customer experience, and we all know how that can set you apart from the crowd—just like a bad one can.

You'll probably also find that CRMs will motivate you to be proactive about how you interact with your clients. In selecting the right platform, ask yourself, "What do I want to achieve with a law firm CRM?" Don't just grab software off the shelf and start using it. Plan and document your processes. Then, determine what you need before investing time and money into a new CRM.

Oh, and make sure it integrates with your call-tracking platform, which leads us to our next point.

DOES YOUR LAW FIRM NEED A CRM AND A CALL TRACKING SOLUTION?

Call tracking is essential for any modern law firm.

Period.

Your law firm just cannot grow without call-tracking software.

That's why we recommend it.

But the ideal situation would be to have both call tracking and a CRM to track your leads.

Call tracking solves several business issues at once:

< **260**   Natalie Fragkouli & Liel Levy >

- It monitors missed calls so you don't lose a client because theirs wasn't answered.

- It determines which advertising channels most often generate your qualified leads.

- It assesses the work of your intake team and improves the quality of customer service.

- It understands all the touchpoints that your lead followed before contacting you.

Obviously, those are all great things you really want.

At the same time, let's look at the many advantages of a CRM for your law firm:[327]

- See the status of every prospective client and keep leads from falling through the cracks.

- Allows your team to quickly sort and prioritize your leads you get from campaigns meant to generate volume via form submissions or lead forms so that your intake team can respond to them in a timely, efficient manner.

- You can easily locate your customer data—no more spreadsheets, email, or sticky notes.

- Smart CRM solutions allow you to extend the power of learnings among customer service agents, routing cases to the right agent, and helping agents answer questions with shared knowledge.

---

327 "7 Signs You Need a CRM System (Customer Relationship Management)," Salesforce, https://www.salesforce.com/solutions/small-business-solutions/crm-basics/customer-relationship-management-system/.

< Measuring Results **261** >

Now, there are integrations that will automatically exchange data between systems. The main tasks of a bundle that combines call tracking with a CRM are:

- Automation of work processes

- Simple reports of qualified leads or different stages of the leads and customer base

- Monitoring of current KPIs

- Tracking the effectiveness of advertising channels in the context of calls and their conversion into transactions

Last but not least, you want your CRM to integrate with your client management system so you can seamlessly transition leads into signed clients. There are a number of case management platforms that have some CRM capabilities you may want to explore.

UNDERSTANDING THE IMPORTANCE OF AVERAGE CLIENT VALUE AND CPA

In this section, we want to discuss one extremely important reason you need to diligently track your leads: CPA (Cost Per Acquisition).[328]

We've talked before about how you must track the ideal CPA of your Google Ads, but let's say you're already doing that.[329]

---

328 "What is Cost Per Acquisition (CPA)? (Updated for 2019)," Big Commerce, https://www.bigcommerce.com/ecommerce-answers/what-is-cost-per-acquisition -cpa-what-is-benchmark-retailers/.

329 "What Law Firms Need to Understand About Google Ads," *Nanato Media*, June 26, 2020, https://nanatomedia.com/blog/what-law-firms-need-to-understand -about-google-ads/.

< **262**   Natalie Fragkouli & Liel Levy >

Maybe you've been running Google Ads long enough that you have some actual metrics that you can use for improving them. And let's say you also have both call tracking and a CRM implemented.

Now that you know where to find your qualified leads and how to generate a report with them, it's time to calculate your *actual* CPA so you can determine what your ROI is.[330] This is the ratio between how much you spent on attracting new clients and how many new clients those activities actually got you during that same time period.

In other words:

Law Firm CPA = Ad Spend/Number of New Clients

Here's an example to help you better understand actual CPA.

Say you spend $5,000 a month on Google Ads for your law firm. For that $5,000 budget, you get one hundred clicks. Out of those one hundred clicks, you get ten leads (phone calls and lead form submissions).

If your close rate is 10 percent, then ten new leads each month will lead to one new client every month.

So, in this scenario, you would have a CPA cost of $5,000. It would take you $5,000 in Google Ads to land one new client.

For most law firms, this is sufficient. They think they have all the information they need to optimize their marketing strategy.

However, there's something extremely important missing.

Insights!

Looking at this equation, how do you know if your online

---

330 "The Marketing Metric You Should Be Tracking (But Probably Aren't) [Free Template]," *Postali*, June 18, 2017, https://www.postali.com/tracking-cost-per-client-acquisition/.

< Measuring Results **263** >

marketing efforts are profitable? You calculate your average client value, too.

What is one client worth to you? If the average fee you get from one case is $15,000, then your average client value is $15,000.

With these numbers, you would be spending $5,000 on Google Ads to get one new client that, on average, earns you a $15,000 fee.

This means you would be making $10,000 from each client you got from Google Ads: $15,000 for the average client value minus the $5,000 cost per acquisition.

This is the way you need to think about profitability with Google Ads. Determine your average client value and then make sure that number is higher than your cost per acquisition.

Don't forget to think long term, as well. Aside from your average profit-per-client, the right lead could literally change your life. One lead that turns into one new client can be worth anywhere from a few thousand to even millions of dollars.

IMPROVE YOUR BUSINESS METRICS TO IMPROVE YOUR MARKETING STRATEGY'S RESULTS (AND FAST)

We mentioned this earlier, but it bears repeating: if you aren't tracking your leads, you're losing at least some of them to competitors.

That could mean losing a lead who would've been worth thousands of dollars. You might even miss out on millions.

There's just no reason to risk that.

< PART 5 >

MEASURING SUCCESS

< CHAPTER 15 >

EVERYTHING YOU NEED TO KNOW TO IMPROVE YOUR LAW FIRM'S INTAKE PROCESS

Is your law firm guilty of taking its intake process for granted? Changing that can be easy and affordable if you know what you're doing. Even better, improving this one step will immediately increase the ROI of your entire law firm's current marketing campaign.

We get it.

Your law firm has a lot of moving parts, even just as far as the marketing department is concerned. There are so many pieces to focus on that it can be tempting to assume the intake process will simply take care of itself.

In fact, many law firms—maybe even most of them—take this very approach.

We've even heard some experts claim that this final step is the easiest part. The theory goes that, so long as you handle all of the other steps of your marketing funnel correctly, this one can't help but succeed.

< **268** Natalie Fragkouli & Liel Levy >

"Clients will be excited to hire you."

Look, we've all known someone who acted like you were lucky just to get to talk to them.

No one likes that person.

And there's no magic formula that suddenly makes that attitude work well for law firms.

If you nail every other step of your marketing funnel, clients should be excited that you'll help them during a difficult time.

But you're still a long way from securing their business.

Don't drop the ball now.

Understand why the intake process is so important, treat it like the priority it is, and watch your law firm's business grow exponentially.

WHY YOU NEED TO TREAT THE INTAKE PROCESS DIFFERENTLY

There are many reasons that the intake process for your law firm is distinct from all the others involved in securing new business.

And we're going to cover many of those below.

For now, let's focus on just one: the intake process is the first time your potential client will actually speak to someone from your firm. Up until that point, they've only engaged with online materials meant for a larger audience. Maybe they've even watched a promotional video for your firm.[331]

But they haven't actually spoken with you.

The intake process is when you prove that their impression of you—based on your marketing funnel—was accurate. It's when

---

331 "Your Law Firm Needs a Video Marketing Strategy," *Nanato Media*, June 20, 2020, https://nanatomedia.com/blog/your-law-firm-needs-a-video-marketing-strategy/.

< Measuring Success **269** >

you show them that you are professional, experienced, and—perhaps most important—caring.

Or is this is the moment you dash their hopes?

Will your intake process convince them that you're just another firm that treats their clients like numbers?

Of course, at some firms, the intake process often isn't the first time their prospects get to speak to them. That's because they never even get to their web form or answer their phone call.

Whatever the case, the result is the same. The prospect takes their business somewhere else and may even tell friends and family about the (lack of) interaction, ensuring those people never become clients, either.

CONSIDER YOUR PROSPECTS' FEELINGS AND ALWAYS PRACTICE EMPATHY

For many companies, the intake process tends to be a fairly straightforward affair.

Very little emotion is involved, which isn't a problem for the prospect. This even tends to be the case for medical practices, though many of the people calling may be looking for help because of fairly sensitive reasons.

Whatever the case, the process is usually the same and it's usually fairly sterile. In many industries, that's perfect.

If you need someone to inspect your roof, you'd probably act surprised if they asked you how you were holding up.

If you called to make your next dentist's appointment, it would probably strike you as odd if the receptionist reassured you that you were making the right decision.

But at your law firm, it's important to keep in mind that your

< **270**   Natalie Fragkouli & Liel Levy >

prospect may not have made the decision just a second ago at the very moment their need for you arose.

Instead, it's very likely that it might have taken this person some time—maybe even days—to build up the courage to finally contact your firm for help. In fact, it's probable that this step will be the most difficult one they take throughout the entire proceeding, including when they actually sit down with you face-to-face to describe their predicament.

So, how do you incorporate this information into your law firm's intake process?

Easy.

Practice empathy.

Empathy has long been the unsung hero of successful salesmanship.[332] It's about more than just making people feel comfortable. It's about putting yourself in their shoes to better understand how they must feel in their current situation.

This is the humane thing to do, but, luckily, it's also great for turning prospects into clients.

Hopefully, practicing this very human trait won't be completely brand-new to you or your staff.

Nonetheless, it's worth touching on some of the basics and specifically how you can be more empathetic during your law firm's intake process.

BE PRESENT

What does it mean to be present?

It means that whoever answers the phones at your office shouldn't be looking at their smartphone at the same time. They shouldn't be surfing the web or going through social media. They

---

332 "Sales," Salesforce, https://www.salesforce.com/quotable/articles/
powerful-selling-skill/.

< Measuring Success **271** >

shouldn't even be trying to multitask by handling other work.

Instead, they should be giving all their attention to the person on the other end of the phone.

The funny thing about giving callers your full attention is that so many people claim they can...while also doing something else. They'll tell you that even though they're reading an email, the person on the line couldn't possibly tell. They're a professional and know how to treat people.

However, we all know what it feels like to call a customer service line or maybe even one of our friends and speak to them while they're distracted. You can simply tell that they're not really present while you're talking.

Of course, those people probably also believe they're doing a great job not letting on.

All this is to say that you need a zero-tolerance policy when it comes to your intake people. They need to be completely present and give their total attention to whoever has trusted your law firm enough to call with what is probably a very sensitive matter.

Imagine what it would feel like (i.e., be empathetic here) to go through a traumatic event, maybe even something that could be your fault. Then, you have to call a complete stranger and explain this difficult moment in your life to them. You might tell this stranger something you haven't even told your family and friends.

Then imagine you can tell that person is just going through the motions as you speak.

"Uh huh."

"Yeah."

"Right."

< **272**   Natalie Fragkouli & Liel Levy >

How does that person feel?

They probably don't feel much like hiring your firm.

Your intake people are the first impression your firm will make with prospects on an actual human level. If those employees signal that they don't care, prospects will assume the same about the rest of your staff but most importantly about the attorney, aka you.

TREAT EACH PROSPECT AS AN INDIVIDUAL

Your intake people should take things one step further, though.

Being attentive is absolutely a requirement and will make it much easier for your prospects to feel at ease.

However, it's just as important that your intake team understands that they have to treat each caller as an individual, too.

We always tell law firms that their intake workers should be answering the phones like they've been waiting for that specific person to call all day. Beginning with this kind of attentiveness and enthusiasm is a great way to practice empathy and let that prospect know that you truly care about their call.

To be fair, this can sometimes be tough to do. Your intake people are fielding these calls all day, every day. If someone calls because they were just in a car accident, the event was most likely a traumatic one. Chances are they haven't been through this kind of jarring experience before. Of course, for your intake person, this might be the third or fourth call of this kind that day. They may hear from dozens of people a week who were recently in car accidents.

That's why you shouldn't take this advice for granted. We know your intake team is made up of perfectly nice, caring people, but it's worth stressing to them that they must treat every prospect as an individual who is going through a completely unique situation.

< Measuring Success **273** >

Similarly, it's easy to assume what the caller's main concern is: they want representation. However, over many years of working with law firms' intake teams, we've learned that this isn't always the case.

For example, if your firm specializes in workers' compensation cases, your intake team probably handles a lot of calls from people who were recently injured on the job. When talking to one of these people, it's perfectly understandable to assume the right thing to do is to ask about their injury.

How serious was it?

Have they seen a doctor?

In short, are they okay?

Now, that's all well and good. We're definitely not suggesting you shouldn't show concern for someone who was recently injured.

But what's the caller's main concern?

They certainly didn't call a law firm so a stranger could double-check they were aware of their injury and that a doctor may be able to help.

Again, that's nice to ask about and you definitely need that information to assess the client's case, but the most pressing issue for them is probably if they'll lose their job or not. They want someone whose opinion they trust to let them know that everything is going to be okay.

If your intake personnel fail to act with empathy, they'll fail to maximize conversions. Even if they truly are concerned for their caller, this won't necessarily show if they can't communicate that concern by anticipating what the prospect is most worried about.

Anticipating isn't always easy, but it can be just as effective for the intake worker to simply let the other person talk and ask relevant questions about what they've said to get to the heart of what's really concerning them.

< **274** Natalie Fragkouli & Liel Levy >

SPEAK THE PROSPECT'S LANGUAGE (LITERALLY AND FIGURATIVELY)

Marketing your firm to Hispanic Americans is a winning strategy, and if you already do so, you probably have staff members who speak Spanish.

While many Spanish-speaking clients will be comfortable communicating with you through a loved one who can translate, making the effort will go a long way toward a winning first impression. The same applies to Hispanic Americans who have no problem speaking English. This is also why we're big proponents of running your law firm's ads in both languages.[333]

Having bilingual intake personnel means you can accommodate people who call whether they prefer English or Spanish.[334] Better still, you can run your ads so that the number you use for those in Spanish use one number and those ads run in English use another.

Think what it will mean to someone who speaks Spanish fluently but may struggle with English when they call and someone answers in Spanish. Think what a competitive advantage this is over other firms who have their intake teams answer in English. When a Spanish-speaking prospect calls your firm, they may actually be taken aback by how much care it shows that you have someone they can communicate with actually answering the phones.

Keep in mind that—according to our experience—60 percent of Spanish-speaking callers will simply hang up the phone if their

---

333 "Bilingual Google Ads," Nanato Media, https://nanatomedia.com/bilingual-services/google-ads/.

334 "Getting Started with Your Law Firm's Hispanic Marketing Strategy," *Nanato Media*, June 20, 2020, https://nanatomedia.com/blog/getting-started-with-your-law-firms-hispanic-marketing-strategy/.

< Measuring Success **275** >

call is answered in English. So, there goes your hard-earned marketing dollars.

DROP THE LEGAL JARGON

Regardless of what language a prospect speaks, none of them are going to be as well-versed as your intake team in legalese.

So, make sure your team knows not to use it on the phone. They should always assume that the person calling is unfamiliar with the kinds of legal terms used inside the courtroom. That doesn't mean talking to the prospect like they're stupid, of course. It means speaking to them as they would talk to a stranger whom they just met at a party and who they know isn't a legal professional.

If you were in this situation, how would you describe legal matters in a way that would ensure the average person would understand them?

You wouldn't use legal jargon.[335] That's for sure.

It's not difficult and it doesn't take any practice. Only a little forethought is required to remember that the person on the phone has probably never worked in a legal field and, at this moment, just wants to speak to someone who can explain their situation to them and provide reassurance that everything is going to be okay.

---

335 Stefan Savic, "The Art Of Client Communication: Avoid Legal Jargon; Give Sufficient Detail, But Don't Drown Them In It," *Above the Law,* August 12, 2016, https://abovethelaw.com/2016/08/the-art-of-client-communication-avoid-legal -jargon-give-sufficient-detail-but-dont-drown-them-in-it/.

< **276**   Natalie Fragkouli & Liel Levy >

RESPECT YOUR LEADS' TIME

Your leads are almost always going to call you with a sense of urgency. Even if you handle tort cases—which don't face the same timelines as, say, a personal injury call—your leads don't want to wait around for days to hear back from you.

According to the 2019 Clio Legal Trends Report,[336] most people will speak to more than one attorney when they need legal representation.

However, it's clear that they'd prefer to hire one right away. Shopping around doesn't feel like a luxury when you need an attorney's help. That's why Clio also reports that 42 percent of people will hire the first attorney they're able to speak to provided they make a good first impression. You can imagine that this percentage is probably even higher when the prospects are people who would prefer to speak with someone in Spanish.

Speaking of Hispanic Americans who primarily communicate in Spanish, we have found that they also prefer to speak with their attorneys in-person—including for the initial consultation. While COVID-19 has made these kinds of in-person meetings less desirable, Spanish speakers have adapted to speaking over the phone or Zoom. The latter is an ideal replacement for in-person meetings because showing your face helps make a personal connection.

Either way, we recommend you make it clear to them if your office is nearby. Over the years, we've also found that Hispanic prospects like knowing that their lawyer's office isn't too far away.

---

336 "2019 Legal Trends Report," Clio, https://www.clio.com/resources/legal-trends/2019
-report/read-online/?cta=masthead-secondary.

< Measuring Success **277** >

WHAT IF THE LEAD DOESN'T CALL YOUR FIRM?

So far, we've talked a lot about how to handle leads when they call your law firm for legal help.

But your firm should have other options for callers to contact your intake team.

Web forms are a prime example,[337] but we also like:

- Live Chat

- Messenger

- WhatsApp

As long as you have someone on your intake team who's responsible for monitoring these channels, there are a number of options for augmenting this important step.

When it comes to web form submissions, we recommend you improve their effectiveness even further by offering the option for prospects to indicate when it would be best to contact them by phone. Otherwise, it's easy to end up in a never-ending game of phone tag, one which may end when one of your competitors gets back to them first.

If your firm uses an auto dialer system, you can simply program them to auto-initiate these calls at the time your prospects requested.[338]

Software can play a big role in your intake process, too. DocuSign is just one example of a platform we've seen work

---

337 Kristen Baker, "Web Forms: The Ultimate Guide," *HubSpot*, https://blog.hubspot.com/marketing/web-forms.

338 Lisa McGreevy, "6 Best Auto Dialer Software for Small Business," *Fit Small Business*, August 8, 2019, https://fitsmallbusiness.com/auto-dialer-software-review/.

< **278**   Natalie Fragkouli & Liel Levy >

wonders for a number of law firms over the years.[339] The list of options is extensive. CRM and case management software can be fantastic for letting prospects sign up remotely through email or even SMS.

Since COVID, we've seen a massive increase in the number of firms that have implemented this kind of technology into their intake processes. However, we wouldn't be surprised if the vast majority of these firms choose to continue using them long after COVID becomes a thing of the past.

Ultimately, the goal of your intake process is to lock down as many qualified prospects as possible, so they can proceed with the next step that turns them into actual, paying clients. This will almost always require more than just having a team of people to answer your phones.

TELEPHONE ETIQUETTE

At Nanato Media, both of our founders have a background in luxury hospitality, so it should come as no surprise that when we model an effective intake process, it resembles the service and personalization you would see from a five-star hotel.

Let's start with some basics.

---

339 DocuSign Developer, https://fitsmallbusiness.com/auto-dialer-software-review/.

INTERACTIVE VOICE RESPONSE SYSTEMS

First, there's Interactive Voice Response (IVR), which has traditionally been a common solution for managing law firms' incoming calls.[340] That said, we've yet to hear someone who looks forward to the prospect of speaking with an automated telephone system, especially when they're calling to speak to an attorney about what is most likely a sensitive topic.

Bottom line: don't use them.

Use live agents to answer your law firm's calls.

AUTOMATICALLY PUTTING CALLERS ON HOLD

Another common intake process for law firms is automatically transferring prospects' phone calls to hold where they are serenaded by absolutely wonderful music until someone can actually speak to them.

Hold music may actually be worse than the IVR alternative.

Instead of paying for clicks to generate calls that will just hang up when they hear your hold music, you might as well donate that money to charity where it can actually do some good.

---

340 Margaret Rouse, "Interactive Voice Response (IVR)," *Search Customer Experience,* https://searchcustomerexperience.techtarget.com/definition/ Interactive-Voice-Response-IVR.

< **280**   Natalie Fragkouli & Liel Levy >

THE GOLDEN RULE REGARDING PHONE CALLS

We can't stress this rule enough.

It might sound trivial, but we promise it will make a difference: answer phone calls before the third ring.

Doing so ensures your prospects are never waiting on the other line for more than fifteen seconds to speak with someone.

Remember, just because you know your firm is the best doesn't mean your prospects are equally aware. Every ring you don't answer gives them one more reason to explore one of their many other options.

IMPLEMENT A TELEPHONE ETIQUETTE POLICY

Taking the above steps will go a long way toward improving your law firm's intake process, but now let's talk about your employees' actual etiquette on the phone.

Here's how simple it can be. When they answer, they should use this script:

Greeting + Name of Your Firm + Their Name + "How can I assist you?"

That's about as complicated as your greeting needs to be.

Obviously, there's more to an effective intake call than the greeting, so here are other important tips:

< Measuring Success **281** >

- Speak calmly and clearly and ensure there is no background noise.

- Ask for the caller's name early on and then use it at least two times in a natural way to personalize the entire call.

- Collect data efficiently.

- Use caller ID but still confirm that the number it reports is a good contact number for them by repeating it to them; make it as frictionless as possible for the caller to share their details.

- Always ask permission before placing a caller on hold, but never leave them on hold for more than a minute. If necessary, get back to the caller and ask for more time.

- Never answer a call and immediately ask to place them on hold. If you have to, answer the call, let the caller speak, and then ask if you can place them on hold.

- When transferring a call, communicate all relevant details to your colleague, so the prospect doesn't have to repeat themselves.

- Always thank the caller for contacting you.

Here's one more tip if you're using a CRM: if the prospect needs your firm's address, offer to send it to them via text message to make it easy for them. You can even offer to send them text or email reminders.

< **282**   Natalie Fragkouli & Liel Levy >

ALWAYS BE CLOSING

The goal of your intake process is to define what the next step is to bring your prospects close to the solution they are looking for: in this case, legal help.

One of the most common mistakes we see intake personnel make is not taking control over the conversation and establishing the next step.

Most of the time, intake calls end with the prospect saying something like, "I'll call again if I need help." Sometimes, they're able to speak these fateful lines before the intake person is even able to collect basic information.

Here are some of the most common phrases responsible for letting this kind of thing happen. Make sure your intake team avoids them at all costs:

- "When would you like to come in or schedule an appointment?"

  - Instead use: "I understand you want to find a solution to your situation, and I'd like to treat this as a priority. Are you available now or this afternoon to talk with the attorney?"

- "You can call us back anytime."

  - Instead use: "Would you prefer for me to follow up with you later today or tomorrow morning?"

And, finally, one of the most shortsighted approaches, which, regrettably, we see all the time:

Prospective client: "What kind of cases do you take?"

< Measuring Success **283** >

Intake agent: "We only take..."

Instead, they should say, "Please tell me about your situation and I'll see how we can help."

Remember, it doesn't matter if you can take the prospect's case or not. They already called. If you take a few minutes to give them some guidance, they'll come back when they do need your help and/or will refer you to someone they know who does.

If they're not a good fit, don't leave them hanging. Refer them to a firm in your network that handles their type of case. Then, call them back a couple of days later and ask if your referral helped them.

IS YOUR INTAKE PROCESS MAKING THE MOST OF YOUR FIRM'S MARKETING BUDGET?

There's just no two ways about it: if your intake process does anything other than bring in every qualified prospect your marketing campaigns attract, you're losing money.

That's how important intake is to your law firm.

<CHAPTER 16 >

THE ULTIMATE GUIDE TO LAW FIRM REVIEW GENERATION

No matter how great your law firm is, if prospects don't believe it, they won't become paying clients. The easiest way to get them excited about hiring you is by showing them what past clients have had to say. Learn to effectively and consistently generate leads and you'll have no trouble getting qualified leads to contact you.

The English bishop, satirist, and writer Joseph Hall once said, "A reputation once broken may possibly be repaired, but the world will always keep their eyes on the spot where the crack was."

That was back in the seventeenth century.

And yet, that quote has arguably never been more relevant.

After all, the internet is known for having a long memory. For more than a decade, experts have tried to remind people that, "The Internet Never Forgets."[341]

"The Internet Never Forgets," *Scientific American*, August 18, 2008, https://www.scientificamerican.com/article/the-internet-never-forgets/.

< **286**   Natalie Fragkouli & Liel Levy >

This is especially important for business owners to keep in mind. Your reputation is no longer limited to word of mouth. If your business starts to suffer because of a bad reputation, you can't hope to simply wait for the memory of that stain to fade.

Once it's online, it stays online.

It's there for every potential client to learn about before they decide whether or not it's worth contacting you for help.

This is why reputation management has become vital for law firms. In a time when Google will show your reputation anytime they show your firm's name, you can't risk leaving your reputation to chance. You either take every step to control public perception, or you risk losing clients before they ever gave you a single click.

WHAT IS REPUTATION MANAGEMENT?

Reputation management refers to a number of different strategies and practices you can use to manage your reputation.[342]

Alright, you probably guessed that.

However, while it's always been wise for business owners to manage their company's reputations, the concept really took off in the Digital Age for reasons we just covered.

More importantly, it's never been more crucial for business owners to be proactive about reputation management. You absolutely cannot assume that you'll simply handle potential problems when they arise. Reputation management for law firms is just as much about two other vital practices:

---

342 "Legal Reputation Management: All You Need to Know About Your Law Firm's Reviews," *Nanato Media*, May 7, 2020, https://nanatomedia.com/blog/legal -reputation-management-all-you-need-to-know-about-your-law -firms-reviews/.

< Measuring Success **287** >

- Proactively stack Google's deck in your favor. You want all kinds of flattering reviews and five-star reviews right next to your law firm's name whenever it shows up in Google. The same goes for Yelp and Facebook.

- Put a plan in place for how you will address negative reviews. You never want to just accept them or find yourself in panic mode when they happen. That doesn't mean you can always get the desired outcome, but you should definitely have a response plan for when they happen.

Reputation management represents as much of a marketing strategy as PPC, SEO, social media, and anything else. In fact, given Google's predilection for showing business reviews, you could argue that reputation management is the most important marketing strategy for your firm.

After all, putting your law firm in front of potential clients won't matter much if, at the same time, those prospects see a less-than-stellar reputation.

WHY REPUTATION MANAGEMENT MATTERS TO YOUR LAW FIRM

According to Bright Local's 2019 Local Consumer Review Survey:[343]

- The average consumer reads ten reviews before feeling ready to trust a business.

- Only 53 percent of people would consider using a business with less than four stars.

---

343 "Local Consumer Review Survey 2020," Bright Local, https://www.brightlocal.com/research/local-consumer-review-survey/.

< **288**   Natalie Fragkouli & Liel Levy >

- The average consumer spends thirteen minutes and forty-five seconds reading reviews before making a decision.

- Among consumers that read reviews, 97 percent read businesses' responses to reviews.

As you can see, prospects put a big premium on what other clients think about your firm. This is known as social proof—because it is so powerful for converting leads.[344]

Simply put, you can use all kinds of different words to advertise your law firm's services, but none of them will carry as much weight as those who've had direct experience with those services as actual clients.

This is even more so the case if you plan on marketing to Hispanic prospects.[345] Hispanic Americans are well-known for sharing their opinions about local businesses with friends and families. In many cases, their tight-knit culture means that their opinions spread far and wide.

So, whether or not you deserve any strikes against your online reputation, once prospects see it, you've lost control of the conversation. Hence, why reputation management is essential to effectively marketing your law firm.

THE THREE TYPES OF CLIENT REVIEWS FOR LAW FIRMS

In a moment, we'll dive into some practical strategies you can use to mold your online reputation and protect it from negative reviews

---

344 Shanelle Mullin, "Social Proof: What It Is, Why It Works, and How to Use It," *CXL*, September 25, 2020, https://cxl.com/blog/is-social-proof-really-that-important/.

345 "Why Law Firms Must Run Spanish Google Ads," *Nanato Media*, March 23, 2020, https://nanatomedia.com/blog/why-law-firms-must-run-spanish-google-ads/.

< Measuring Success **289** >

that may not accurately reflect your level of service. Obviously, these are very important for building your law firm's business, especially if you market to Hispanic Americans. As it turns out, Hispanic people are *highly* influenced by customer reviews.[346]

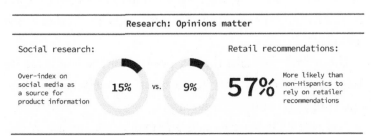

Research: Opinions matter

Social research:

Over-index on social media as a source for product information   **15%**   vs.   **9%**

Retail recommendations:

57% More likely than non-Hispanics to rely on retailer recommendations

Source: Univision & Media Predict, 2018

First, let's define what online client reviews entail.

For the most part, there are three types of online client reviews that you need to know about:

- First-Party Reviews: These are client reviews that are collected and displayed on your own website without any input from you or your staff members.

- Third-Party Reviews: These client reviews are collected by third-party websites like Google, Facebook, Yelp, and others. Again, your firm has nothing to do with these reviews.

- Testimonials: This kind of customer feedback is usually pulled from a personal email or a third-party review but is displayed on your law firm's website for prospects to see.

---

346 Kathy Whitlock, "Engaging the Powerhouse US Hispanic Online Shopper," *Univision*, https://corporate.univision.com/blog/2018/08/16/engaging-the-powerhouse-u-s-hispanic-online-shopper/.

< **290**   Natalie Fragkouli & Liel Levy >

Each of these three types of client reviews can play a role in marketing your law firm.

THE BENEFITS OF FIRST-PARTY REVIEWS

Still, we want to briefly touch on the importance of First-Party Reviews because they usually don't get as much attention as the other two.

The reason we make them a priority for the law firms we partner with is because they help to diversify your reviews, which helps with your firm's local search.

You also don't need to have an email or an account with a third party.

Finally, you can display these flattering reviews right on your website (just like testimonials).

SHOULD YOUR LAW FIRM SOLICIT CLIENT REVIEWS?

Before we dive further into using reputation management strategies for your law firm, we want to note that nothing we say should be understood to overwrite your state's Bar Association's rules about reviews and soliciting reviews.

While we've successfully used these strategies with a number of law firms from all over the country and across every major practice area, please be sure you check with your state's guidelines before proceeding with your own plan.

With that said, let's talk about a very hot topic when it comes to reputation management: soliciting online reviews.

< Measuring Success **291** >

THE MOST IMPORTANT PLATFORM FOR CLIENT REVIEWS

It should come as no surprise that the most important place you want to show off your clients' positive reviews is through...*GOOGLE!*

Obviously, that's where the vast majority of your prospects will head when they're looking for help from an attorney like yourself.

Great, so go ahead and start spamming your email list for those positive, new-business-winning reviews, right?

That seems to be the guiding wisdom of a lot of firms, but let us assure you, Google doesn't appreciate that kind of approach. And if Google doesn't appreciate a certain approach, you probably shouldn't take it.

Now, that said, Google *is* okay with you soliciting reviews, as long as you aren't "soliciting reviews from customers in bulk."[347]

In other words, it's okay for you to remind clients how helpful their testimonial would be, but if Google notices a sharp uptick in reviews from out of the blue, expect trouble.

WHATEVER YOU DO, DO NOT ASK FOR REVIEWS ON YELP

On the other hand, Yelp does not like businesses asking their clients for reviews.[348]

Like at all.

"If we find indicators of systematic review solicitation, we will apply a search ranking penalty to affected Yelp business pages. Businesses can avoid this review solicitation penalty by complying with Yelp's policies.

347 "Google Review Policy: What Business Owners Can and Can't Do to Get More Google Reviews," Boast, https://boast.io/google-review-policy-what-business-owners-can-and-cant-do-to-get-more-google-reviews/.

348 "What is Yelp's Review Solicitation Penalty?" Yelp Support Center, https://www.yelp-support.com/article/What-is-Yelp-s-review-solicitation-penalty.

< **292** Natalie Fragkouli & Liel Levy >

"Extreme attempts to manipulate a business's reputation and inflate search ranking by soliciting or purchasing reviews on Yelp may lead to a *Consumer Alert* on the business's Yelp page."[349]

In other words, Yelp will make it clear to your potential clients that your company—a law firm—tried to bypass their rules to misrepresent themselves to people who need their help.

Not a great look for a law firm.

It should also come as no surprise that Yelp will drop your rankings on their platform—by a lot. In one case of Yelp punishing a business for soliciting reviews, "...the business went from being listed in sixth place in Yelp's search results to not being in the first five pages of results for their main keyword."[350]

That could go a long way toward hurting your firm's business, especially if you're depending mainly on organic search to bring you traffic.

To make matters worse, Yelp doesn't believe in a simple kiss-and-make-up approach.

Once you've been caught, you need to quit soliciting reviews—obviously.

But then, you have to complete a Compliance Verification form (doesn't that sound like fun?).

After that, you'll need to wait between thirty and forty-five days for Yelp to finish their review and conclude your firm is, in fact, no longer soliciting reviews.

---

349 "What are Consumer Alerts?" Yelp Support Center, https://www.yelp-support.com/article/What-are-Consumer-Alerts.

350 Joy Hawkins, "How Does Yelp's Review Solicitation Penalty Work?" *Search Engine Land*, June 14, 2018, https://searchengineland.com/how-does-yelps-review-solicitation-penalty-work-299893.

< Measuring Success **293** >

HOW FACEBOOK FEELS ABOUT REVIEWS

Facebook has taken a very unique approach to customer reviews.[351] It's one that you won't find on any other platform, but one that you should still understand because of how important Facebook has become to law-firm marketing (especially among Hispanics, who *love* social media[352]).

Instead of collecting customer reviews, Facebook now requests recommendations. Users are prompted with either a yes or a no and then they're allowed to leave an explanation for their choice.

Although this probably won't apply much to your firm, Facebook will also allow users to provide "rich endorsements," which means they can upload images of their experience with your business.

At the same time, Facebook has also made it so that their recommendations lend themselves to easy reporting if users suspect they're not 100 percent credible. So, while that doesn't mean you can't solicit reviews from your users for Facebook, it does mean you don't want them to stretch the truth on your behalf.

SHOULD YOU USE INCENTIVES TO GAIN MORE CLIENT REVIEWS FOR YOUR LAW FIRM?

We've covered this a bit previously, but it's such a common question across every single platform that we really want to give our opinion on the entire concept.

---

351 Jamie Pitman, "Facebook Is Switching Review Ratings to Recommendations," *Bright Local*, August 22, 2018, https://www.brightlocal.com/blog/facebook-switching -reviews-to-recommendations/.

352 Adrianna Lynch, "What the cultural evolution of US Hispanics means for marketers," *Digital Commerce 360*, November 7, 2019, https://www.digitalcommerce360. com/2019/11/07/what-the-cultural-evolution-of-us-hispanics-means -for-marketers/.

< **294**   Natalie Fragkouli & Liel Levy >

Here's what we tell the law firms we partner with: incentiv-ize your team to provide the best possible service, and positive reviews will follow. There's no need to risk consequences for your online presence by toying with the rules set forth by platforms.

CHECK YOUR STATE'S BAR ASSOCIATION'S RULES

We also want to make this guideline completely clear to you one more time. No matter what Google, Yelp, Facebook, or anyone else has to say, your state's Bar Association definitely has an opin-ion on the matter and it's worth listening to.

Because, actually, it's not really an opinion, so much as it's a law.

As a lawyer, you should appreciate how important those rules are.

In case you don't, here are some examples to help with that.

In 2019, a law firm in Pennsylvania was sued after it was dis-covered that they were soliciting positive online reviews.[353] Well, it's a little worse than that. They actually:

> "...orchestrated a scheme of soliciting positive online reviews from people who had never used the law firm's services. Nonlawyer employees were encouraged to solicit friends and family to write the reviews and given time off for each positive review they secured, the suit alleged."

Ooooooh boy. Never do that. Aside from the lawsuit you'll face, you're really going to need reputation management after that.

---

353 Debra Cassens Weiss, "Firm Settles Suit Alleging it Solicited Fake Online Reviews that Tricked Woman into Becoming Client," *ABA Journal*, August 13, 2019, https://www.abajournal.com/news/article/firm-settles-suit-alleging-it-solicited-fake-online-reviews-that-tricked-woman-into-becoming-client.

< Measuring Success **295** >

While there's no state where that kind of plan is a good one, laws can fluctuate quite a bit throughout the country.

New York is a prime example. Its Bar Association has stated that a lawyer can give their clients a $50 credit toward their legal bills in exchange for an online review.[354] The only stipulation is:

- The credit against the lawyer's bill is not contingent on the content of the rating.

- The client is not coerced or compelled to rate the lawyer.

- The ratings and lawyer reviews are done by the clients and not by the attorney.

Obviously, this is not the case throughout the country, so again, be sure to check what your Bar Association has to say on the matter before you risk courting any negative publicity for your firm.

MAKE YOUR LAW FIRM'S REVIEW POLICY TRANSPARENT

One last note about garnering those valuable reviews from your prospects before we move on: make sure you have a policy in place and make sure it's transparent. Creating such a policy does no one any good if it's vague or difficult to interpret. Don't expect your Bar Association to give you the benefit of the doubt in that case, either.

IS REVIEW GATING A GOOD IDEA?

No.

It is not a good idea to "review gate" and the truth is that it never was.[355]

---

354 "Ethics Opinion 1052," *New York State Bar Association*, March 25, 2015, https://nysba.org/ethics-opinion-1052/.

355 Greg Sterling, "Study: Killing 'Review Gating' Doesn't Hurt Scores and Grows Overall Volume." *Search Engine Land*, October 31, 2019, https://searchengineland.com/study-killing-review-gating-doesnt-hurt-scores-and-grows-overall-volume-324310.

< **296**   Natalie Fragkouli & Liel Levy >

Ever.

No matter what any experts may have told you, the practice was never a good idea and almost never showed positive results, either.[356]

For those of you who are lucky enough to never have been pitched this "service," review gating was the practice of sending clients who had positive things to say right to platforms that would publish those flattering reviews.

What about bad reviews?

Well, if you thought someone might leave you a bad review, you simply sent them down a very, very different path. For example, many firms would solicit reviews directly and then, once they realized a former client would not be flattering, they'd corral them into some kind of "reconciliation" process—a step that usually amounted to little more than consumer fraud.

Under no circumstances should you go anywhere near review gating or any marketing agency that pitches you the idea. It holds no real prospect of working favorably, and it could go a long way toward ruining your law firm's reputation forever.

HOW TO HANDLE NEGATIVE REVIEWS OF YOUR LAW FIRM

Look.

We're not saying your law firm would ever deserve a negative review.

But unless you're literally brand new to the field, like you just passed the bar and never did any sort of internship in law school

---

356 "Does Review Gating Impact Star-Ratings?" *GatherUp*, October 17, 2019, https://gatherup.com/blog/does-review-gating-impact-star-ratings/.

< Measuring Success **297** >

and have never actually talked to another attorney before, the reality is that you're going to have unsatisfied clients.

Even if you employ a rigorous vetting process, you're still going to end up with clients every now and then who were never going to be happy no matter what you did for them.

So, accept that you're going to get a negative review from time to time and get busy creating a strategy for what you'll do about it.

Even if you have ninety-nine amazing reviews, prospects are still going to seek out the one negative review to show them the "worst-case scenario" they can expect if they hire you.

The first step toward dealing with these is to simply keep a close eye on them. Don't let a negative review go unnoticed until you finally make time for your annual check.

The second step is to respond.

While we understand that it would feel amazing to really give the reviewer a piece of your mind and maybe even say some of those things you kept to yourself back when they were still a client, we recommend the high road.

It's not so much that you want to change that past client's opinion of your services. Instead, think about the impression you want to give a prospect who's going to be reading your response. Respond compassionately to the aggrieved party and invite them to contact you if they'd like to discuss the matter further.[357] If possible, tactfully add context to the negative review if you think it'll help your prospects understand why the criticism isn't completely accurate.

Google pays a lot of attention to which businesses respond to reviews and favors them for local rankings as it feels more confident about showing a business that is responsive to users who interact with their GMB listing.

---

357 Nina Solis, "How to Respond to Negative Online Reviews," *Broadly*, September 7, 2017, https://broadly.com/blog/how-to-respond-to-negative-reviews/.

< **298**   Natalie Fragkouli & Liel Levy >

That's one more very good reason to respond to client feedback.

WHAT CAN YOU LEARN FROM YOUR CLIENT'S REVIEWS?

It's easy to solely pay attention to those reviews that make your law firm look incredible, but we encourage you to also look at how many mention your process—not just your results.

If your firm is like most, you'll find that even satisfied clients very rarely say positive things about the experience itself.

That may be because working with a lawyer often makes people nervous. Perhaps your firm isn't providing a superior customer service experience.

Whatever the case, if you're not seeing the actual process getting brought up in a flattering light again and again, that's where there's a real opportunity for your firm to improve. You want reviews that talk about how comfortable your staff made clients feel. You want prospects to know they'll be in good hands throughout the entirety of their time with you.

HOW TO SHOW STAR RATINGS FOR YOUR SITE IN THE GOOGLE SEARCH RESULTS?

As we mentioned, Google is one of the best places to show off just how much former clients love your firm.

The easiest way to get started with doing this is by using a plugin that allows you to generate first-party reviews. Then you

< Measuring Success **299** >

can pull those reviews from different sites and display them on your website. You also want a plugin that makes them visible to users and includes the schema markup this requires.[358]

It's just as important that you tell Google to aggregate your star ratings so there's no reason for the search engine to suspect that you're suppressing any reviews that aren't flattering.

Similarly, avoid including your firm's ratings on every page of your site. Instead, put reviews for practice areas on the practice area page. If you try putting them on your home page or other general pages, you may earn a Google Search Console warning or even a ranking penalty.

HOW TO SELECT REPUTATION MANAGEMENT SOFTWARE

Reputation management platforms will make it much easier for your firm to reach out to clients and ask for reviews. Look for one that also tracks your reviews across multiple sites.

Those two traits aren't hard to find these days. The one that we really think makes the best platforms stand out is automatically scanning reviews for specific words before producing a sentiment analysis. At Nanato Media, we entrust Yext for reputation monitoring.[359] Among other things, it has an AI-powered sentiment analysis tool and also helps you craft a personalized response to your reviewers, something you now know is extremely important.

---

358 Neil Patel, "How to Boost Your SEO by Using Schema Markup," *Neil Patel*, https:// neilpatel.com/blog/get-started-using-schema/.

359 "Yext Reviews," Yext, https://www.yext.com/products/reviews/monitor-respond/.

< **300** Natalie Fragkouli & Liel Levy >

DOES YOUR REPUTATION MANAGEMENT SOFTWARE INCLUDE THE FOUR MOST IMPORTANT FEATURES?

There are all kinds of reputation management platforms on the market.[360] As we just mentioned, we love Yext, but there may be a better option for your particular needs.

Whatever the case, there are four features you absolutely must have in any software you use to monitor your firm's reputation.

A DASHBOARD

The main benefit of a dashboard is that it lets you see a variety of information all on a single screen. For reputation management software, this means that you can see all of your reviews from multiple websites, manage your online reviews, and track key metrics.

Without a dashboard, properly managing your reputation is quickly going to become more cumbersome than necessary.

REPORTING AND GOAL SETTING

You also want a platform that combines data from multiple review sites and presents it to you in a unified inbox, so you don't need to track reviews on a site-by-site basis. Again, this would be much too time consuming to be practical for most firms. Reputation management software should make your life easier.

AUTOMATIC NOTIFICATIONS

You want your reputation management software to immediately notify you of important events, such as a new review being published. These notifications can occur within the program itself or by sending you a text or email. Whichever you prefer, what

---

360 "Reputation Management Software," Capterra, https://www.capterra.com/reputation-management-software/.

< Measuring Success **301** >

matters most is that you're able to read your reviews right away so you can address them as necessary.

INTEGRATIONS

You'll find review generation and reputation management much simpler if your platform can integrate with your law firm's case management system and CRM.[361] Bring all of those together in one platform that's easy to manage, and you'll have a much easier time letting prospects know how great your law firm is.

ACTIVELY PURSUE REVIEWS TO BOOST YOUR FIRM'S BUSINESS

With all it takes to run a successful law firm, it can be easy to assume that simply doing your best work—and demanding the same of your staff—means you'll develop the kind of reputation that automatically generates business.

Of course, it's not that simple. While it's never been easier to show off your satisfied clients' flattering reviews, you still need to do some work.

---

361 "CRM 101: What is CRM?" Salesforce, https://www.salesforce.com/crm/what-is-crm/.

< CONCLUSION >

START PROFITING FROM A PROVEN DIGITAL MARKETING STRATEGY

At the very beginning of the book (remember all the way back then?), we promised that we would give you all the information you need to build a successful digital marketing strategy based on proven tactics we've been using for years.

Since we made that promise, we've covered some extremely important territory. You should now feel very comfortable when it comes to the fundamental building blocks of digital marketing strategies. Foundational elements like:

- The difference between SEO and PPC

- The essential business metrics

- How to use Facebook ads

You should also understand how all of the methods we covered fit with one another and how each one is able to strengthen the others.

< **304** Natalie Fragkouli & Liel Levy >

Feeling good about this?

Then there's just one last step to the process.

GET STARTED BUILDING YOUR LAW FIRM'S DIGITAL MARKETING STRATEGY ASAP

If there's one final recommendation we can make before ending this book, it's that you get started right away.

While you've now earned a high-level understanding of how to digitally market a law firm online, that knowledge isn't worth anything if you don't put it to use.

As countless studies have shown, the longer you wait to do so, the more you risk two costly consequences:

- Forgetting What You Learned: Look, we did our best to make all of this information as interesting, accessible, and memorable as possible. Nonetheless, despite our best efforts, we know you'll start forgetting a lot of what you just learned if you don't begin using it ASAP.

- Losing Your Momentum: That wouldn't be such a big deal if it weren't for the second consequence, which is that your enthusiasm will start to wane the longer you wait to get going. Even the idea of coming back to reference this book will become formidable as the days go by. Soon, you'll begin relying on the same strategies that have underwhelmed you in the past—even though you now know better.

< Conclusion **305** >

So, *please* get started right now.

Even if it's something as simple as starting your first Google Ads account or signing up for Local Service Ads, get going today.

OR LET EXPERIENCED PROFESSIONALS CREATE AND EXECUTE A DIGITAL MARKETING STRATEGY FOR YOU

Maybe you already have a million things on your plate.

You certainly wouldn't be the first law firm owner facing a fully booked calendar.

You also wouldn't be the first without the prospect of free time in the foreseeable future.

That's why we won't take it personally if you call us for help. We know even with the detailed roadmap to success that we just outlined for you, there's not a whole lot you can do if you don't have the time to execute it.

As we mentioned at various points throughout the book, we also know there's a bit of a learning curve to these strategies. It's just part of gaining the experience you need to be successful.

Again, that takes time.

If you don't want to wait, or you simply don't like the idea of trial and error, we're always here to help. Feel free to give us a call.

Whether you just need clarification about a certain point in this book, or you're interested in securing our professional services, we'd absolutely love to hear from you.

< ACKNOWLEDGMENTS >

This book was a labor of love. Much of that labor was contributed by people we love, so we'd like to take a moment to acknowledge them right now.

First and foremost, this book would not have been possible if not for our partners—the many law firms that have entrusted us over the years with their marketing strategies and allowed us to be an extension of their business. Thank you for believing in us, but most importantly, thank you for believing and recognizing the Hispanic market.

To our Nanato Media family, your passion and dedication to the work we do is what inspired this book. Themos, Gil, Tannya, Liz, and Elisa—gracias!

To our publishing team: John, your understanding of our voice and tone was instrumental in creating this book; thank you for being part of our team. To Skylar, Rikki, Emily, Katie, Rachael, and everyone else behind the scenes at Scribe who guided and helped us make this book a reality in what feels like a record amount of time—thank you.

Nathaniel and Juliana: you make Mommy and Daddy so proud every day, and we hope that one day when you are old enough to read this book, you will feel proud of us, too.

Last but not least: to you, our reader, thank you for taking the time to read this book. Kudos for making it to this section, even though you did not know you were going to be mentioned. But this is it. This is the end of the book.

Now go and put into practice what you've learned.

< GLOSSARY >

A

A/B Testing: The process of simultaneously running an experiment between two or more variants of a landing page to see which one performs best.

Ad Copy: The text in your ad. This is the description that calls the searcher to an action.

Ad Extension: These expand your ads and show users more reasons they should click. Ad extensions add useful business data below your ad, such as locations, additional links, prices, and more. This makes ad extensions a good idea for just about every advertiser.

Ad Fatigue: This occurs when your campaign frequency gets too high, causing your target audiences to see the same ads again and again, and therefore becoming less responsive to them.

< **310** Natalie Fragkouli & Liel Levy >

Ad Frequency: How many times each user sees your ads.

Ad Preview and Diagnosis Tool: This tool shows a preview of a Google SERP for a specific term, so you can see which ads and extensions are appearing for it. Once you enter a search keyword and other criteria (e.g., location, language, etc.), the tool tells you whether or not your ad will be eligible to appear in that situation.

Ad Placement: Where your ad shows up.

Ad Rank: This is what determines your ad's position in the auction: CPC bid x Quality Score.

Ad Reach: This is how many people you'll be targeting with a specific ad, which is extremely important because, among other things, you have to keep an eye on whom you'll be targeting.

Ambicultural: Someone who is Ambicultural is able to functionally transit between Latino and American cultures. This gives Ambicultural individuals a unique position in the consumer landscape.

Americanizado: The term means "to Americanize," making this a very accurate term for Hispanic people who were born in the US, just like their parents and grandparents. Many have family roots that go back even further. English is their native language. They speak little, if any, Spanish. Despite their heritage, Americanizados participate in very few Hispanic cultural practices.

< Glossary **311** >

Automatic Bidding: With this type of bidding, you choose your goals and Google automates the bidding based on the strategy you choose: Maximize Clicks, Target Impression Share, Target CPA, Target ROAS, Maximize Conversions, and Maximize Conversions Value.

Average Conversion Rate: Seven percent for Google Ads run on the Search Network and 1.8 percent for Display. You can determine your conversion rate in Google Ads[362] by dividing the number of conversions your ad has received by the total number of clicks it earned.

Average Lifetime Value of Client: The amount you expect to earn from a client.

B

Bidding Script: These types of scripts allow you to automate the bidding process while maintaining a great deal of control and flexibility over your campaign. By automatically integrating helpful third-party datasets, you can increase available data, too. The result can be better, more effective bidding, and Google Ads campaigns that produce greater ROIs.

---

362 "Conversion Rate: Definition," *Google Ads Help*, n.d., https://support.google.com/google-ads/answer/2684489?hl=en.

< **312**   Natalie Fragkouli & Liel Levy >

Bidding System: When you select each keyword for your ad campaign, you can choose how much you're willing to pay whenever a customer searches for that keyword and clicks your ad. This is your keyword's maximum cost-per-click, or max CPC, bid amount. Some advertisers prefer manual bids because of the control it gives them, while others are happy to let the Google Ads system make bids on their behalf.

Branded Ads: Ads targeting users who search for a specific brand name. This could be the name of the company running the ad or the name of one of their competitors.

Broad Match: This type will show your law firm's ad when a specific keyword is searched for, as well as variations of it and related keywords.

Budget Script: These scripts automatically check if an item (e.g., keyword, ad, ad group, campaign, or account) exceeds your budget.

Buyer Persona: Your ideal, most desired client.

C

Call-Only-Ads: Ads that allow mobile users to call the business by tapping their screens without leaving the search page.

Click Fraud: These are illegitimate clicks on ads, which can come from multiple sources, such as competitors, click farms, bots, etc.

< Glossary **313** >

Content Targeting: This is when you target users by search behavior (keywords in search queries they completed in Google), locations they have visited (where users searched for those on Google Maps), or specific websites.

CPA: Cost Per Acquisition is a marketing metric that represents the total cost spent to acquire one paying customer at a marketing campaign or channel level.

Law Firm CPA = Ad Spend/Number of New Clients

CPC: Cost Per Click is how much you're spending on average when a prospect clicks your PPC ad.

Cost Per Result: How much each lead is costing you, similar to cost per conversion in Google Ads.

CRM: Customer Relationship Management is the process in which a business manages interactions with peers, leads, prospects, and clients.

CRO: Conversion Rate Optimization is the systematic process of increasing the percentage of website visitors who take a desired action—filling out a form, becoming customers, or otherwise.

Cross-Screen Viewing: This is when someone has the TV on while still engaging with content on their mobile device. Common examples are people checking their phones between innings, during commercials, or simply when the action on-screen slows down.

< **314** Natalie Fragkouli & Liel Levy >

CTA: Call-to-Action. This is any type of content—a phrase, paragraph, or closing remark in a video—designed to get a specific response from the prospect (e.g., a phone call, a form submission, live chat session, etc.).

CTR: This stands for Click Through Rate, which is the number of clicks your ad receives divided by the number of times your ad is shown:

clicks ÷ impressions = CTR.

D

Dayparting: The practice of scheduling ads for certain times of day and/or certain days of the week, depending on when they're most likely to convert target audiences.

Demographics: These are identifiers like gender, household income, etc.—all traits you may want to target when running PPC ads.

Dynamic Number Insertion: With this feature, your leads will see a different phone number to call depending on what channel they're using to find it *and* where they're located when they do it.

< Glossary **315** >

E

Engagement Custom Audiences: This specific type of custom audience targets users who have interacted with your law firm's content through one of Facebook's services or apps.

Exact Match: In the past, this approach meant that Google would only show your ad to users who typed the *exact* keywords or phrases you specified. That recently changed, so that Google may still show your ads if the searcher uses synonyms, similar variations, or the plural version of your specific keywords.

F

Facebook Lead Ad: When a qualified prospect sees this type of ad, they can just tap on it and a form will immediately pop up. Better still, this form arrives prepopulated with the qualified prospect's contact information—taken directly from their Facebook profile.

Facebook Pixel: This small piece of code allows you to track people who visit your website from Facebook ads. As a result, you can run retargeting campaigns that help you earn their business even after they've left your site.

Facebook Post Boost: As long as you have a business page, you can boost posts from your Facebook Business page so it appears before more people.

< **316** Natalie Fragkouli & Liel Levy >

First-Party Reviews: These are client reviews that are collected and displayed on your law firm's website *without* any input from you or your staff members.

G

GMB: Google My Business. This is your Google business listing, which can show up in the SERPs and Maps.

Google Display Network (GDN): This is Google's network of sites that will display its user's ads (e.g., those of your law firm). Currently, there are more than two million sites on GDN.

Google Keyword Planner: This tool shows how popular a keyword is, how much competition there is for it, and what you should plan on spending whenever you earn a click for it.

Google Search Console: This tool allows webmasters to check indexing status and optimize visibility of their websites.

Google Search Network Ads: Ads that appear on Google's SERP.

Google Trends: This tool shows the relative popularity of search terms. It even eliminates repeated searches from the same person over a short period, so the reported popularity isn't affected by small groups of people.

< Glossary **317** >

H

Heatmap: Website heatmaps show the most popular (hot) and unpopular (cold) regions of web pages using colors on a scale from red to blue. By aggregating this kind of user behavior, website heatmaps provide an at-a-glance understanding of how users interact with an individual web page. This includes everything from what they click on to what they scroll through to even what they ignore. This type of data aggregation helps site owners identify trends so they can optimize for greater future engagement.

Highly Relevant Keywords: These are keywords that are 100 percent relevant to your law firm's specific market, and hence, the ones that are most likely to earn your ad clicks.

Hispano: A term that refers to Hispanic Americans who emigrated to the United States more than ten years ago but still prefer to speak Spanish. Generally, Hispanos do speak some English, though. They still partake in many Hispanic cultural practices, as well.

I

Ideal CPA: To get this amount, first take how many leads you need before you have a client and multiply it by your current CPA. Then take this number and subtract it from the average lifetime value of a client. This will give you your profit margin, which will help you decide what you want your ideal CPA to be.

< **318**   Natalie Fragkouli & Liel Levy >

Impression Share: The number of impressions your ad receives divided by the *estimated* number of impressions you were eligible to receive.

IVR: Interactive Voice Response. This is an automated telephone system (to be avoided by law firms).

K

Keyword-Level Tracking: When a visitor arrives on your landing page by following an online search, they will be assigned a unique phone number for the entirety of their stay. That specific number sticks with them for as long as they're on your landing page. They're the only ones who can see that specific number while they are online with you.

Keyword Matching: Keyword match types help you control which searches in Google will trigger your ad to display for a user. So, you could use broad match to show your ad to a broad audience, or you could use exact match to focus on specific groups of prospects.

L

Landing Page: A landing page can be any page on your site, from blog posts to the home page to anything else. As long as someone lands there, Google counts it as a landing page in Analytics.

< Glossary **319** >

However, in PPC, the term has a much more specific definition. It refers to a page on your site that is designed to convert visitors into leads. It is usually a standalone web page, created for a marketing or advertising campaign. It's where a visitor "lands" after they click a link in an email or ads from Google, Bing, YouTube, Facebook, Instagram, Twitter, or similar places on the web. It's the digital version of a traditional sales letter, though its goal could be a number of different actions (e.g., the prospect providing their email address).

Latinoamericana: Someone who is Latinoamericana emigrated to the United States within the last ten years. They speak Spanish but almost no English.

Latinx: A person who is of Latin American origin or descent. The term is used as a gender-neutral or non-binary alternative to the traditional identifiers—Latino or Latina. It isn't meant to apply to everyone as an identity category, though, nor is it meant to refer to any particular sexuality.

Instead, it gives people greater options for how they decide to express themselves. Individuals who have historically been marginalized because the Spanish language has such gendered dynamics see this alternative spelling as one that fosters inclusivity and openness.

Lookalike Audiences: This is an audience you create based on whom you're already marketing to successfully.

< **320**   Natalie Fragkouli & Liel Levy >

M

Manual Bidding: With this bidding method, you set your own maximum cost-per-click (CPC) and set a bid for each keyword you are targeting.

Modified Broad Match: You can "lock" certain keywords or even phrases into place by using the "+" parameter. By doing this, you can keep your ads focused on a relatively broad audience while increasing your control over who is able to see those ads.

Multichannel Attribution: This one decision will show you every single touchpoint that led your lead to make a phone call or submit a form.

N

Nueva Latina: A Nueva Latina is someone with equal footing in American and traditional Hispanic cultures. They're second-generation Americans who prefer English but can speak at least some Spanish.

Negative Keywords: A set of keywords that you tell Google (or other networks) you do not want your ads showing up for when people use those keywords.

O

Omnichannel Strategy: A seamless strategy across all available channels (e.g., online and offline).

< Glossary **321** >

Organic Traffic: This is traffic that comes to your site through unpaid means. A common example is using blogs that rank well on Google. When people find and click website links, they end up on your site, even though you're not paying directly for that traffic.

P

Phrase Match: This approach will ensure that your ads appear only when prospects search for your key phrase using the keywords you want in the exact order you determined. Queries can still include other words before or after your specified phrases.

PPC: Pay Per Click (Paid Digital Marketing Strategy) refers to when you buy ads that will display on sites and search engines. Think of them as digital billboards.

Q

Q&A: In marketing, Q&As refer to prerecorded or written assets that involve experts answering participants' questions—typically common questions that the viewer or reader will also have.

Qualified Lead: A qualified lead is someone who matches one of your buyer personas and is currently in need of an attorney who offers your services.

Quality Score: Google assigns this score to PPC ads. This score will affect both the rank and CPC of these ads.

< **322** Natalie Fragkouli & Liel Levy >

R

Remarketing: These are ads that let you remarket prospects who have previously interacted with your firm's site or mobile app. Remarketing ads can be strategically positioned so they get right in front of prospects as they browse Google or any of its many partner websites.

Reputation Management: This is a strategy of proactively stacking Google's deck in your favor. You want all kinds of flattering reviews and five-star reviews right next to your law firm's name whenever it shows up in Google. The same goes for Yelp and Facebook.

This term can also refer to putting a plan in place for how you will address negative reviews. You never want to just accept them or find yourself in panic mode when they happen. That doesn't mean you can always get the desired outcome, but you should *definitely* have a response plan for when they happen.

Responsive Ads: With these ads, you can automatically adjust their size, appearance, and format to fit available ad spaces. So, the same responsive ad may appear as a small text ad in one place and a large image ad in another. To create this kind of ad, you need to enter its assets (i.e., headlines, descriptions, images, and logos).

Retargeting Ads: A specific type of paid traffic that is used to retarget people who have already come to your website.

Review Gating: This is the process of soliciting customer feedback and sending satisfied customers down one path and others with negative sentiment down another.

ROAS: Return on Ad Spend—a marketing metric that represents the overall efficacy of your digital advertising campaign.

ROI: Return-on-Investment is the ratio of how much you spend to how much you get back on your marketing campaigns.

S

Schema Markup: This is code (semantic vocabulary) that you put on your law firm's website to help search engines return more informative results to their users.

SEO: Search Engine Optimization is a wide range of practices used to improve a website's standing in search engines so as to increase traffic.

SERP: Search Engine Results Page.

Smart Bidding: This advanced bidding strategy uses machine learning to optimize your bids so that they maximize your law firm's conversions, as well as their conversion value across your campaign or entire bidding portfolio. This strategy also includes four subsets of its own.

Smart Display Campaigns: You provide a set of assets, and Google will mix and match them at scale.

< **324**   Natalie Fragkouli & Liel Levy >

Social Proof: A psychological and social phenomenon that describes how people will often copy the actions and behaviors of those around them.

Standard Display Campaigns: You can manually choose the targeting, bidding, and ad formats.

T

Tracking Pixels: Code that follows visitors after they leave your site or social media account, so that when they go to other sites, display ads in the network you're using (e.g., Google Display Network, Facebook, etc.) will pop up.

Telephone Etiquette: How your intake team should be answering the phone:

> Greeting + Name of Your Firm + Their Name + "How can I assist you?"

Testimonials: This kind of customer feedback is usually pulled from a personal email or a third-party review but is displayed on your law firm's website for prospects to see.

Third-Party Reviews: These client reviews are collected by third-party websites like Google, Facebook, Yelp, and others. Again, your firm has nothing to do with these reviews.

< ABOUT THE AUTHORS >

LIEL LEVY

Liel gained experience with marketing to the US Hispanic market at an early age through his family advertising agency in Los Angeles. He holds an Honors BA degree in Hotel Management from the world-renowned Les Roches University in Spain and has over a decade of experience in management roles across some of the world's most prestigious hotel brands, including The Ritz Carlton, Four Seasons, and Mandarin Oriental. His customer service skills and management experience have driven his success with helping law firms shift to a multicultural and client-centered approach. Liel is now the producer and co-host of "In Camera Podcast," which is dedicated to the good, bad, and controversial in legal marketing. He is a regular speaker at the Google Digital Coaches program, and co-founder of Nanato Media, helping law firms across the nation dominate their Hispanic markets.

< **326**   Natalie Fragkouli & Liel Levy >

NATALIE FRAGKOULI

Natalie is an MBA and former lecturer on Corporate Strategy and Business Marketing at the University of West London in the UK. Her passion for marketing in the digital era led her professional trajectory in the US, where she has specialized in legal marketing to the US Hispanic market for more than ten years. She has created and managed in-house digital marketing teams that have generated thousands of Hispanic leads for law firms around the nation. Natalie worked directly with Google Mexico and pioneered attorney PPC. She was even the first marketer to earn the Google Premier badge in the legal marketing field. She co-founded Nanato Media with an in-house approach in mind to give every law firm access to highly targeted and cost-effective digital marketing strategies in Spanish that yield real business results.

Made in United States
North Haven, CT
15 December 2023

45827756R00211